GRAVES
of our
FOUNDERS

Volume III

Their Lives, Contributions, and Burial Sites

JOE FARRELL • LAWRENCE KNORR • JOE FARLEY

Mechanicsburg, PA USA

Published by Sunbury Press, Inc.
Mechanicsburg, Pennsylvania

SUNBURY PRESS
www.sunburypress.com

Copyright © 2024 by Joe Farrell, Joe Farley, and Lawrence Knorr.
Cover Copyright © 2024 by Sunbury Press, Inc.

Sunbury Press supports copyright. Copyright fuels creativity, encourages diverse voices, promotes free speech, and creates a vibrant culture. Thank you for buying an authorized edition of this book and for complying with copyright laws by not reproducing, scanning, or distributing any part of it in any form without permission. You are supporting writers and allowing Sunbury Press to continue to publish books for every reader. For information contact Sunbury Press, Inc., Subsidiary Rights Dept., PO Box 548, Boiling Springs, PA 17007 USA or legal@sunburypress.com.

For information about special discounts for bulk purchases, please contact Sunbury Press Orders Dept. at (855) 338-8359 or orders@sunburypress.com.

To request one of our authors for speaking engagements or book signings, please contact Sunbury Press Publicity Dept. at publicity@sunburypress.com.

FIRST SUNBURY PRESS EDITION: October 2024

Set in Adobe Garamond | Interior design by Crystal Devine | Cover by Lawrence Knorr | Edited by the authors.

Publisher's Cataloging-in-Publication Data
Names: Farrell, Joe, author | Farley, Joe, author | Knorr, Lawrence, author.
Title: Graves of our Founders : Volume III : Their Lives, Contributions, and Burial Sites / Joe Farrell Lawrence Knorr Joe Farley.
Description: First trade paperback edition. | Mechanicsburg, PA : Sunbury Press, 2024.
Summary: Joe Farrell, Joe Farley, and Lawrence Knorr have traveled across the eastern USA to the graves of over 200 founding fathers (and mothers) responsible for the birth of the United States of America. Included in this first volume are biographies and grave information for 53 of these luminaries who made significant contributions to the Revolutionary cause.
Identifiers: ISBN 979-8-88819-251-1 (softcover).
Subjects: HISTORY / United States / Revolutionary Period (1775-1800) | BIOGRAPHY & AUTOBIOGRAPHY / Political.

Designed in the USA
0 1 1 2 3 5 8 13 21 34 55

For the Love of Books!

Contents

Introduction. 1

Thomas Jefferson The Founder of the Virginia Dynasty. 5
Andrew Adams Connecticut's Chief Justice. 24
Samuel Adams Boston's Radical Revolutionary. 28
Ethan Allen Leader of the Green Mountain Boys. 35
John Armstrong Sr. The Hero of Kittanning 41
Crispus Attucks The Boston Massacre. 46
John Barry The Commodore 51
Dr. Josiah Bartlett First Vote for Independence. 61
Richard Bassett Senator #1 67
Edward Biddle Speaker of the Pennsylvania Assembly 72
John Blair Jr. Grand Master of Virginia 78
Richard Bland Planter and Pamphleteer. 83
Elias Boudinot President During the Treaty of Paris 88
Carter Braxton Most Descendants 95
David Brearley Judge and Master Mason 100
Pierce Butler The British Soldier Who Became a Founder 104
Charles Carroll of Carrollton The Catholic Signer 108
William Clingan Chester County Continental Congressman 115
George Clinton "The Father of the Empire State". 120
Jonathan Dayton Youngest Constitution Signer 130
Eliphalet Dyer ". . . an honest, worthy man . . ." 134
William Floyd Major General in the Congress. 139
Christopher Gadsden "Sam Adams of the South". 144
Nathan Hale "But One Life" 150
Edward Hand Lancaster's Major General 156
John Hanson President of the United States in Congress Assembled 161
George Robert Twelves Hewes "The Shoemaker and the Tea Party" . . . 166
Stephen Hopkins "Greatest Statesman of Rhode Island" 175

James Armistead Lafayette Lafayette's Double Agent 184
Henry Laurens First President of the Recognized USA. 188
Benjamin Lincoln Received the Surrender at Yorktown. 195
James Lovell Teacher, Orator, Signer, Spy 202
George Mason "The Father of the Bill of Rights" 207
John Mathews "The Disagreeable One" 217
Frederick Augustus Conrad Muhlenberg The First Speaker. 222
John Peter Gabriel Muhlenberg Major General Who Was a Minister. . 229
James Otis Jr. "Founding Firebrand" 237
Thomas Paine "The Mouthpiece of the American Revolution" 243
William Paterson Author of the New Jersey Plan. 251
Timothy Pickering Radical Federalist 257
Charles Cotesworth Pinckney XYZ Affair 264
Molly Pitcher (Mary Ludwig) Sergeant Molly. 271
Peyton Randolph The First President 277
George Read Triple Signer 284
Joseph Reed President of Pennsylvania 288
Paul Revere "Listen, my children, and you shall hear . . ." 293
George Ross Lawyer, Colonel, and Congressman. 300
Edward Rutledge Youngest to Sign the Declaration 304
John Rutledge "The Dictator" 309
James Smith York's Radical Revolutionary 316
Haym Solomon Financier of the Revolutionary War 320
John Sullivan Irish General 325
Artemas Ward First Commander-in-Chief. 333

Sources. 339
Index 343

Introduction

Welcome to *Graves of Our Founders Volume Three*. This work aims to examine the lives and contributions of the amazing men and women who, using their courage and talents, established the country we love. Our original plan called for a four-volume series, with each covering approximately fifty founders, and that goal remains. We are also creating regional and topical volumes based on this content. The book *Before George* is about the patriots who were the Presidents of Congress before the US Constitution. We have also published *Pennsylvania Patriots* and *Chesapeake Patriots*, two of our regional volumes. *New Jersey Patriots* and *New York Patriots* will soon follow.

Over the past decade, we have made trips to numerous cemeteries to produce twelve volumes of the popular Keystone Tombstones and two titled Gotham Graves. This series covering the founders follows the same format of those works and involved more effort in both time and research. Our travels to visit the graves of those we have identified as founders have taken us to more than the thirteen original states. Accessing information about some of the lesser-known individuals who made contributions to the creation of the United States at times has been challenging. We hope that our efforts in meeting those challenges will please our readers.

The first question we had to answer regarding this series was who to include. In other words, who qualifies as a Founder? The standard we settled on resulted in the inclusion of signers of either the Continental Association, the Declaration of Independence, the Articles of Confederation, or the Constitution. In addition, we have also identified non-signers of the above-referenced documents who made significant contributions to the creation of the United States of America. Among those are the major generals, other military heroes, financiers, thought leaders, and otherwise legendary people associated with the Revolution.

Paul Revere is an example of the latter, immortalized by Henry Wadsworth Longfellow in his poem, but did not sign any important documents or lead large armies. He appears in this volume.

We all agree that our visits to the gravesites and the research on the founders have been rewarding and educational. However, in some cases, the visits have been sobering, shocking, and shameful. The well-known founders such as Washington, Jefferson, Hamilton, and Madison are at rest in well-maintained graves accessible to the public. Unfortunately, this is not the rule. Too many of our nation's founders are interred in neglected places and left unattended and thus are subject to decay. Some are inaccessible, and others cannot be located at all due to the development of the land and poor record keeping. One of our goals in doing this series and including photographs of the graves is to bring this problem to light and hopefully spurn action to address this issue before it is simply too late.

Considering the condition of many of these graves, we have established a website, www.adoptapatriot.com, where one can find information on all the people we have identified as founders. We continue to update this site as we come across new information. In addition, the website includes a Wall of Shame where we highlight those gravesites that we have concluded are in the worst shape due to neglect or are in remote difficult-to-reach locations or where the founder is under memorialized given their contributions to the nation. It is our sincere hope that many of these graves will be restored, renewed, or relocated.

One thing we have learned about the founders in writing this series, and we are confident that most of them would agree with us, is that they were products of their times and not perfect nor infallible. They disagreed on many of the issues they faced, and none may have been as hotly debated as slavery. As a matter of fact, on our many trips, we have had some heated debates as to how the various founders dealt with slavery on both public and personal levels. It is difficult to reconcile men who undertook a war against the most powerful army in the world, proclaiming that all men are created equal while, at the same time, many of these same men held other men, women, and children in bondage. The contradiction is obvious and quite difficult to excuse. Nevertheless, we have attempted to tell each founder's story truthfully and deal with the slavery issue on a case-by-case basis. There are several chapters in this volume, including those on Thomas Jefferson and Carter Braxton, where we hope our readers will find that we have met that standard.

As the country celebrates the 250th anniversary of the Declaration of Independence, we view these volumes as timely reminders of the founders' sacrifices and contributions to create this nation. We should never forget those who put their lives and fortunes on the line and succeeded in establishing the greatest country the world has ever known. We remain inspired by the words of Marcus Cicero:

> POOR IS THE NATION HAVING NO HEROES
> SHAMEFUL THE ONE THAT HAVING THEM FORGETS

Thomas Jefferson
(1743–1826)

The Founder of the Virginia Dynasty

Buried at Monticello Graveyard
Albemarle County, Virginia

This founder had many talents and interests. He was an inventor, an architect, a scientist and a gifted writer. He served the nation in multiple roles, first as a member of the Continental Congress, then as Governor of Virginia, as the United States minister to France, followed by a term as Vice-President and finally as the third President of the United States. He was also the first of three Virginians elected to the highest office in the land. All three served two terms in what is known as the Virginia Dynasty. He is best known as the principal author of the Declaration of Independence. It is ironic that the man who put pen to paper and wrote, "We hold these truths to be self-evident: that all men are created equal; that they are endowed by their Creator with certain inalienable rights, that among those are life, liberty and the pursuit of happiness" was a slave owner. This contradiction has made him one of the more controversial founders in recent times. His name was Thomas Jefferson.

Jefferson was born on April 13, 1743, in Shadwell, Albemarle County, Virginia. His father was Peter Jefferson, a successful tobacco planter and surveyor. Like the majority of Virginia planters, he owned slaves to work his fields and as his wealth increased, he purchased more land and more slaves. His mother was Jane Randolph Jefferson, who came from one of

Thomas Jefferson

Virginia's most distinguished families. When Jefferson was fourteen, his father died, and the young boy inherited an estate of about 5,000 acres.

As detailed by Winston Groom in his work *The Patriots: Alexander Hamilton, Thomas Jefferson, John Adams and the Making of America* Jefferson's education began when he was a young boy. At the age of five, he was enrolled in a local English school and by the time he was nine, he was studying French, Latin and Greek under the tutelage of a Scottish clergyman. After his father's death, he was instructed on the classics by Reverend Maury. At the age of 17 he enrolled in the College of William and Mary in Williamsburg. Here, he met the law professor George Wythe, a man who would remain an influence on Jefferson until the day he died. After two years in college, he studied law under Wythe, who sponsored his 24-year-old student to be a member of the Virginia Bar in 1767. He also regularly attended sessions of the House of Burgesses where he heard Patrick Henry forcibly denounce the Stamp Act.

After successfully passing the Virginia Bar examination, Jefferson began to practice law. He specialized in land cases or what is today known as real estate law. He also took on several cases on behalf of slaves who were seeking their freedom. In these cases, he found little, if any, sympathy for his arguments in Virginia. In one case, he argued that "Everyone comes into the world with a right to his own person. This is what is called personal liberty and is given him by the author of nature . . . Under that law, we are all born free." The judge was not convinced and ruled against him.

In 1768 Jefferson began work on the mountain home he would call Monticello. He designed the home itself and guided the builders, which included some of his slaves. During this time, he also spent a considerable amount of time reading from his book collection. He was especially attracted to the ideas of writers that, as a group, became known as the Enlightenment. These writers abandoned the idea of absolute faith in popes and kings. Instead, they saw a world ruled by logic and science. Jefferson would promote these ideas for the rest of his days.

In 1770, Jefferson met Martha Wayles Skelton. He fell in love, describing her as "distinguished for her beauty, her accomplishments and her solid merit. In 1772, the couple was wed. The years they were married were one of the happiest periods of Jefferson's life, according to his biographer Dumas Malone. The marriage would last ten years until Martha's death and produce six children, only two of which, Martha and Mary, survived to adulthood.

As told by Fawn M. Brodie in her work, *Thomas Jefferson: An Intimate History*, eighteen months after they were wed, Martha's father died and she inherited, among other things, 135 slaves. These included Betty Hemings and ten of her twelve children. The majority of them became favored house servants. Betty herself was given a cabin, and Jefferson noted in his account book payments to Betty for "pullets" and "fowls," which indicated special treatment. Later, Madison Hemings would write of his grandmother, "She had seven children by white men and seven by colored—fourteen in all." Brodie also adds that Martha's father had fathered three of what were her half-white sisters.

During this time, the work continued on Monticello and its gardens which was noted by Jefferson in the Garden Book he kept to record the status of his agriculture. Here, he detailed what had been planted, and it was a long list that included plum, peach, cherry and apple trees. There were also cabbages, radishes, carrots, peas, beans and potatoes. He also planted grape vineyards used to produce what his biographer described as a "respectable wine."

His first written political work to be widely praised was in 1774, titled *A Summary View of the Rights of British America*, which provided directions to Virginia's delegated serving in the First Continental Congress. In the document, he maintained that while Virginia did not want separation from the mother country, he wrote that King George III was "no more than the Chief officer of the people, appointed by the laws, and circumscribed with definite powers to assist in working the great machine of government." The work appeared in pamphlet and was purchased by both George Washington and John Adams. While he was not listed as the author, it became known that he had authored the work that was a repudiation of Parliament's authority over British Americans. Adams called it "a very handsome public paper." It brought Jefferson to the attention of people throughout the colonies.

In the spring of 1775, the battles at Lexington and Concord not only resulted in "the shot heard round the world" but brought a total war with England closer to reality. As a direct result a Second Continental Congress met in Philadelphia that May. Jefferson represented Vigilante as one of that colony's delegates. Initially, this meeting produced what was called the "olive branch," which was sent to King George in hopes of avoiding an all-out conflict. The king was unimpressed and simply ignored it.

In August, Jefferson returned to Monticello to spend time with Martha, who was suffering from health problems. He was also greeted with the news that British Governor Dunmore had announced that any slave who would join the British army in the fight against the colonies would earn his freedom. This edict brought with it the fear of a slave uprising.

Thomas Jefferson (1743–1826)

In late March of 1776, Jefferson's mother passed away as a result of a stroke. For weeks after, he battled depression, which he ultimately overcame. That June, he was back in Congress in Philadelphia, where the delegates were debating whether to negotiate with England or declare independence. While the debate raged, Congress agreed that a declaration should be drafted in case the result was a vote for independence. Jefferson was assigned to a five-man committee, including Benjamin Franklin, John Adams, Roger Sherman, and Robert Livingston, which were assigned the task of producing a draft document.

The committee assigned Jefferson the task of writing what would be his most famous work, The Declaration of Independence, according to A. J. Langguth, in his book *Patriots*, Jefferson never intended the work to be original. His rivals would point to his debt to other writers like John Locke. He was also clearly influenced by the writings of his fellow Virginian, George Mason. In a recent work by David Fleming, *Who's Your Founding Father: One Man's Epic Quest to Uncover the First, True Declaration of Independence*, the author argues that the Mecklenburg Declaration signed on May 20, 1775, in North Carolina, was plagiarized by Jefferson when he composed his far more famous declaration. While Jefferson may have utilized many of these sources, it was he who put pen to paper and organized the arguments for independence that achieved the goal of expressing what thousands of Patriot essays written by the likes of Samuel Adams, John Adams, and Thomas Paine had been grouping for.

On July 1, 1776, the delegates, with Jefferson's declaration ready, took up Richard Henry Lee's resolution that the American states declare themselves independent. John Dickinson rose and argued that independence should be delayed until the states were confederated, the boundaries of the new nation fixed and a pact could be reached with France. John Adams hoped that some other delegate would rise to answer Dickinson, but none did, so Adams rose and repeated the arguments he had long made favoring independence. By this time, nine of the thirteen colonies publicly favored independence. During the debate, a dispatch arrived from General George Washington reporting that the British were poised to attack American positions in New York. That alarm may have swayed the delegates that Adams's arguments had failed to convince, and on July 2, 1776, with no dissenting votes, Congress declared that the colonies were free and independent states. Had the vote gone the other way, Jefferson's work would have been long forgotten.

After the Declaration was approved, Jefferson angered many of his colleagues. Congress requested he accompany Benjamin Franklin to France to seek aid for the Continental Army. Since Jefferson spoke French, he was a natural choice. He refused and resigned his seat in Congress. At the time, his wife was pregnant and in poor health. She had a history of problems when it came to childbearing, and this obviously influenced Jefferson's decision. Jefferson never informed those in Congress of her condition. His wife suffered a miscarriage.

As noted in *Patriots*, John Adams accepted another term in Congress. On returning to public service, he was leaving his wife, Abigail Adams, for the sixth time. Adams was upset with Jefferson's choice, writing that the country was not yet secure enough "to excuse your retreat in the delights of domestic life."

Jefferson returned to public service when he was elected Governor of Virginia in 1779. By this time, the British army had turned their attention to the American South. They had gained control over Georgia and South Carolina and were now fighting in North Carolina. There was little doubt that Virginia would be their next target. It was at this point in 1780 when Jefferson reluctantly began his second term as governor. By 1781 Jefferson's biographer Dumas Malone would record that his personal problems and the affairs of Virginia were so great that "reading about them" became painful. In April, his wife gave birth to a daughter who died at the age of five months. In May, a British force led by none other than Benedict Arnold captured the city of Richmond.

By this time, British General Cornwallis had also entered Virginia. He set up his headquarters at Elk Hill, located about 40 miles from Richmond. Jefferson had considerable holdings at Elk Hill, which Cornwallis destroyed. The English commander eliminated all the crops, burned the barns, and took the cattle and hogs as well as any horse that could be of service. Those not capable of service, including young colts, were killed.

Thomas Jefferson (1743–1826)

June 2 was the last day of Jefferson's second term as governor. With the British soldiers on the march against the outnumbered Patriots, the state treasury virtually empty, and the political situation verging on collapse, Jefferson chose not to run for another term. Cornwallis sent his favored Calvary officer, Banastre Tarleton, to search for Jefferson and other Virginia lawmakers. Jack Jones, a captain in the Virginia militia, rode to Monticello to warn him of the approaching British calvary. Jefferson sent his wife and two daughters to a friend's plantation. He then mounted his favorite horse and rode to a vantage point with a good view of Charlottesville. Using a spyglass, he saw that the city was filled with British cavalry. Jefferson rode off to join his family. The British arrived at Monticello within minutes of Jefferson leaving. They questioned slaves regarding where Jefferson had gone. They searched the house to no avail. They waited for eighteen hours, thinking he might return.

Jefferson, meanwhile, moved his family to Poplar Forest, another plantation he owned located about 70 miles south of Monticello. Here he waited until the danger passed when Washington arrived and defeated Cornwallis at Yorktown. Jefferson's critics and his political enemies would point to his fleeing the British as evidence of cowardice. Actually, the future president had acted prudently. It is likely that if the author of the Declaration of Independence had been captured, he would have been treated unkindly. He could have been sent to London to languish in the Tower of London or hanged.

After the American victory in the Revolution, a state delegate called for an investigation of the final months of the Jefferson administration. Jefferson believed Patrick Henry, who was by now a political opponent, was behind the call for an inquiry. The complaint centered on the ease with which the British had invaded Virginia. Jefferson responded in writing to questions posed by the General Assembly. In the end, he was exonerated.

On May 8, 1782, Jefferson's sixth child was born, a daughter named Lucy Elizabeth. Martha Jefferson was ill after the birth and was confined to bed. She died on September 6, 1782, with Jefferson at her side. Others at the bedside included a number of the house slaves, among them the nine-year-old Sally Hemings and the forty-seven-year-old Betty Hemings both of which had been inherited from Martha's father. Jefferson took the death hard. He went to his room, where he stayed for weeks. He followed that with hours riding on horseback. He had lost the woman he adored, and there was nothing he could do to change it.

In the fall of 1782, the Continental Congress renewed their plea for Jefferson to go to France to represent the new country. With Martha gone, he no longer felt restrained, and he welcomed the opportunity. He accepted and would head to Europe for the first time in his life.

In 1784, Jefferson sailed to France as Minister Plenipotentiary to the Court of Versailles, joining Benjamin Franklin and John Adams. He felt prepared. He spoke French; he had studied the culture and the French philosophers. He viewed his goal to diplomatically achieve important, lasting treaties with France on both the commercial and military levels. His view was that a strong partnership with France would protect the new country of the United States from any aggressive British moves or policies.

In his five years of service in France, his diplomatic efforts produced only two treaties, one with Prussia and the other with Morocco. He was also responsible for a Consular Agreement with France in 1789. He also attempted to deal with the Barbary pirates of North Africa, who were seizing American ships and citizens and then demanding ransom for their return. His experience here convinced him that only a war could respond to these actions.

In 1787 Jefferson was still in France witnessing the beginnings of the French Revolution, much of which he agreed with, while the Constitutional Convention was meeting in Philadelphia. George Washington sent Jefferson a draft of the Constitution that the gathering Washington presided over had adopted. While he found some of the provisions to his liking, he was concerned about the power given to the executive branch and the lack of a Bill Of Rights. Despite his misgivings, Jefferson wrote to his friend Madison, saying that if the states "approve of the proposed Constitution in all its parts, I shall concur in it cheerfully, in hopes that they amend it whenever they find it work wrong."

As the French Revolution evolved, so did Jefferson's view. As detailed by H. W. Brands in this work *Founding Partisans* in May of 1789, Jefferson wrote to his friend Madison, "The revolution of this country has advanced thus far without encountering anything which deserves to be called a difficulty. There have been riots in a few instances in three or four different places, in which there may have been a dozen or twenty lives lost. But nothing inordinate or worrisome to lovers of liberty."

Just three months later, after the fall of the Bastille, Jefferson would write to Maria Cosway, a married woman he fell in love with during his days in France, "We have been in the midst of tumult and violence. The cutting off of heads is become so much a' la mode, that one is apt to feel in the morning whether their own is on their shoulders." By this time, Jefferson had been granted his request to return to America. He left Paris on September 27, 1789, and headed to the United States, a country now governed by the First Congress and the first president, George Washington. Jefferson was accompanied on his trip home by his daughters Patsy and Polly and the slaves James Hemings and his sister Sally.

In 1787, when she was 14 years old, Sally Hemings traveled to Paris with one of Jefferson's daughters. Once in France, she was legally free because slavery was illegal in that country. She worked for Jefferson as a paid servant. At some point during her 26-month stay in Paris, Jefferson began having intimate relations with Hemings, who was the half-sister of Jefferson's departed wife, Martha. Jefferson was thirty years older than Hemings. According to one of Hemings' sons, at first his mother had refused to return to America with Jefferson. He claims that Jefferson offered her extraordinary privileges and promised that her children would be freed at the age of 21. It was on this basis that she agreed to return to America.

Evidence that includes modern DNA analyses shows that Jefferson impregnated Hemings multiple times during their time together at Monticello. Many historians agree that Jefferson fathered six of her children. Four of these children reached adulthood and were freed when they reached their 21st birthday. Confirmation of Jefferson's relationship with Hemings has affected his standing with a number of historians and Americans in general. In a 2001 Gallup poll on the Greatest Presidents in American History, Jefferson received one percent of the vote.

The historian Henry Wiencek, among others, noted that Jefferson was not the reluctant benevolent slave owner that many scholars had painted him to be. He writes that Jefferson's early efforts relative to emancipation ceased once he realized that the profits from slavery enabled him to live an extravagant lifestyle and maintain his beloved Monticello. In *Who's Your Founding Father*, David Fleming quotes the Virginia abolitionist, "Never did a man achieve more fame for what he did not do." In a review of Wiencek's book, *Master of the Mountain: Thomas Jefferson and His Slaves*, the *New York Times* referred to Jefferson as the "Monster of Monticello." New York's city hall removed a statue of Jefferson, whose stature has certainly suffered in many corners in recent times.

Upon his return to the United States, Jefferson learned that President Washington had nominated him to serve as the country's first Secretary of State. Jefferson was unsure that he wanted the position, and he wrote Washington that he was concerned about "criticisms and censures of a public . . . sometimes misinformed and misled." He added that his preference would be to remain as an ambassador. Washington responded that he "knew of no person" better suited for the office. Jefferson accepted Washington's judgment and became a member of the nation's first cabinet.

As Secretary of State, Jefferson defined the responsibilities of American diplomats living abroad. He also played a major part in negotiating the Compromise of 1790 from Philadelphia to what would become the District of Columbia in exchange for the acceptance of Secretary of the Treasury Alexander Hamilton's financial plan. Jefferson quickly grew to view Hamilton as a political rival who wanted to place too much power in the executive branch. Jefferson believed this threatened to destroy the liberty that had been one by the Revolution.

While all may have seemed well within the cabinet, that was hardly the case. Winston Groom, in his work *The Patriots*, describes an evening when Jefferson invited his fellow cabinet members to his home. The after-dinner conversation turned to politics and the British form of government. Vice President John Adams said, "If some of its defects and abuses (of the British system) were corrected, it would be the most perfect Constitution of government ever devised by man." That comment appalled Jefferson, who wasn't made any happier when Hamilton said, " It was the most perfect model of government that could be found and that the correction of its vices would render it an impracticable government." That evening, Hamilton also noticed portraits hanging in Jefferson's dining room, and he asked his host who the men were. Jefferson identified Sir Francis Bacon, Isaac Newton, and John Locke, describing them as the three greatest men the world had ever produced. Hamilton replied, " The Greatest man ... that ever lived was Julius Caesar." The evening convinced Jefferson that Hamilton and Adams intended to install a British style of government in America.

As time went on Jefferson grew not only to dislike his job but also living in Philadelphia. He also disagreed with President Washington's position that America should remain neutral relative to world affairs. Jefferson wanted to ally with France. Washington wanted Jefferson to stay on the job, but despite the president's wishes, Jefferson submitted his resignation on January 31, 1793. With reluctance, Washington accepted it on New Year's Day and offered "my most earnest prayers for your happiness accompany you in your retirement." John Adams didn't exactly share Washington's view, writing to his wife Abigail, "Jefferson went off yesterday and good riddance to bad ware." He added that he knew Jefferson had talents but that he believed "his mind is now poisoned with passion, prejudice and faction." Little did Adams know at the time that Jefferson would be his main rival in the next two presidential elections.

Jefferson returned to Monticello as the de facto head of the opposition party. He kept himself busy building his estate, tending his gardens and horseback riding. He also remained very interested in current affairs. His two protégés and future presidents, James Madison and James Monroe, carried on a steady correspondence with him dealing with the news of the day.

When President Washington announced that he would not seek a third term, Jefferson became the leading candidate of the Democratic-Republican Party for the highest office in the land. In August of 1796, he received a letter from Tennessee Senator William Cocke telling him that the people of his state wished him to be the next President, with New York's Aaron Burr serving as his Vice President. At the time, potential presidents did not campaign for the office only acknowledging their willingness to serve after others put their names forward. Jefferson's name was indeed put forward, and he found himself facing the Federalist candidate, John Adams.

In his farewell speech Washington warned against the factions forming in the country. His wish was not granted. The election of 1796 would be the first to pit two political parties against each other, and it would turn into a bitter fight. The Federalists painted Jefferson as a coward who had abandoned his post as Governor of Virginia during the Revolution and with the violence surrounding the French Revolution. This was false.

Meanwhile Jefferson's party was accusing Adams of favoring a monarchy. Federalists also accused Jefferson of being an atheist and being too pro-French. Jefferson's effort may have been hurt when the French ambassador publicly backed him shortly before the election. In a close election, Adams received 71 electoral votes, which was one more than he needed. Jefferson won 68 electoral votes and became the Vice President. Thus, we had two rivals elected to the highest offices in the land. It was clear that the founders had made an error in setting the election system, a fact that would become even clearer in the turbulent election of 1800.

Prior to the vote by the electoral college, Madison had told Jefferson that the possibility existed that he would finish second and that he needed to be prepared to accept the Vice Presidency. That was fine with Jefferson, who said, "It is not the less true, however, that I do sincerely wish to be second on that vote rather than the first." On March 4, 1797, both Jefferson and Adams were inaugurated. On that day, Jefferson told Madison, relative to Washington, "The President is fortunate to get out just as the bubble is bursting, leaving others to hold the bag." Later at the White House, Adams told Jefferson that he wanted his participation in decision making. Remembering this conversation, Jefferson would later write, "He never after that said one word to me on the subject, or even consulted me on any measures of the government."

One of the reasons Adams may have decided to marginalize Jefferson was the Vice President's attitude toward the French nation, which remained favorable. That nation was a major problem, perhaps the only one Adams inherited from Washington. The French were preying on American merchant ships. In addition, France was at war with Great Britain and was upset that the Americans had signed the Jay Treaty with the former mother country. In addition, in a move Jefferson objected to, after the execution of Louis XVI, America decided to cease the repayment of Revolutionary War debts to France, saying the debt was owed to a different regime.

The tensions between the former allies became known in history as America's Quasi-War with France. At the time many were convinced it would turn into a real war. By July of 1798, Adams declared that the country needed to prepare to defend itself. Congress agreed and passed bills creating a standing army, which Jefferson opposed. In addition, the Marine Corps and the Department Of Navy were established. Funds were directed to build three twenty-two gun frigates with plans to build an additional eighteen warships. Jefferson favored these moves but not to fight France. He was convinced that he could win the presidency in 1800 and saw the warships as being necessary to defeat the Barbary pirates.

Pulitzer Prize author Edward J. Larson, in his work *A Magnificent Catastrophe,* described the election of 1800 as tumultuous and as America's first presidential campaign. It certainly was unlike any other, as we had a sitting President and Vice President in two different parties fighting to win the highest office in the land. The Federalist Party candidates were President John Adams and Charles C. Pinckney of South Carolina. The Democratic-Republicans nominated Jefferson and Aaron Burr from New York. While these were the candidates, another prominent American, Federalist Alexander Hamilton, would play a significant role in determining the election results.

The main issues included the effects of the French Revolution and the Quasi-War. The Federalists wanted to maintain close ties with England and were in favor of a strong federal government. The Democratic-Republicans wanted more power placed in the hands of the states and criticized the taxes the Federalists had levied. They also made the Alien and Sedition Acts that had been passed by the Federalists an issue. These acts made it more difficult for immigrants to become citizens and made it easier to prosecute those who were critical of the federal government.

On December 14, 1799, George Washington passed away. Both Washington and Hamilton had considerable influence on the Adams cabinet members. With Washington's death, Adams became more independent and, in Hamilton's view, too independent. As a result, Hamilton schemed, behind the scenes, to have Pinckney elected to the highest office in the land. Hamilton believed that Pinckney would be more open to his influence.

While Hamilton hoped his activities on Pinckney's behalf would only be known to fellow Federalists who shared his views, he made the mistake of writing a 54-page letter in which he made the case that Adams was unfit to hold the highest office in the land. The Democratic-Republicans obtained a copy of the letter and immediately began reprinting it in their newspapers. The letter, which showed that there were major divisions in the Federalist Party, became a major factor in the election. When the electoral votes were cast, Jefferson and Burr each received 73 votes compared to 65 for Adams and 64 for Pinckney. The tie resulted in the election being decided by the House of Representatives.

The Constitution required the House to wait until February 11 to begin casting ballots. In the weeks that led up to that date, there were rumors and intrigue. Jefferson's party feared that the Federalists would pass legislation that would place the Federalists in charge of the executive branch. According to Jefferson, he verbally informed Adams that a move to install a temporary executive would result in "resistance by force and incalculable consequences." In addition, some feared that the Federalists would make a deal with Burr to preserve some of their power and influence in return for making him president. Burr distanced himself from the fray, allowing things to take their course. The fact that he did not publicly endorse Jefferson may have contributed to Jefferson's distrust of his running mate.

The voting began with each state casting one vote, with the winner being the candidate securing a majority of the state delegations. Neither Jefferson nor Burr were able to gain a majority on the initial 35 ballots. Jefferson was winning the backing of the state delegations controlled by his party, but the Federalists were backing Burr. Once again, Alexander Hamilton played a large role in the outcome. He had a strong dislike of both men but preferred Jefferson. He believed that under either man, the country was heading towards disaster, and he believed his party would share in the blame if Burr were elected. Hamilton convinced several Federalists to change their votes, and Jefferson was elected on the 36th ballot.

On March 4, 1808, Jefferson's second cousin, Chief Justice John Marshall, swore him in as the third President of the United States. Taking office, Jefferson faced the challenge of dealing with the 83-million-dollar national debt. His Secretary of the Treasury, Albert Gallatin, developed a plan to eliminate the debt in sixteen years. Among the moves Jefferson made was a reduction in both the nation's army and navy. By the end of his two terms in office, the debt was reduced to $57 million.

Jefferson's crowning achievement during his first term was the Louisiana Purchase. He instructed James Monroe and Robert R. Livingston to negotiate with France to purchase New Orleans and surrounding areas. At the time, Napoleon needed funds to continue his wars. In April of 1803, he surprised the American negotiators by offering to sell 827,987 square miles of territory for 15 million dollars. The United States accepted the offer doubling the size of the United States. The purchase gave the country access to some of the most fertile land of its size on the planet. It also opened the door to westward expansion.

As detailed in Brian Kilmeade and Don Yeager's work, *Thomas Jefferson and the Tripoli Pirates*, Jefferson was the first President to go to war with a foreign country. From his days as Secretary of State, Jefferson had firsthand experience dealing with the North African Ottoman provinces of Algiers, Tunis, Tripoli, and the Sultanate of Morocco. Barbary corsairs and crews from these countries preyed on merchant ships in the Mediterranean, capturing their crews and either enslaving them or holding them for ransom. Jefferson had long opposed paying ransom or tribute, and when he became President, he was determined to address the problem.

After Jefferson was inaugurated, Yusuf Karamanli, the Pasha Of Tripoli, demanded payment of $225,000 from the United States. Jefferson refused to comply. The Pasha responded by cutting down the flagstaff in front of the American Consulate, which was the Barbary way of declaring war. The war would last until 1805. The decisive Battle of Derna resulted in the American flag being raised for the first time in victory on foreign shores. On June 10, 1805, Karamanli signed a treaty ending the hostilities.

In 1804 Jefferson ran for re-election, replacing Aaron Burr with George Clinton as his running mate. The Federalists nominated Charles Cotesworth Pinckney. Jefferson's party pointed to a very strong economy, the Louisiana Purchase, and lower taxes as the administration's achievements. Jefferson won in a landslide the vote in the electoral college was 162-14.

Jefferson's second term was marked by difficulties due to the wars in Europe. The country's relations with England suffered, and the relationship between Jefferson and the British diplomat Anthony Merry contributed to the deterioration. In 1805 Napoleon became less cooperative relative to trading rights. Jefferson's response was the Embargo Act of 1807, which targeted both England and France. This act was largely both unpopular and ineffective and led to a drastic decline in exports. Jefferson abandoned the policy after a year.

Although Jefferson had replaced Burr in his second term, his dealings with his former Vice President were not over. Seeing he had no future with Jefferson, Burr ran for Governor of New York in 1804. He was soundly defeated. During the campaign, Alexander Hamilton made some disparaging remarks relative to Burr's character, and Burr challenged the former Secretary of the Treasury to a duel and mortally wounded him. Killing Hamilton effectively ended Burr's political career.

As detailed in the work of James E. Lewis Jr. titled *The Burr Conspiracy*, Burr set his sights on the western part of the country. In the fall of 1806, he and sixty men headed down the Ohio River. Historians differ on his intentions. Some say he had enticed supporters with a plan to liberate Spanish Mexico. Others with promises of land in the Orleans territory. There were rumors that his real intention was to establish his own empire in the western part of the country. Burr had consulted with the Louisiana Territory Governor James Wilkinson, who reported the plot to Jefferson. Jefferson ordered that Burr be arrested for treason. Burr was captured and sent to Virginia to be tried by a court presided over by John Marshall.

Reactions to the arrest and trial captivated many. John Adams, in a letter, remarked that he had never believed Burr to be a fool, but if he really was guilty of the accusation, he must be an "Idiot or a Lunatic."

Joe Farley and Thomas Jefferson

Senator William Plumerias remarked that "Burr is capable of much wickedness, but not of so much folly." Some, including Adams, felt that if Burr were acquitted, he could still become president. He was indeed found not guilty, but his political career was over.

Jefferson was succeeded in office by two fellow Virginians, James Madison and James Monroe. He was said to be the founder of what is called the Virginia Dynasty. After he left office, he continued to

Grave of Thomas Jefferson

correspond with both men. As a matter of fact, the Monroe Doctrine was influenced by the advice Monroe sought from Jefferson.

Jefferson spent his final days at his beloved Monticello. In July of 1825, his health began to deteriorate. By June of the next year, he was confined to his bed. On July 3, he was overcome by a fever, and he had already declined an invitation to attend an anniversary celebration of his Declaration. The next day, on the 50th anniversary, he passed away, with his last words being, "Is it the fourth?" or "This is the fourth." John Adams died later that same day. After Jefferson passed, a gold locket was found around his neck. It contained a lock of his wife Martha's hair. He was laid to rest at Monticello.

Since his death, Jefferson's reputation among historians has risen and fallen in cycles. Currently, it would be at low tide. Historians and many Americans have serious questions about how, as a slaveholder, he failed to live up to the words he had written in 1776. Not to mention that one current author in his book, *Who's Your Founding Father*, questions whether Jefferson should be credited with writing the Declaration. As noted earlier, New York City removed a statute that had been erected to honor Jefferson. Things were far different in the 20th Century when Jefferson was selected to be one of the four presidents on Mount Rushmore. During those years, it was not unusual for the Democratic Party conventions to be decorated with gigantic posters depicting the man who founded their party. On April 29, 1962, President John F. Kennedy hosted a dinner at the White House honoring the Nobel Prize winners from the Western Hemisphere. Shortly into his welcome, Kennedy said, "I think this is the most extraordinary collection of talent, of human knowledge, that has ever gathered together at the White House, with the possible exception of when Thomas Jefferson dined alone."

Andrew Adams
(1736–1797)
Connecticut's Chief Justice

Buried at West Cemetery
Litchfield, Connecticut

**Continental Congress • Signer of the Articles of Confederation
Militiaman**

Perhaps the least famous of the Founders named Adams, Andrew was a Continental Congressman from Connecticut who signed the Articles of Confederation. He was also a colonel in the Connecticut Militia and rose to be the Chief Justice of the Supreme Court in Connecticut. Unfortunately, no known portrait survives.

Andrew Adams, the son of Samuel Adams (1703-1788) and his wife, Mary (née Fairchild) Adams (1698-1803), was born in Stratford, Connecticut, on January 7, 1736. No, this was not the famous Samuel Adams of Boston, who was active in the Sons of Liberty. This Samuel Adams was a lawyer from Connecticut who was no relation to the Boston Adamses. In addition to practicing law, this Samuel Adams was a judge in Fairfield County.

Young Andrew first received the traditional "classical education" in local schools and then followed in his father's footsteps into the law, attending Yale, where he graduated in 1760. He then studied law under his father and first practiced with him in Stamford. By 1764, Adams opened his practice in Litchfield, Connecticut, and soon became one of the leading attorneys there.

Andrew Adams (1736–1797)

York Courthouse where the Articles of Confederation were approved

Adams married Eunice Buel, the youngest daughter of Judge Samuel and Abigail (Peck) Canfield of New Milford, Connecticut. The couple had one child, a son named Andrew.

In 1772, Adams was named the king's attorney for the County of Litchfield. He and his family moved there in 1774, where he spent the rest of his life. Adams was also a Freemason in Litchfield as a member of St. Paul's Lodge No. 11.

Adams became involved in politics and was elected to several minor positions in the Litchfield area. As the tensions began to rise between the colonies and Great Britain, Adams was appointed to the Connecticut Council of Safety for two years. When hostilities broke out at Lexington and Concord, Adams volunteered for the Connecticut militia and rose to the rank of colonel during his service. In 1776, Adams was elected to the Connecticut House of Representatives, serving until 1781. He was the speaker in 1779 and 1780.

On October 11, 1777, Adams was elected to the Second Continental Congress, then meeting in York, Pennsylvania, and negotiating the Articles of Confederation. Adams was unable to attend that year, instead joining in 1778 when the Congress returned to Philadelphia. There, on July 9, 1778, at Independence Hall, Adams was one of the first to sign the Articles of Confederation as a delegate from Connecticut. During his remaining time in Congress, Adams was consulted about military affairs in New England and was proactive in seeking funding.

When Adams returned to Connecticut the next year, Governor Trumbull named him to the Connecticut Executive Council and appointed him as a judge on the Connecticut Supreme Court. He also continued to serve in the Connecticut Militia until the end of the war.

In 1793, Adams rose to Chief Justice of the Connecticut Supreme Court. He also earned his LL.D. (Doctorate in Law) degree from Yale in 1796.

Andrew Adams died at the age of 61 in Litchfield, Connecticut, on November 26, 1797. He was interred at what was then called the "East Cemetery" in Litchfield but is now known as West Cemetery. As of 1909, historian Dwight C. Kilbourn had visited Adams' grave and noted it was "a rapidly crumbling marble slab." The stone read:

> In memory of the Hon. Andrew Adams, Esq., Chief Judge of the Superior Court, who died November 27, 1797, in the 63d year of

Grave of Andrew Jackson

Andrew Adams (1736–1797)

his age. Having filled many distinguished offices with great ability and dignity, he was promoted to the highest judicial office in the State, which he held for several years, in which his eminent talents shone with uncommon lustre, and were exerted to the great advantage of the public and the honor of the High Court in which he presided. He made an early profession of religion, and zealously sought to protect its true Interests. He lived a Life and died the Death of a Christian. His filial Piety and paternal tenderness are held in sweet Remembrance.

A new granite memorial has since been placed next to the decrepit memorial.

Samuel Adams
(1722–1803)

Boston's Radical Revolutionary

Buried at Granary Burial Ground
Boston, Massachusetts

**Continental Association • Declaration of Independence
Articles of Confederation • Governor**

Samuel Adams was an American statesman, political philosopher, and Founding Father, who signed three of the four founding documents. His role in the origins of the American Revolution cannot be overstated. He was a zealot for independence and a thorn in the side of the British. He spoke out against British efforts to tax the colonists and pressured merchants to boycott British products. John Adams, the second President, said of his cousin Sam that he embodied "steadfast integrity" and "universal good character." The Royal Governor of Massachusetts, Thomas Hutchinson, felt differently, saying there existed no "greater incendiary in the King's dominion or a man of greater malignity of heart" . . . as any passionate activist, he was controversial, but for sure, he was an ardent Patriot.

Adams was born in Boston on September 27, 1722. He was one of twelve children born to Samuel Adams Sr. and Mary Adams. Only three of these children lived past the age of three. The parents were devout Puritans, and the family lived on Purchase Street on the south end of colonial Boston. Samuel Sr. was a prosperous merchant, church deacon, and leading figure in Boston politics.

Samuel Adams (1722–1803)

Samuel Adams

Samuel Jr. attended the Boston Latin School and then entered Harvard College at the age of fourteen in 1736. He supposedly was preparing for the ministry but exposure at Harvard to the ideas of philosophers like John Locke, who held that certain rights and liberties were inherent to humanity and that government should reflect the truth, shifted his interest toward politics. He graduated in 1740 but continued as a graduate student, earning a master's degree in 1743. In his thesis, he argued that it was lawful to resist the supreme magistrate if the commonwealth could not otherwise be preserved.

After Harvard, Adams decided to go into business. His business ventures were failures, and finally, his father made him a partner in the family's malthouse. His lack of interest and understanding of business led to its shutting down.

In 1748, Adams and some friends established a political newspaper called *The Independent Advertiser*. Sam became a frequent contributor to this newspaper, which became an outlet for his beliefs. His writings argued that people must resist any encroachment on their constitutional rights.

In October 1749, he married Elizabeth Checkley. Over the next seven years, she gave birth to six children, but only two survived to adulthood. In July 1757, Elizabeth died soon after giving birth to a stillborn son. Adams married again in 1764 to Elizabeth Wells but had no children.

In 1756, he got his first steady job when the Boston Town Meeting elected him tax collector. He often failed to collect taxes and was held liable for the unpaid tax. He often paid with his own funds, and friends often chipped in to bail him out.

The British government was in deep debt after the French and Indian War and passed two measures to tax the colonies. The first, the Sugar Act of 1764, taxed molasses and refined sugar, and Adams was a powerful figure in opposition. He denounced the act, being one of the first to cry out against taxation without representation. Then, in 1765, Parliament passed the Stamp Act, a tax on all legal and commercial documents, newspapers, and court documents. This was like pouring gasoline on a fire and led to the founding of the Sons of Liberty which would play a role throughout the American Revolution. Their motto became "No Taxation without Representation." Adams made frequent use of colonial newspapers and suggested a boycott of British goods. There were frequent riots and violent attacks to intimidate tax collectors. Officials blamed Sam Adams for inciting the violence.

According to the modern scholarly interpretation of Adams, he supported legal methods of resisting parliamentary taxation, such as petitions, boycotts, and nonviolent demonstrations, but opposed mob violence. All the pressure generated by Adams's various activities resulted in the repeal of the Stamp Act in early 1766. The city of Boston rejoiced.

In 1767, Parliament struck again with the Townshend Acts, a series of laws that taxed goods imported to the colonies. The colonists saw the acts as an abuse of power and organized a boycott of British goods. In his letter that became known as the "Massachusetts Circular Letter," Adams urged the other colonies to join in the boycott. In response to protests and boycotts, the British sent troops to occupy Boston and quell the unrest. This resulted in frequent clashes between citizens and troops. In March 1770, after years of agitation, British troops found themselves backed into a corner amid a mob and fired, killing five civilians. Adams called it The Boston Massacre. He wanted the accused soldiers to receive a fair trial, convincing his cousin John Adams to take up their defense. He wanted to demonstrate that Boston was not controlled by a lawless mob. After the defendants were acquitted of murder, however, he wrote a condemnation of the outcome.

In 1772, Adams was behind the formation of the Committees of Correspondence, which connected the town meetings of Massachusetts to one another. Soon similar committees were formed in other colonies as well. In 1773, Parliament passed the Tea Act, which granted the East India Company a monopoly on the tea trade. Sam Adams was a key figure in organizing opposition, resulting in the famous Boston Tea Party in December 1773. His exact role in this event is unsure. Adams never revealed if he went to the wharf or if he was involved in the planning, but he worked to publicize and defend it.

This pain-aggression spiral continued as Parliament responded to the Tea Party by passing a series of four laws in 1774 known as the Coercive Acts or Intolerable Acts. The four acts were intended to punish Massachusetts and send a message to the other colonies. They were the Boston Port Act, Massachusetts Government Act, Administration of Justice Act, and Quartering Act. These oppressive acts sparked strong colonial resistance including the meeting of the First Continental Congress. Adams worked to coordinate resistance to the Coercive Acts, and in June 1774, he proposed the meeting in Philadelphia and was chosen as one of five delegates to represent Philadelphia. Friends bought him new clothes and paid his expenses for his first trip outside Massachusetts.

The Congress met from September 5 to October 26 in Carpenters' Hall with delegates from twelve of the colonies. Georgia did not participate. Sam Adams worked for colonial unity and was a force for the formation of a colonial boycott known as the Continental Association. They agreed to meet again in May. When Adams returned to Massachusetts, he served in the Massachusetts Provincial Congress, which created the first Minuteman companies—militiamen ready for action at a moment's notice. Admiral Montague, the British Governor of Newfoundland and officer in the Royal Navy, upon reading of the events of the Continental Congress, said, "I doubt not but that I shall hear Mr. Samuel Adams is hanged or shot before many months are at end. I hope so, at least."

The Boston Town Meeting selected Adams to attend the Second Continental Congress and added John Hancock to the delegation. Believing rumors that they were to be arrested for treason, Adams and Hancock left Boston in February 1775 and were in Concord on April 19, 1775, when British troops first clashed with local militia, igniting the Revolutionary War. After the battles at Lexington and Concord, General Gage, the commanding officer, issued a proclamation granting a pardon to all who would "lay down their arms and return to duties of peaceable subjects." He, however, excepted Hancock and Adams.

At the Second Continental Congress in Philadelphia, Adams signed the Declaration of Independence. He also nominated George Washington to be Commander in Chief of the Continental Army. His inflammatory rhetoric continued in a speech in Philadelphia where he castigated Americans who sided with the crown. "If ye love wealth better than liberty, the tranquility of servitude than the animating contest of freedom—go from us in peace," he said. "We ask not your counsels or arms. Crouch down and lick the hands which feed you. May your chains set lightly upon you, and may posterity forget that ye were our countrymen." Adams served on military committees in Congress and was particularly concerned with punishing loyalists, i.e., Americans who continued to support the British. He was appointed to the Board of War and was the Massachusetts delegate to the committee appointed to draft the Articles of Confederation. The resulting Articles were sent to the states for ratification in November 1777. Adams urged ratification from Philadelphia, and it was ratified by Massachusetts and signed by Adams in 1778, but it took until 1781 for all states to ratify.

Sam Adams took a two-month break from Congress to return home to Boston and move his family to Dedham, Massachusetts. His home on Purchase Street had been destroyed and vandalized, and all the furnishings had been stolen. He returned to Boston in 1781 after retiring from Congress and never left Massachusetts again.

The remainder of Adams's career was devoted to state rather than national politics. In the 1780s, Adams served as President of the Massachusetts Senate. In January 1788, he was elected to the Massachusetts ratifying convention. He was initially opposed to ratification of the Constitution, but he and Hancock listened to the debate carefully and eventually agreed to support it with the promise that some amendments be added. Even with their support, it barely passed 187 to 168. From 1789 to 1793, he served as Lieutenant Governor under John Hancock. When Hancock died in office, Adams assumed the Governorship. Following that, Adams was elected to three consecutive one-year terms. He retired from politics after his tenure as Governor in 1797. He died at the age of eighty-one on October 2, 1803, and was interred at the Granary Burying Grounds in Boston.

Samuel Adams is a controversial figure in American history. Disagreement about his significance and reputation began before his death and continues to the present. Supporters of the Revolution praised

Grave of Samuel Adams

Adams, but Loyalists viewed him as a sinister figure who used propaganda to incite ignorant mobs. Some on each side claim that without him, there would not have been a revolution. For Adams, personal happiness had never been the supreme goal. He preferred virtue. While other men in Congress and the Army found ways to improve their fortunes, Adams returned to Boston in 1781 even poorer than when he left for the first Continental Congress. Some have dubbed his life as a riches to rags story. He wrote no memoir, resisting even calls to assemble his political writings. He was rare for his ability to keep a secret, any number of which he took to the grave, including the backstory of the Boston Tea Party.

Ethan Allen
(1738–1789)

Leader of the Green Mountain Boys

Buried at Green Mountain Cemetery
Burlington, Vermont

Ethan Allen is a Revolutionary War hero who was a general in the Continental Army best known as the founder of the famous Green Mountain Boys. He is also known for his tireless and controversial effort to make Vermont independent from Britain, other colonies, and perhaps even from the U.S.

Allen was born in Litchfield, Connecticut, on January 21, 1738, the first born to Joseph and Mary Allen. The family moved to Cornwall, and the Allens had seven more children, five boys and two girls. He began studies under a minister in the nearby town of Salisbury and hoped to gain admission to Yale. That plan was changed when his father died in 1755. He volunteered for militia service during the French and Indian War but saw no action and returned to Cornwall. He met and married Mary Brownson after a short courtship and took part ownership with his brother Heman in an iron furnace in Salisbury. There he bought a small farm and kept developing his iron business. The marriage was an unhappy one. They had five children, two of whom survived to adulthood. Mary died in 1783.

During his time in Salisbury, Allen met Thomas Young, a doctor. They had common interests in philosophy and political theory and decided to collaborate on a book. Young had convinced Allen to become a

Ethan Allen

Deist, i.e., the philosophical position that rejects revelation as a source of divine knowledge and asserts that reason and observation of the natural world are sufficient to determine the existence of god. The book was intended as an attack on organized religion. They worked on it until 1764, when Young moved away, taking the manuscript with him.

In the late 1760s, New Hampshire Governor Benning Wentworth sold land grants west of the Connecticut River. Allen bought grants for about 1000 acres. New York had issued land grants to much of the same land, and the dispute rose to the attention of the New York Supreme Court in 1770. New York won the suit, and Wentworth's grants were declared fraudulent. After the trial, Allen met with other grant holders at Catamount Tavern in Bennington. At this meeting, the settlers formed a militia group to defend their land. They called themselves The Green Mountain Boys and chose Allen as their leader. For the next four years, they fought against New York authorities to keep their land. The New

York legislature branded Allen and others as outlaws and offered a reward for their capture.

It was well known throughout New England that there were cannon and artillery at the British forts at Ticonderoga and Crown Point. Following the Battles of Lexington and Concord, a Connecticut militia asked Allen if he and his men would help them capture the forts. He agreed, and the Green Mountain Boys joined 60 men from Massachusetts and Connecticut in a meeting in Bennington on May 2. They planned a dawn raid for May 10. Not long after the Connecticut expedition was launched, the Massachusetts Committee of Safety launched its own expedition with Benedict Arnold in command. On the afternoon of May 9, they met, and Arnold asserted his right to command. The men refused to follow Arnold, and privately Allen and Arnold reached a deal that they would both lead the attack.

The British at Ticonderoga and Crown Point were not aware that war had broken out and were not expecting an attack of any kind. On May 10, 1775, Allen, Arnold, and the Green Mountain Boys stormed the fort at Ticonderoga and captured it with almost no resistance.

The victorious Americans quickly made plans for a strike against Crown Point. Led by Captain Seth Warner, a detachment of the Green Mountain Boys captured the small garrison there. The capture of Fort Ticonderoga and Crown Point proved to be important in the Revolutionary War because it secured protection from the British to the north and provided vital cannon for the colonial army.

When the Continental Congress found out about the capture of the fort, there was concern that it may have ruined any chance at reconciliation with Britain. Congress asked Allen to take the cannon and artillery to the southern end of Lake George so that inventory could be taken. Allen refused the request and argued that removing the weapons from the fort would leave the fort defenseless and leave the colonists in the western territories vulnerable to attack. As long as the cannon and artillery remained at the fort, they could be used to control traffic on Lake Champlain.

The cannon and artillery from Ticonderoga were eventually retrieved by Henry Knox and taken to Boston, where they were used to fortify Dorchester Heights and other areas around the city. Once Dorchester Heights was fortified, the British were forced to evacuate Boston.

On June 22, Allen and Seth Warner appeared before Congress in Philadelphia, where they argued for the inclusion of the Green Mountain Boys in the Continental Army. Congress agreed to establish a regiment of the Green Mountain Boys and agreed to pay them army rates for their service at Ticonderoga. When the regiment met, they held a vote to determine command. Seth Warner was elected to lead the regiment. He was viewed as a more stable and quieter choice than Allen.

Allen took the rejection in stride and wasted no time in joining Brigadier General Richard Montgomery's invasion of Canada. Operating an independent command ahead of the main body, he botched an attack on Montreal and was captured on September 25. He spent the next two and a half years as a British prisoner, enduring harsh conditions in British castles, New York City jails, and on prison ships. Allen was the type of Yankee the British loved to hate. He was a natural-born leader, brilliant, fearless, crude, bullheaded, arrogant, impulsive, egotistical, confrontational, physically imposing, and principled. General Prescott, the military governor of Montreal, put Allen in irons for 30 days and, with great fanfare, sent him to London to be executed. He arrived at Falmouth, England, after crossing under filthy conditions and was imprisoned in Pendennis Castle, Cornwall. In the meantime, Prescott was captured trying to escape Montreal. King George, fearing for Prescott's fate, decreed that American prisoners should be sent back to America and treated as prisoners of war.

Meanwhile, in January 1777, Vermont declared its independence from Great Britain and land claims from New York and New Hampshire to become the Republic of Vermont, which existed for fourteen years. Though an ally to the American colonies, the Continental Congress did not recognize them, referring to them as "The New Hampshire Grants." Remarkably, slavery was outlawed in the republic.

In August 1777, Allen, while in custody in New York, learned of the death of his young son Joseph due to smallpox. In May 1778, he was exchanged for Colonel Archibald Campbell and reported to George Washington at Valley Forge. He would see no further action in the war.

Allen spent the next several years involved in Vermont's political and military matters and served as commander of the state's militia with the rank of Major General. During this time, some in Vermont negotiated a unification with Quebec, which was agreeable to the British, but following the surrender at Yorktown, Vermont sided with the Americans.

Ethan Allen (1738–1789)

Statue of Ethan Allen at Fort Ticonderoga

On February 16, 1784, Allen married Frances "Fanny" Montresor Brush Buchanan after a brief courtship, and they had three children. That same year, Allen recovered the Deist manuscript from the estate of Thomas Young and had it published as *Reason- The Only Oracle of Man*. It is considered the first work published in the United States that openly attacked Christianity. The book was a financial and critical failure and undermined Allen's reputation as an iconic American Patriot.

On February 12, 1789, Allen died at his home in Burlington after suffering an apoplectic fit. He was buried in Green Mountain Cemetery in Burlington. The exact location of his remains within the cemetery is unknown. The magnificent columnar monument marking his grave may or may not actually be over his remains. Attempts have been made to settle the issue, including subsurface radar scans to detect remains, but the scans have remained inconclusive. The uncertainty has fueled an ongoing local controversy over the true burial site.

Vermont finally achieved statehood in 1791, after Allen's death.

Grave of Ethan Allen

John Armstrong Sr.
(1717–1795)

The Hero of Kittanning

Buried at Old Graveyard,
Carlisle, Pennsylvania.

Military • Continental Congress

John Armstrong was a Presbyterian from Northern Ireland who emigrated to Pennsylvania to utilize his surveying skills on behalf of the Penn family. He planned the city of Carlisle and served as a military commander before and during the French and Indian War. When the American Revolution began, he was a brigadier general in the Continental Army and then the Major General of the Pennsylvania Militia. Upon retiring from active duty in 1777, he was elected to the Continental Congress where he continued his advocacy for George Washington and later for the U.S. Constitution.

John Armstrong was born on October 13, 1717, in Brookeborough, County Fermanagh, in what is now Northern Ireland. The names of his parents and exact birthplace are lost to history, though there is some belief his father's name was James, and his parents married in 1704. He was one of fifteen children who included Margaret (1737-1817, the wife of Reverend George Duffield (1732-1790); and Rebecca (1738-1828), who was the wife of James Turner (1737-1803).

Armstrong learned surveying and civil engineering in Ireland before emigrating to Delaware and then Pennsylvania in the 1740s. The exact date of his arrival in Pennsylvania is unknown, but he married Rebecca Lyon Armstrong (1710–1797), the daughter of Archbald and

John Armstrong, Sr.

Ann Armstrong, in 1747. According to one biographer, the Armstrongs settled in the Kittatinny (Cumberland) Valley, west of the Susquehanna River. Armstrong worked as a surveyor for the Penns and laid out the first plan for the town of Carlisle, where he was an initial settler.

In 1749, Armstrong got involved in politics and was elected to the Pennsylvania Assembly representing the newly formed York County, which included the new town of Carlisle at that time.

He later surveyed the boundaries of Cumberland County, which was carved out of York County in 1750. In 1751, he was returned to the Pennsylvania Assembly, this time representing the newly formed Cumberland County. He then served in a series of appointed positions, including as a justice of the peace and as a magistrate or judge. In 1754, he was selected as a delegate for Pennsylvania to travel to Albany to negotiate with the colony of Connecticut regarding removing its settlers from the province. There had been a dispute between the colonies regarding borders.

John Armstrong Sr. (1717–1795)

During the French and Indian War, Armstrong served in the British military and used his surveying skills to assist with logistics, cutting trails through the forests for supply routes. He also planned a series of forts in the wilderness of western Pennsylvania.

In 1756, as the commander of Pennsylvania provincial forces, he led British and Pennsylvania troops against the natives in retaliation for the defeat of General Braddock. At Kittanning, a native stronghold along the Allegheny River, Armstrong defeated a large force of Delaware Indians led by chief "Captain Jacobs." Upon the death of the chief in battle, Armstrong's decisive victory led to the rise of Teedyuscung in his place. The new chief, realizing his precarious position, sued for peace. Armstrong, who was injured in the battle and lost seventeen men, became an instant celebrity among the colonials, known as the "Hero of Kittanning."

After the battle, back in Carlisle, Armstrong became a judge in the Court of Common Pleas and was the sole judicial authority for most of the region. He was well-respected for his temperament on the bench.

When General Forbes launched his expedition against Fort Duquesne in 1758, Colonel Armstrong led 2700 Pennsylvania troops. Seeing this large force, the French vacated and destroyed their fort. During this campaign, Armstrong became good friends with a young Virginia militia commander named Colonel George Washington.

In 1763, as part of the campaign against Chief Pontiac, General Armstrong led colonial forces against native Delaware and Monsey towns along the West Branch of the Susquehanna, burning them and destroying their corn.

During the years before the American Revolution, Armstrong continued in service to his community and congregation. In 1773, he was one of the founding trustees of what would become Dickinson College in Carlisle. When its namesake, John Dickinson, could not serve as president, Armstrong served in his place.

At the outbreak of the American Revolution, Armstrong was appointed a brigadier general in the Pennsylvania militia. On March 1, 1776, the Continental Congress gave him the same rank in the Continental Army. George Washington initially sent him to Charleston,

South Carolina where he utilized his engineering talents to construct the defenses there. Upon the arrival of General Charles Lee in early April, Armstrong returned to Pennsylvania. There, he was elevated to Major General of the Pennsylvania Militia. Meanwhile, in Charleston, Armstrong's defenses enabled Lee's rebels to withstand the Battle of Sullivan's Island in June 1776.

In charge of Pennsylvania forces, Armstrong saw action following the British invasion of Philadelphia in 1777. At the Battle of Brandywine on September 11, Armstrong's troops held the far left of the American line and guarded the army's supplies. Though the Americans lost, Armstrong was able to escape with the supplies after dark.

The following month, at the Battle of Germantown, Amstrong's forces led the American right, attempting to circumvent the British left to attack their rear. While the attack was going well, there was confusion in the fog leading to a friendly-fire incident between Adam Stephen's men and Anthony Wayne's troops. Despite marching to the center of Germantown, Armstrong's forces had to withdraw.

Following Germantown, with the opposing armies encamped, his health failing, and his old wounds complaining, Armstrong retired from active command at age sixty. He returned home to Carlisle.

On November 20, 1778, Armstrong was elected by the Pennsylvania Assembly to the Continental Congress. He was also re-elected the following year. His tenure of actual service was February 1779 to August 1780.

In a letter to his friend General Horatio Gates, Armstrong complained of the pride and politics of the various representatives who were not focused on the needs of the army. He felt serving in the military was easier. Armstrong also continued a steady correspondence with his friend, George Washington, offering advice and support.

Following his year and a half in Congress, Armstrong returned home to Carlisle and enjoyed a quiet retirement. He participated in numerous civic roles and was an ardent supporter of the new U.S. Constitution. However, it was his son John Jr. who attended the Confederation Congress during its waning months in 1787 and 1788, not him.

John Armstrong Sr. (1717–1795)

The grave of John Armstrong

John and Rebecca Armstrong were the parents of James Armstrong (1748–1828), who married Mary Stevenson (1766–1813), the daughter of George Stevenson, Esquire; and John Armstrong Jr. (1758–1843), who married Alida Livingston (1761–1822), the sister of Robert R. Livingston of the "Committee of Five" and Edward Livingston. John Jr. later became a Continental Congressman, U.S. Senator, and a controversial Secretary of War under President James Madison during the War of 1812.

John Armstrong Sr. died on March 9, 1795, at his home in Carlisle, Pennsylvania. He was laid to rest in the Old Graveyard in Carlisle. His passing was barely noted in the newspapers. One, *The American Minerva* of New York, merely stated, "Died on Monday the 9th instant, Gen. John Armstrong, in an advanced age, being a resident in this town for many years past."

Rebecca Armstrong passed away on November 16, 1797, joining her husband in the Old Cemetery.

In 1800, Pennsylvania created Armstrong County and put its seat at Kittanning.

Crispus Attucks
(1723–1770)

The Boston Massacre

Buried at Granary Burying Ground
Boston, Massachusetts

On March 5, 1770, in the city of Boston, a group of British soldiers were confronted by an ever-growing number of local citizens. The crowd that gathered was angry because one of the soldiers, Private White, had used the butt of his musket to deliver a blow to the head of a young local named Edward Garrick. Tension between the crowd, which continued to draw more Bostonians, and the soldiers continued to grow. Church bells rang out, arousing the curiosity of the locals. Among those joining the crowd was an American of African and Native American descent named Crispus Attucks.

Attucks was born in 1723 in Framingham, Massachusetts. Town histories describe him as a slave of Deacon William Brown. In 1750, Brown took out advertising offering a reward of ten pounds for the return of a runaway slave named Crispus. Whether he was a runaway slave or a free man in 1770 has been long debated by historians.

Attucks worked as a sailor and a whaler, and much of his adult life was spent at sea. On March 5, 1770, he was a member of the crew of a whaling ship that had docked in Boston Harbor. He was scheduled to leave Boston on a ship headed to North Carolina.

Some say that Attucks was the leader of a group of sailors who joined the crowd jeering the British soldiers. As the crowd grew, Private White

Crispus Attucks (1723–1770)

Crispus Attucks

believed that reinforcements were needed. As told in *The Boston Massacre: A Family History* by Serena Zabin, the additional soldiers arrived and were led up King Street by Captain Thomas Preston. The street was too narrow for both the crowd and the advancing soldiers. Their bayonets poked people as those gathered attempted to get out of the way. One word many in the crowd agreed they heard was "fire." Was it a command to the soldiers, or was it the taunts of the crowd saying, "You dare not fire." No one knew then, and no one knows now.

One of the witnesses, Jane Crothers, said she saw some in the crowd threatening to kill White as they threw snow, wood and ice at him. She said she heard a civilian ask Preston if he intended to open fire on the crowd. According to Crothers, Preston replied, "Sir, by no means, by no means." She later testified that she saw a man in a dark coat behind the soldiers who encouraged them to fire, saying, "Fire, by God, I'll stand by

"Boston Massacre, March 5th, 1770" by John H. Bufford based on a drawing by William L. Champney, ca.1856 Boston.

you." Again, according to Crothers, the man slapped one of the soldiers on the back, and he opened fire.

Others on the scene told different stories. Thomas Wilkinson. He said he saw nothing being thrown but heard this order given to the soldiers, "Fire, damn your Bloods, Fire." He said at this time the soldiers fired calmly and deliberately. When the dust cleared, five colonists were killed and six others wounded. Attucks took two bullets to the chest and is believed to have been the first to die. His body was taken to Faneuil Hall, where it would lay in state until March 8. At that time, he and the other victims were laid to rest in Boston's Granary Burying Ground. John Hancock and Samuel Adams, among other notable figures, are also buried here. At the time of his death, Attucks was appropriately 47 years of age.

John Adams successfully defended the soldiers who were brought to trial. The man who would become the second President of the United States called the crowd "a motley rabble Of saucy boys, negroes and mo-lattoes, Irish leagues and outlandish Jack Tarrs. Adams charged Attucks

Crispus Attucks (1723–1770)

with having "undertaken to be the hero of the night," and with having precipitated a conflict by his "mad behavior." It was Sam Adams, a cousin of John Adams, who named the incident the "Boston Massacre," ensuring the event would not be forgotten.

In 1858, Boston area abolitionists established "Crispus Attucks Day" to commemorate him. Abolitionists at the time pointed to Attucks as a hero of the Revolution and lauded him for playing a heroic role in the history of the United States. In 1886 the spot where Attucks fell was marked by a circle. In 1888, a monument standing 25 feet tall honoring

Grave marker at the Granary Burial Grounds for Crispus Attucks and others killed in the Boston Massacre.

Attucks and the other victims was erected on the Boston Common. In 1940, Attucks was honored with 1 of the 33 dioramas at the American Negro Exposition in Chicago. In 2002, the scholar Molefi Kete Asante listed Attucks as one of the 100 Greatest African Americans. There are multiple schools around the country named in his honor. Martin Luther King Jr. made a reference to Attucks in the introduction to *Why We Can't Wait* As an example of a man whose contribution to history provided a potent message of moral courage.

John Barry
(1745–1803)

The Commodore

Buried at St. Mary's Catholic Churchyard,
Philadelphia, Pennsylvania.

Military

John Barry was an Irish-born naval commander during the American Revolution who after the war became the first commodore in the new United States Navy. Many of his contemporaries dubbed him "The Father of the United States Navy," an epithet he shares with John Paul Jones, Joseph Hewes, and John Adams.

John Barry was born March 25, 1745, in a modest thatched-roof cottage at Ballysampson on Our Lady's Island in Tacumshane parish, County Wexford, Ireland. Barry's father was a tenant farmer who was soon evicted by his British landlord. The family next moved to nearby Rosslare on the coast where Barry's uncle was a fisherman. Young Barry soon found himself a ship's cabin boy thanks to his uncle and progressed from seaman, to able seaman, to a mate.

Barry grew to be six-feet four-inches in height, an imposing figure in those times. He was also intelligent. He learned navigational skills by combining mathematics, astronomy, and meteorology.

Around 1760, at the age of fifteen, he came to Philadelphia to find employment in the growing merchant trade. By twenty-one, he was a master seaman and earned command of his ship, *Barbados*. Barry

Commodore John Barry

developed a reputation as a fair captain who cared about the men working for him. He was also a devout Christian, beginning each morning by reading passages from his Bible.

"Big John" Barry made no less than nine trips to the West Indies without incident. This reliability, along with his personable nature, led to success in the shipping business. He moved up to a brigantine named the *Patty and Polly*, and then to a schooner named the *Industry*. During this time, Barry married Mary Clary (or Cleary) at Old St. Joseph's chapel in Philadelphia on October 24, 1768.

By 1772, Barry's abilities drew the attention of Meredith and Clymer, one of the premier mercantile businesses in Philadelphia. Reese Meredith hired him to command the *Peg*, a much larger vessel. Upon developing a friendship with Robert Morris, the financier, Barry moved to Willing, Morris, and Cadwalader where he took command of the 200-ton merchant ship *Black Prince*. During this time, Barry set the record (for the 18th century) of traveling 237 miles in 24 hours on a return voyage from England. Unfortunately, while at sea, Barry's wife passed away suddenly at only 29 back in Philadelphia on February 8, 1774. This loss affected Barry greatly.

At the outbreak of the American Revolution, Barry, a patriot from the start, sold his merchant ship *Black Prince* to the cause, outfitting his ship into a warship named *Alfred*, which became the flagship of commander Esek Hopkins. He was assigned to equip other ships for war, overseeing rigging, the piercing of gunports, strengthening of bulwarks, procuring powder and canvas, and loading provisions. Congress recognized this contribution by awarding him a Captain's commission. It was signed by John Hancock, President of Congress, on March 14, 1776, giving him command of his first warship, the brig *Lexington*. Three weeks later, on April 7, 1776, Barry was credited with the first capture of the war, the British sloop *Edward*, caught off the coast of Virginia after a one-hour battle. Barry reported to Congress:

> In sight of the Cape of Virginia
> April 7, 1776
> to the Marine Committee
>
> Gentlemen: I have the pleasure to acquaint you, that at 1:00 P.M. this day, I fell in with the sloop, *Edward* belonging to the *Liverpool* frigate. They killed two of our men and wounded two more. We shattered her in a terrible manner as you will see. I shall give you a particular account of the powder that was taken out of her, as well as my proceedings in general. I have the pleasure to acquaint you that all our people behaved with much courage. This victory had a tremendous psychological effect in boosting American morale, as it was the first capture of a British warship by a regularly commissioned American cruiser.

Barry brought the captured *Edward* into Philadelphia. On June 28, in what became known as the Battle of Turtle Gut Inlet, the brig *Nancy* ran aground while trying to elude the British blockade. Laden with barrels of powder, Barry ordered them rowed ashore during the night, leaving only 100 barrels aboard by dawn. A fuse was lit, and when the British sailors boarded in the morning, the powder exploded. Barry continued to captain the *Lexington* until October 18, 1776, capturing several more vessels during that time.

Next, Barry was given command of the 32-gun *Effingham*, a new frigate under construction in Philadelphia. Tories in Philadelphia offered Barry the tremendous sum of 15,000 guineas in gold or 20,000 pounds sterling plus a commission as a captain in the Royal Navy if he would hand over the *Effingham* to the British when it was ready to sail. Barry emphatically refused "the eyedee of being a treater."

With the *Effingham* under construction, Barry volunteered for the Continental Army. He served with a company of Marines under General John Cadwalader, who had been a part-owner of the shipping company with which he had been affiliated. As Cadwalader's aide-de-camp, Barry participated in the Battles of Trenton and Princeton. Washington chose Barry as a courier to convey the wounded through British lines and to carry a dispatch of a flag of truce to General Cornwallis.

On July 7, 1777, Barry married again, this time taking an attractive and popular Sarah "Sally" Keen Austin as his bride at Old Christ Church. The Reverend William White, rector, and founder of the American Episcopal Church officiated, though Sarah eventually converted to Barry's Catholic faith.

Later in 1777, as the British threatened Philadelphia, Barry had to scuttle the *Effingham*. He then took up command of a smaller craft, the USS *Delaware*. He focused on the destruction of the British hay forage in the region and disrupted shipping in the lower Delaware Bay, often running past British batteries. On March 8, 1778, Barry surprised two British armed sloops and a fortified schooner with seven small craft, including rowboats, barges, and longboats, capturing all three of the enemy vessels.

Later in 1778, Barry was given command of the 32-gun frigate USS *Raleigh* out of Boston. He captured three prizes during this time but learned his beloved brother Patrick was lost at sea with his ship *Union*, which was never heard from after leaving France. Barry's luck also seemed to run out in late September 1778 when the British frigate

John Barry (1745–1803)

Washington presents Barry with his commission

Unicorn and ship-of-the-line *Experiment* chased the *Raleigh* to Penobscot Bay in Maine. For two days, the *Raleigh* battled *Unicorn* until the foretopmast was cracked. Now in unfamiliar waters, cornered near Wooden Ball Island, Barry planned to save his crew and burn his ship. However, a traitorous crewmember prevented the destruction of the ship and the escape of all the crew. Barry did manage to get away with 88 men, two-thirds of his men, but the *Raleigh* was captured by the British.

While awaiting his next command, Barry wrote a signal book to improve communications between ships at sea. It was published first in 1780.

Barry was next in command of the 36-gun frigate *Alliance* in 1780. That December, he was assigned to convey Colonel John Laurens on a diplomatic mission to join Ben Franklin in France. Laurens was initially reluctant to go, but after being convinced by Alexander Hamilton and the Congress, he arrived on March 1781. Along the way, Barry engaged in battle with and subdued two British sloops of war and captured several prizes.

Barry's most famous naval battle happened off Newfoundland on May 28, 1781. The *Alliance* battled with two British sloops, *Atlanta* and *Trespassey*. The Alliance opened up and gained the initial advantage but was then becalmed. The two sloops managed to get in front and behind *Alliance* and rake her with fire causing considerable damage to the rigging and steerage. Undeterred, Barry continued the defense of his ship until he was struck in the left shoulder by canister projectiles. He continued to lead his men for another twenty minutes until he passed out from the loss of blood. He was then taken below to the ship's surgeon.

After the *Alliance*'s flag was shot away, the second in command, Lieutenant Hoysted Hacker, came to Barry while his wounds were being dressed. He urgently requested permission to surrender due to their dire position. Said Barry angrily, "No, Sir, the thunder! If this ship cannot be fought without me, I will be brought on deck. To your duty, Sir."

The crew raised a new flag, and the fight continued. As Hacker returned to the deck, luck turned for the better as the wind picked up. This filled *Alliance*'s sails, allowing her to swing about. The following broadsides on the inferior British vessels were devastating, resulting in the surrender of both ships.

This four-hour battle cost the British two ships, one dead captain, eleven dead sailors, and twenty-five wounded. Captain Edwards, the surviving British commander, came to the deck of *Alliance* to surrender, as was customary. He was led to Barry's cabin where he presented his sword. Barry received it, and then returned it saying, "I return it to you, Sir. You have merited it, and your king ought to give you a better ship. Here is my cabin, at your service. Use it as your own."

Barry continued at the helm of *Alliance* for the remainder of the war. While cruising the shipping lanes between Bermuda and Cape Sable, he captured four British ships. Off the Straits of Florida, while returning from Havana on March 1783, he encountered three British frigates seeking to intercept him while he escorted the *Duc de Lauzon* which was transporting 72,000 Spanish pieces of eight bound for the Continental Congress. Off Cape Canaveral, *Alliance* battled the British frigate, *Sybil*, shattering her rigging, masts, and hull. It was the last naval battle of the war.

John Barry (1745–1803)

The grave of John Barry

In the years immediately after the war, Barry returned to the maritime trade, and from 1787 to 1789 he helped to open commerce to China and the Orient while captaining the merchant ship *Asia*. While the Barrys had no children, they raised their nephews Michael and Patrick Hayes, who had been brought to Philadelphia from Ireland. They were the sons of Barry's deceased sister Eleanor. Young Patrick accompanied his uncle on these journeys to the Far East.

In the 1790s, under the direction of President George Washington, the United States Navy was reinstated in response to trouble with the Barbary Pirates. On June 5, 1794, Secretary of War Henry Knox informed Barry he had been selected senior Captain of the Federal Navy by the President with the advice and consent of the Senate. Barry immediately set about to construct and equip the first frigates of the United States Navy including his flagship 44-gun frigate the USS *United States*. The ship was ready for service in 1797. That year, on February 22, Barry was issued Commission Number 1 by President George Washington, backdated to June 4, 1794, dubbing him "Commodore." Barry was the first commissioned naval officer in the U.S.A. and its first flag officer.

Barry commanded the American fleet during the undeclared Quasi-War with France from 1798 to 1800. He captured several French merchant vessels and transported commissioners William Richardson Davie and Oliver Ellsworth to France to negotiate a new alliance.

Commodore Barry's last action in active service was as the squadron commander at Guadeloupe from 1798 to 1801.

Under the Adams administration, Barry requested a Department of the Navy be formed distinct from the Department of War. This was achieved, and government-funded naval facilities were established.

The popular Barry was so well-regarded President Jefferson retained his services despite reorganizing the military establishment. Barry was also responsible for training many of the naval heroes of the War of 1812, leading his contemporaries to declare him "The Father of the American Navy."

Later in life, Barry was socially active as a member of the Friendly Sons of St. Patrick, the Hibernian Fire Company, and the Society of the Cincinnati. He had also always been a member of the Charitable Captains of Ships Club providing relief to widows and orphans of lost sailors.

Barry remained the head of the United States Navy until his death from complications of asthma on September 12, 1803, at his country home "Strawberry Hill" a few miles outside of Philadelphia. Two days later, he received his country's salute in a full military burial in Philadelphia's Old St. Mary's Churchyard.

Barry was well-regarded by his peers, including John Paul Jones, who bequeathed to Barry, upon his death, the gold sword he had received when knighted by French King Louis XVI. Barry wore the sword during the Quasi-War. When he died, he gave the sword to Jones' favorite lieutenant, Richard Dale. The sword is now displayed at Jones' tomb at the U.S. Navy Academy in Annapolis, Maryland. Barry's Bible is showcased nearby, resting on the altar in the chapel.

Physician and friend Benjamin Rush eulogized Barry: "He fought often and once bled in the cause of freedom, but his habits of war did not lessen in him the peaceful virtues which adorn private life."

Commodore John Barry is memorialized in a multitude of ways:

- The U.S. Revenue Cutter *Commodore Barry*.
- Commodore Barry Park in Brooklyn, New York.

John Barry (1745–1803)

- Four U.S. Navy ships: USS Barry (DD-2) (1902–1920); USS Barry (DD-248) (1921–1945); USS Barry (DD-933) (1956–1983); USS Barry (DDG-52) (1992–present).
- World War II liberty ship SS John Barry.
- A large portrait of Commodore Barry at the Rhode Island State House in Providence.
- Title 16 of the Rhode Island Statutes (§ 16-20-3 – Days of special observance) requires observing September 13 as Commodore John Barry Day.
- Commodore Barry Bridge, which crosses the Delaware River from Chester, Pennsylvania to Bridgeport, New Jersey.
- John Barry Hall at Villanova University.
- Commodore Barry Club (Philadelphia Irish Center) Emlen Street & Carpenter Lane, Mount Airy, Philadelphia, Pennsylvania.
- Barry Township, Schuylkill County, Pennsylvania.
- Commodore John Barry Elementary School in Philadelphia, Pennsylvania.
- Commodore John Barry Elementary School in Chicago, Illinois.
- Commodore John Barry Division of Ancient Order of Hibernians, Annapolis, Maryland.
- John Barry Bar, Grand Hyatt Muscat, Muscat, Oman.
- September 13, Commodore John Barry Day in New Jersey public schools.
- Commodore John Barry Memorial Plaque at Staten Island Borough Hall.
- Plaques at Port Canaveral, Boston Common, and Old St. Mary's Church in Philadelphia.
- A life-sized bronze statue stands in Franklin Square in Washington, D.C.
- Barry Hall is one of six military barracks facilities at the United States Merchant Marine Academy.
- An entrance to the United States Naval Academy commemorates him.
- A large statue of Barry stands directly in front of the formal entrance to Independence Hall in Philadelphia, Pennsylvania.

GRAVES of our FOUNDERS

- A statue of Barry overlooks the Crescent Quay in Wexford town in Ireland. It was a gift to the village from the United States and was delivered by a United States Navy destroyer USS John R. Pierce (DD-753). The statue was unveiled in 1956, and each year a parade and wreath-laying ceremony takes place at the statue to celebrate "Barry Day," commemorated by the Irish Naval Service and the Minister for Defence.

Dr. Josiah Bartlett
(1729–1795)

First Vote for Independence

Buried at Plains Cemetery
Kingston, New Hampshire

**Continental Congress • Signer of the Declaration of Independence
Signer of the Articles of Confederation**

The first to vote for independence from Great Britain was the delegate from New Hampshire, who was also a physician. Dr. Josiah Bartlett said "Aye," and was then the second to sign the document after President John Hancock. Bartlett later signed the Articles of Confederation and served as the first governor of New Hampshire and Chief Justice of the New Hampshire Supreme Court.

Josiah Bartlett was born on November 21, 1729, in Amesbury, Massachusetts, the fifth child and fourth son of Deacon Stephen Bartlett, a shoemaker, and his wife Hannah (née Webster) Bartlett. Stephen was the son of Richard and Hannah (Emery) Bartlett, and according to one genealogical study, the Bartlett line can be traced back to John Bartlett, Sr., who came to Newbury, Massachusetts, in 1634, on the ship *Mary and John*. Josiah's maternal grandfather was said to be "wealthy in landed property."

Young Josiah study Latin and Greek in his teens but likely due to the family's circumstances, received a limited education. Soon, he was apprenticed to a relative, Dr. Nehemiah Ordway, with whom he studied medicine. At just twenty years of age, in 1750, and after three years of

Dr. Josiah Bartlett

studies, Josiah moved to Kingston, New Hampshire, and started medical practice. At the time, Kingston was a frontier community where his services were greatly needed, being the only doctor in the county. With the proceeds, in 1751, he purchased land and a farm.

Josiah married his first cousin, Mary Barton Bartlett (1730-1789), the daughter of his uncle Joseph and his wife, Sarah (née Hoyt) Bartlett, on January 15, 1754. Mary was from nearby Newton, New Hampshire. Together, the Bartletts had eleven children: Mary (1754), Lois (1756), Miriam (1758), Rhoda (1760), Hannah (1762, did not survive), Levi (1753), Josiah (1765, did not survive), Josiah (1768), Ezra (1770), Sarah (1773), and Hannah (1776, did not survive). Three sons and five grandsons later became physicians.

In years past, the Kingston area was the center of an epidemic of "throat distemper," serious for adults and often fatal for young children.

In 1754, the illness was back, and Bartlett experimented with therapies and drugs, discovering that Peruvian bark aided recovery, saving many.

Josiah Bartlett next became involved in politics. In March 1757, he was elected as a selectman for the town of Kingston, a position he held until 1775 when the town's government was dissolved by the royal governor at the outset of the Revolution.

In 1763, Bartlett was behind several real estate ventures, settling the town of Warren, New Hampshire, where Bartlett was the original grantee. He served in the same capacity for the villages of Wentworth and Sudbury, and was the proprietor for Salisbury and Perrystown (now Sutton).

In 1765, Bartlett was elected to the colonial assembly and joined in a three-year partnership for a medical practice with Dr. Amos Gale in Kingston.

In 1767, Bartlett became the colonel of the county militia, was appointed justice of the peace by Governor John Wentworth, and was asked to propose reforms to provincial laws.

The governor and Bartlett continued their close collaboration in 1770 when Wentworth asked Bartlett to help establish a system of equitable taxation for the colony. Following the Boston Massacre in March 1770, Bartlett was commissioned a lieutenant in the 7th New Hampshire Regiment in November.

By 1774, the friendship with Governor Wentworth was greatly strained. That year, in response to the Intolerable Acts following the Boston Tea Party, Bartlett was appointed to a committee of correspondence and attended the First Provincial Congress, held in Exeter, New Hampshire, after Wentworth dissolved the colonial assembly. This body sent delegates to the new Continental Congress in Philadelphia.

As tensions mounted later that year, the Bartlett home was destroyed by fire, allegedly set by Tories. After moving his family to their farmhouse, he commenced on reconstruction. Bartlett was selected as a delegate to the Continental Congress but declined so he could attend to his family and home. While still in New Hampshire, Bartlett alerted the state militia about a raid on British arms and gunpowder at Fort William and Mary in Portsmouth Harbor on December 14 and 15, 1774. Bartlett helped prepare for the British response. Angered at Bartlett's behavior and attendance at the Second Provincial Congress in January 1775, Governor Wentworth revoked Bartlett's various positions prior to being expelled.

Bartlett was elected to the Third Provincial Congress in the Spring of 1775 and wrote letters of support to Massachusetts following the clashes at Lexington and Concord. On August 23, 1775, Bartlett was elected as a delegate to the Second Continental Congress, and through early 1776, was the only representative from New Hampshire in Philadelphia, forcing him to participate on all of the committees. Bartlett wrote often to his wife. In one of the letters, he worried about potential outcomes, but left the results to higher powers:

> Kind Providence will order all things for the best, and if Sometimes affairs turn out Contrary to our wishes, we must make our selves Easy & Contented, as we are not Certain what is for the best.

During the second session, Bartlett was joined by delegates William Whipple and Matthew Thornton. On July 1, 1776, when the draft of the Declaration of Independence was circulating, Bartlett wrote to John Langdon, then the President of New Hampshire:

> The affair of Independency has been this day determined in a Committee of the whole House; by next Post, I expect you will receive a formal declaration with the reasons; the Declaration before Congress is, I think, a pretty good one. I hope it will not be spoiled by canvassing in Congress.

When the question of declaring independence from Britain was proposed, the vote was processed from the northernmost colony to the southernmost. Thus, New Hampshire was called first, and Bartlett the first delegate. He voted in the affirmative and became the first to vote for independence.

During the remainder of July 1776, Bartlett was very interested in what form the new government would take. He shared with John Langdon the arrival of the constitutions of Virginia and New Jersey, which he suggested would be good models for New Hampshire.

On August 2, 1776, when many of the delegates signed the Declaration of Independence, Bartlett was the second to sign, following John Hancock, the President of Congress. Bartlett returned to New

Hampshire in December 1776 and declined another term in Congress. Instead, he joined the militia as a doctor under General John Stark. At the Battle of Bennington in August 1777, he cared for wounded soldiers.

In 1778, Bartlett was named to a legislative committee in New Hampshire to consider the adoption of the Articles of Confederation. Bartlett reluctantly agreed to again join the Continental Congress in Philadelphia, where he signed the Articles of Confederation on behalf of New Hampshire and then returned home.

In 1779, Bartlett served as a judge on the Court of Common Pleas and as a member of the State Executive Council. Bartlett was elected to the New Hampshire State Legislature and named a delegate to the state's constitutional convention.

Despite not being a lawyer, Bartlett was appointed a justice on the State Superior Court in 1781. In 1782, he was appointed to the New Hampshire Supreme Court. In 1784, he presided over the inaugural session of the new state legislature. In 1788, Bartlett was named Chief Justice of the New Hampshire Supreme Court and was a delegate, and part-time chairman, of the state's convention to adopt the U.S. Constitution. Bartlett supported ratification, which occurred June 21, 1788. The legislature then named Bartlett as one of the state's first Senators, but Bartlett declined, his wife had failing health and passed away on July 14, 1789.

In 1790, Bartlett was selected as the Chief Executive of New Hampshire ("governor") under the new state constitution. He was re-elected three times. In 1792, he was the state's first popularly elected governor. He started the New Hampshire Medical Society, and upon his retirement as governor, became the society's first president.

Less than a year after his final term as governor, Bartlett suffered a stroke on May 19, 1795, and died in Kingston at age 65. He was buried next to his wife in the family sarcophagus at the Congregationalist Church in Kingston (now Plains Cemetery).

Bartlett's son of the same name (1768–1838) served in the US House of Representatives in the Twelfth Congress (1811–1813). A distant relative, Roscoe Gardner Bartlett also served as a Congressman more recently (1993–2013).

The town of Bartlett, New Hampshire, is named after Josiah. Relatives still live in the home at 156 Main Street in Kingston, now a historic landmark. A bronze statue of Bartlett stands in the town square in Amesbury, Massachusetts, and his portrait hands in the New Hampshire State House in Concord. It was drawn from the original by John Trumbull. Bartlett's name dons an elementary school, and he is the subject of a historical marker on New Hampshire Route 111 in Kingston. The Bartlett School operated in Amesbury, Massachusetts, and is now known as the Bartlett Museum, a nonprofit corporation.

The main character in the NBC drama series *The West Wing* was President Josiah Bartlet. Though a fictional character with a slightly different spelling, this Josiah played by Martin Sheen claimed lineage to the signer of the Declaration of Independence.

Grave of Dr. Josiah Bartlett

Richard Bassett
(1745–1815)

Senator #1

Buried at Wilmington & Brandywine Cemetery,
Wilmington, Delaware

U.S. Constitution

Richard Bassett, a native of Delaware, was an attorney, politician, Revolutionary War soldier, signer of the U.S. Constitution, U.S. senator, Chief Justice of the Court of Common Pleas, governor, and a United States circuit judge. According to Senate records, he is ranked as senator #1 in United States history.

Richard Bassett was born April 2, 1745, in Cecil County, Maryland, the son of Arnold Bassett, a farmer and tavern-keeper, and his wife, Judith (née Thompson) Bassett. After being abandoned by his father, Bassett was raised by Peter Lawson, a relative of his mother, from whom he later inherited his Bohemia Manor estate.

Bassett attended preparatory schools and then pursued a career in the law, studying in Philadelphia. He was admitted to the Delaware bar in 1770 and practiced law in Kent County, near Dover. He also prospered as a planter and eventually came to own Bohemia Manor and homes in Dover and Wilmington. Focusing on religious and charitable pursuits, he rose among the local gentry and was known for his hospitality and philanthropy.

Bassett married twice, first to Mary Ennals and second to Betsy Garnett. He fathered several children, including Anne "Nancy" Bassett, who later married James Asheton Bayard II. Bassett was a devout Methodist, held religious meetings at Bohemia Manor, and supported the church financially.

A natural politician, Bassett was elected by his fellow citizens of Kent County in 1774 to serve on the Boston Relief Committee. This group sought to collect contributions for those suffering from the hardships of the Coercive Acts passed by Parliament. Bassett soon found himself in the company of Caesar Rodney, his brother Thomas, and John Haslet, who would command Delaware's regiment in the Continental Army. Bassett served on the Kent County Council of Safety and was a member of the state constitutional convention in 1776. He was also a state senator and representative.

Bassett was integrally involved with military affairs, planning the mobilization in Delaware. He helped to organize Haslet's regiment and selected officers based on merit. Haslet's regiment was later judged among the best under Washington's command. Bassett was also effective in raising troops for Washington's Flying Camp and helped organize Captain Thomas Rodney's Dover Light Infantry, which saw action in the Trenton-Princeton campaign late in 1776. When the British entered the Chesapeake Bay in the summer of 1777 with their sights on Philadelphia, Bassett volunteered for service and joined General Caesar Rodney to delay the British advance. After the British left Philadelphia, Bassett returned to Kent County, where he assumed command of the Dover Light Horse cavalry unit.

The service in the military hardened Bassett, who became more serious and direct as a leader rather than the affable socialite. He filled several political roles, including as a member of the Delaware Legislative Council in 1782 and the Delaware House of Representatives in 1786. Also, that year he represented Delaware at the Annapolis Convention.

The following year, he was a delegate to the Constitutional Convention. Though a relatively quiet delegate, Bassett strongly supported the Great Compromise designed to protect the rights of the small states. It called for a national legislature that gave an equal voice to all thirteen states in a Senate composed of two senators from each but based representation in a House of Representatives on population. Bassett signed the U.S.

Constitution and was then a key member of the Delaware ratifying convention making Delaware the first state.

Bassett returned to his law practice in Wilmington from 1787 to 1789, at which point he was elected as a U.S. senator on March 4, 1789, serving until March 3, 1793. Among the first U.S. senators, he is listed as the first U.S. senator on the seniority ranking due to being first alphabetically. In the Senate, Bassett was allied with the moderate wing of the Federalist party being organized by Vice President John Adams. In that capacity, he voted in favor of the president's power to remove governmental officers and against Hamilton's plan for the federal assumption of state debts. Reflecting the continuing concerns of the small states, Bassett was the first to vote for locating the new national capital away from New York and Pennsylvania in an independent federal district on the banks of the Potomac River.

Bassett was a member of the Delaware state constitutional convention in 1792, playing a principal role, along with John Dickinson, in drafting a new constitution for Delaware.

From 1793 to 1799, Bassett served as the first chief justice of Delaware's court of common pleas. In 1796 he served as a member of the Electoral College in the presidential election, casting his votes for John Adams.

From 1799 to 1801, Bassett served as the fourth governor of Delaware. His focus was on the revitalization of the Delaware militia and worked to establish a continental army.

On February 18, 1801, President John Adams nominated Bassett to the U.S. Circuit Court through one of his "midnight appointments." He was confirmed by the U.S. Senate on February 20 and served until the court was abolished on July 1, 1802, by Jeffersonian Republicans.

Bassett spent the rest of his life on his plantation known as Bohemia Manor in Cecil County, Maryland. He died there on September 15, 1815. Said Reverend Henry Boehm of the place,

> This mansion, let it be remarked, which was distinguished for its antiquity, for the splendid paintings that adorned its walls, for the hospitality that reigned there, and as the home of Bishop Asbury

when he preached on Bohemia Manor, was burned down many years ago.

Bassett was initially interred in a vault at Bohemia Manor in Cecil County, Maryland. An elaborate funeral was held at the estate, but no religious services were performed at the vault due to the large turnout. Some years later, after the fire, the vault was broken into, and the graves disturbed. In 1865, Bassett's remains were moved to Wilmington and Brandywine Cemetery in Wilmington, Delaware.

Recalled his friend, Reverend Henry Boehm,

> ... at one time, Governor Bassett was a very fashionable man, and being rich, had his good things in this life. But after his conversion, he was as humble and teachable as a little child. At this remote period, it is impossible to have a correct idea of the position he once occupied and the influence he exerted in favor of the church of his choice, in whose annals he should ever have a prominent place.

The tomb containing the body of Richard Bassett

In person, Governor Bassett was a stout-built man of medium height and looked as if he was made for service. His countenance was full of benignity, his eye was very expressive, and his voice strong and musical. He was distinguished for benevolence and was given to hospitality. He had three homes, residing part of the time in Dover, then on Bohemia Manor, and then in Wilmington. He has entertained over one hundred persons at one time. His heart was as large as his mansion.

Bassett was the grandfather of U.S. Senators from Delaware; Richard H. Bayard and James A. Bayard Jr. Bassett Street in Madison, Wisconsin, is named after him.

Edward Biddle
(1738—1779)

Speaker of the Pennsylvania Assembly

Buried at St. Paul's Cemetery,
Baltimore, Maryland

Continental Association

Edward Biddle, a native of Pennsylvania, represented that state in the First and Second Continental Congresses and signed the Continental Association. He was connected via marriage to the Ross family of Philadelphia and an uncle of Richard and Nicholas Biddle.

Edward Biddle was born in 1738 in Philadelphia, Pennsylvania, one of ten children of William Biddle (1698-1756) and his wife, Mary (née Scull) Biddle (1709-89). William's grandparents, William and Sarah Kempe Biddle, were Quakers who emigrated from Birlingham Parish, Worcester, England, in 1681 and settled in Mount Hope, New Jersey. Mother Mary was the daughter of Nicholas Scull, the surveyor-general of Pennsylvania.

Edward's father moved to Philadelphia before Edward's birth. Edward's brothers were Judge James Biddle, President Judge of the first judicial district, Commodore Nicholas Biddle, and Charles Biddle, Vice-President of the Supreme Executive Council of Pennsylvania.

Biddle's education was in the common schools, studying Latin and other languages, literature, philosophy, and other subjects. He then attended the Academy of Philadelphia (now the University of Pennsylvania) from 1752 to 1755, working as a tutor in English for a while.

Edward Biddle (1738–1779)

Edward Biddle

With the outbreak of the French and Indian War in 1754, Biddle joined the Pennsylvania militia as an ensign. He wrote a letter to his father in Philadelphia, describing the alarm in Reading on November 16, 1755,

> My Dearest Father:—I am in so much horror and confusion I scarcely know what I am writing. The drum is beating to arms and bells ringing and all the people under arms. Within these two hours, we have had different though too certain accounts all corroborating with each other, and this moment is an express arrived, dispatched by Michael Reis, at Tulpehocken, eighteen miles above this town, who left about thirty of their people engaged with about an equal number of Indians at the Reis'. This exclaim against the

Quakers and some are scarcely restrained from burning the houses of those few who are in this town. Oh, my country! My bleeding country! I commend myself to the divine God of armies. Give my dutiful love to my dearest mother and my best love to brother Jemmy.

I am, honored sir, your most affectionate and obedient son,

E. Biddle.

Sunday, 1 o'clock. I have rather lessened than exaggerated our melancholy account.

Biddle served for the duration of the war, present at the taking of Forts Duquesne and Niagara. He was promoted to captain in 1763 and received five thousand acres of land for his service.

Biddle, at 23, married Elizabeth Ross on June 6, 1761. The couple had two daughters, Abigail and Catherine, who lived to adulthood. Elizabeth was the sister of George Ross, who was later a delegate to the Continental Congress and signer of the Declaration of Independence. The famed seamstress Betsy Ross was the wife of Elizabeth's nephew.

After Biddle returned from the war, he read law at the offices of George Ross. By 1767, Biddle was admitted to the bar, and the couple moved to Reading, Pennsylvania, where he practiced law. In 1768, Biddle was elected to the American Philosophical Society. He also became interested in politics and was elected to represent Berks County in the Pennsylvania Provincial Assembly, serving until that body was abolished during the Revolution and then the rebel assembly. Biddle drafted legislation to remove settlers from land that had not yet been purchased from the Indians and lobbied against taxation without representation from Britain by drafting petitions to King George III. He was elected the 28th Speaker on October 14, 1774, replacing James Galloway. Biddle served on seven committees, including the Committee of Correspondence.

As the Revolution loomed, on July 22, 1774, the Pennsylvania Assembly sent a split delegation to the Continental Congress, including moderates Galloway, Humphreys, and Rhoads, and radicals Biddle, Mifflin, Morton, and Ross. Biddle attended sessions from September 5

Edward Biddle (1738–1779)

to October 26, 1774. During his time in the Congress, Biddle was a member of the committee that drafted the Declaration of Rights and signed the Continental Association. He also oversaw the printing of the resolutions that passed Congress.

On January 23, 1775, Biddle traveled to Philadelphia from Reading. While crossing the Schuylkill River, he fell overboard into the ice-cold river. Forced to sleep in wet clothes, he caught cold and developed chronic rheumatism, leading to his deteriorating health and loss of sight in one eye. Biddle attended Congress from May 10 through July 1775 and signed the Olive Branch Petition. He did not attend Congress for the remainder of 1775 or during 1776.

Wrote John Adams to his wife, Abigail, on July 23, 1775,

> There is a young gentleman from Pennsylvania, whose name is Wilson, whose fortitude, rectitude, and abilities too, greatly outshine his master's. Mr. Biddle, the Speaker, has been taken off by sickness, Mr. Mifflin is gone to the camp, Mr. Morton is ill too so that this province has suffered by the timidity of two overgrown fortunes. The dread of confiscation or caprice, I know not what, has influenced them too much, yet they were for taking arms and pretended to be very valiant.

In a letter to fellow Connecticut delegate Joseph Trumbull, Silas Deane wrote in September 1775,

> The Congress is well-nigh full, little Business has yet been done, but This Week it will be seriously entered upon, and I wish in Vain, that Mr. [Thomas] Mifflin [of Pennsylvania] was here. Mr. Biddle continues dangerously ill, Mr. [James] Willson [sic; should be Wilson] at Fort Pitt on an Indian Treaty, and Mr. [Thomas] Willing [of Pennsylvania] a Constant attendant on Congress, will give Mr. Mifflin a proper Idea of the representation of this Colony, to whom present my sincerest respects.

In his memoir, General James Wilkinson wrote,

I took Reading in my route and passed some days in that place, where I had several dear and respected friends, and among them Edward Biddle, Esq., a man whose public and private virtues commanded respect and excited admiration from all persons; he was Speaker of the last Assembly of Pennsylvania under the Proprietary government, and in the dawn of the Revolution devoted himself to the cause of his country, and successfully opposed the overbearing influence of Joseph Galloway. Ardent, eloquent, and full of zeal, by his exertions during several days and nights of obstinate, warm, and animated discussion in extreme sultry weather, he overheated himself and brought on an inflammatory rheumatism and surfeit, which radically destroyed his health, and ultimately deprived society of one of its greatest ornaments, and his country of a statesman, a patriot, and a soldier; for he had served several campaigns in the war of 1756, and if his health had been spared would, no doubt, have occupied the second or third place in the revolutionary armies.

Back home, in Berks County, Biddle served on the Committee of Correspondence from 1774-1775 and the Committee of Observation and Inspection from 1774-1776. He was again appointed to serve in Congress in 1778 but declined due to rapidly failing health.

At only 41, Edward Biddle died in Chatsworth, Maryland, at his daughter's home near Baltimore, on September 5, 1779. He was buried in St. Paul's churchyard in Baltimore. Wrote a "Friend of Justice" in *The Pennsylvania Packet*, eulogizing Biddle, "The name of Col. Biddle will always be dear to those who knew the critical situation of our affairs in the year 1774. No difficulties or dangers appalled him. His eloquence in the counsels of our State, as well as in Congress, flashed like lightning with equal force upon the dignified Tory and temporizing Whig."

Joseph Reed, President of the Supreme Executive Council for Pennsylvania, remarked,

> On Thursday last, after a very lingering illness, died at Baltimore, in the forty-first year of his age, that great lawyer, Hon. Edward

Biddle, of Reading, in this State. In early life, as captain in our provincial forces, his military virtues so highly distinguished him that Congress designed him to high rank in the American army, which, however, his sickness prevented; his practice at the bar for years having made his great abilities and integrity known, the county of Berks unanimously elected him one of their representatives in Assembly, who soon made him their speaker and a delegate in Congress, and the conduct of the patriot did honor to their choice. As a public character, very few were equal to him in talents or noble exertion of them, so in private life, the son, the husband, the father, brother, friend and neighbor, and master had in him a pattern not to be excelled. Love to his country, benevolence, and every manly virtue rendered him an object of esteem and admiration to all that knew him.

John Blair Jr.
(1732–1800)

Grand Master of Virginia

Buried at Bruton Parish Churchyard
Williamsburg, Virginia

Signer of the US Constitution • US Supreme Court

John Blair, Jr., was a lawyer from Williamsburg, Virginia, whose family had close ties to the College of William and Mary and the colonial government. Blair represented Virginia at the US Constitutional Convention and signed the resulting document. He was then appointed one of the first Associate Justices of the US Supreme Court.

Blair was born in Williamsburg, Virginia, on April 17, 1732. He was one of twelve children of John Blair, a member of the Virginia House of Burgesses, and his wife, Mary (née Monro), the granddaughter of Reverend John Monro of St. John's Parish, King William County, Virginia. The elder Blair served in the Virginia colonial government as a burgess, on the Governor's Council, and as acting Royal Governor on four occasions. Dr. Archibald Blair, the paternal grandfather, was also a member of the House of Burgesses. His brother, Reverend James Blair, was the founder and president of the College of William and Mary. Upon Reverend James's passing, John Senior inherited most of the estate.

Both father and son were graduates of the College of William and Mary. Young John completed his degree in 1754. He then went to London to study law at the Middle Temple in 1755. Blair married his

John Blair Jr. (1732–1800)

John Blair, Jr.

cousin, Jean Balfour (1736–1792) in Edinburgh, Scotland, while visiting in 1756. The couple had two children. Blair was admitted to the Virginia bar in 1757.

One of Blair's first assignments was an appointment as representative in the House of Burgesses for the College of William and Mary at a time when his father was on the Governor's Council. Blair served in this capacity from 1766 to 1799. He also served other roles in the colonial government through 1780.

Blair became involved in the patriot cause in Virginia, joining George Washington and others in 1770 and 1774 in the declaration of nonimportation agreements in response to unjust taxes imposed by the British Parliament. Blair also joined in supporting the people of Boston in 1775 following the Intolerable Acts.

In 1776, Blair helped to prepare the Virginia Declaration of Rights and the new Virginia Constitution. During the American Revolution, Blair served as a judge in several state courts and was a highly respected jurist, staying out of public political debates. He also served on Governor Patrick Henry's Privy Council of advisors from 1776 to 1778. In 1782, as a judge on the Virginia Court of Appeals, Blair ruled that courts could declare legislative acts unconstitutional. The case, *The Commonwealth of Virginia v. Caton el al* helped set precedence for the US Supreme Court's later case, *Marbury v. Madison*.

Throughout his life, Blair was a devout Freemason. He was a Master of the Williamsburg Lodge and organized the formation of the Grand Lodge of Virginia in 1777. Blair was elected the Grand Master of the Virginia Lodge on October 13, 1778.

As an adherent of James Madison and proponent of national union, Blair joined the Constitutional Convention of 1787, but there is no account of his speaking or serving on any committees. He signed the document with quiet approval. He then pushed for its ratification by Virginia.

On September 24, 1789, President George Washington nominated Blair to the US Supreme Court as one of the five associate justices serving with Chief Justice John Jay. He had sought "the first characters of the Union" for the body. Blair wrote in response to Washington, "When I considered the great importance, as well as the arduous nature of the duties, I could not but entertain some fears." Nevertheless, he "determined to make an experiment, whether I may be able to perform the requisite services, with some degree of satisfaction, in respect both to the Public and my self."

The Senate confirmed him two days later, and Blair served until October 25, 1795, when he resigned. Only thirteen cases were decided by the court over those first six years. Blair was a proponent of the supremacy of the Constitution, where appropriate, in all matters legal in the new country. Blair wrote regarding one decision, "The constitution of the United States is the only fountain from which I shall draw; the only authority to which I shall appeal."

James Sullivan, attorney general of Massachusetts, wrote to United States Senator William Bingham, "I think the President has been very fortunate in the appointment of Judges. We are much pleased with Judge

John Blair Jr. (1732–1800)

Grave of John Blair

Blair who has been with us. His candor ease politeness and learning are acknowledged and I am no less pleased with his independence."

Blair's resignation was due to health reasons. At the time of his resignation, he wrote the president. "A strange disorder of my head, which has lately compel'd me to neglect my official duties, . . . has for some time past made me contemplate the resignation of my office, as an event highly probable . . . I return you now the commission by which I have been so highly honoured."

Upon learning of Blair's retirement, Senator William Plumer from New Hampshire wrote, "I consider him as a man of good abilities, not indeed a Jay, but far superior to Cushing, a man of firmness, strict integrity and of great candour."

After Jean's death in 1792, Blair became a widower and returned to Williamsburg following his resignation, spending the rest of his life there. In 1797, Blair wrote to his sister about another health episode, "I happened to be employed in some algebraical exercises . . . when all at once a torpid numbness seized my whole face and I found my intellectual powers much weakened, and all was confusion. My tongue partook of the distress, and some words I was not able to articulate distinctly, and a general difficulty of remembering words at all."

Blair passed away on August 31, 1800, and is buried in the churchyard of Bruton Parish Church in Williamsburg. He was 68 years old.

Blair Street in Madison, Wisconsin, was named in his honor. John Blair House remains in the town of Williamsburg as a historic site, part of which was the original house of James Blair.

Richard Bland
(1710–1776)

Planter and Pamphleteer

Buried at Jordan Point Plantation, on the Jordan Point Manor
Prince George County, Virginia

Signer of Continental Association • Continental Congress

Richard Bland was a wealthy plantation owner from Prince George County, Virginia, who was orphaned at a young age. Raised by his aunts and uncles, Bland was very close to cousins Peyton Randolph and Thomas Jefferson via his late mother's Randolph line. Bland was a longtime member of the Virginia House of Burgesses who was an early patriot, challenging the right of the British Parliament to impose taxes. Bland was elected to the First Continental Congress, where he was one of the oldest members. He signed the Continental Association.

Bland was born May 6, 1710, at either Jordan's Point Plantation in Prince George County, Virginia, or Bland House in Williamsburg, Virginia. He was the oldest son of Richard Bland, a wealthy planter, and his second wife, Elizabeth (née Randolph), a sister of Richard and William Randolph. The elder Bland owned a thousand-acre plantation along the James River, about sixty-five miles north of the Chesapeake Bay. Both parents were from old Virginia families.

In 1720, during Richard's tenth year, his mother died on January 22 and his father on April 6. Richard and his four siblings were orphaned and raised by their uncles, William and Richard Randolph. These men

Richard Bland

acted as guardians, looked after the plantation, and raised and educated the children. During this time, Richard became very close to his first cousin, Peyton Randolph, a relationship that would last throughout his life.

The heir to an incredible estate, Blair was educated at the College of William and Mary and Edinburgh University in Scotland. He studied law, though he never practiced in court as an attorney. He was admitted to the Virginia bar in 1746.

Bland was married three times: first to Anne Poythress in 1730 until her death in 1758; for only eight months in 1759 to Martha Massie, a widow who passed away that same year; and lastly in 1760 to Elizabeth Blair Bolling, until her death in 1775. Richard and Anne had twelve children, including six sons and six daughters.

Bland first served as a justice of the peace in Prince George County. He was made a militia officer in 1739 and was often referred to as "Colonel" Bland in later years. Bland was elected to the Virginia House of Burgesses in 1742, serving 33 years until 1775. He wrote several pamphlets over these years pertaining to the clergy and to colonial government.

In 1766, in response to the Sugar Act of 1764 and the Stamp Act of 1765, he penned the pamphlet *An Inquiry into the Rights of the British Colonies*, questioning Parliament's right to impose taxes on the colonies. Wrote Bland:

> The Question is whether the Colonies are represented in the British Parliament or not? You affirm it to be an indubitable Fact that they are represented, and from thence you infer a Right in the Parliament to impose Taxes of every Kind upon them. You do not insist upon the Power, but upon the Right of Parliament to impose Taxes upon the Colonies. This is certainly a very proper Distinction, as Right and Power have very different Meanings, and convey very different Ideas; For had you told us that the Parliament of Great Britain have Power, by the Fleets and Armies of the Kingdom, to impose Taxes and to raise Contributions upon the Colonies, I should not have presumed to dispute the Point with you; but as you insist upon the Right only, I must beg Leave to differ from you in Opinion, and shall give my Reasons for it.

Around this same time, James Otis, Jr. made similar arguments in Massachusetts. John Adams later paraphrased Otis, summarizing the protest as "Taxation without Representation is Tyranny." Bland, Otis, and others made similar arguments for this ancient concept, harkening back to chapter 12 of the *Magna Carta*, "(n)o scutage or aid is to be levied in our kingdom, save by the common counsel of our kingdom."

As tensions increased with the British, Bland was appointed to Virginia's Committee of Correspondence in 1773. In response to a call for a Continental Congress to convene in Philadelphia in October 1774, Bland was elected on August 5, though he still hoped for reconciliation with Britain. He then traveled to Philadelphia with his fellow Virginia delegates. Bland attended what became known as the First Continental Congress in October 1774. John Adams described Bland as a "learned, bookish man" in his diary. Concepts from Bland's pamphlet made it into Congress's Declaration of Rights on October 14, 1774. The Congress then signed the Continental Association on October 20, 1774.

Following the Battles of Lexington and Concord, Bland returned for the May 1775 session of Congress but declined to accept the appointment to another term on account of his health. Instead, he returned to Virginia with Peyton Randolph, now convinced the path to independence was necessary. There, he joined an eleven-man Committee of Safety that governed the colony following the collapse of the royal government. Bland also attended the Virginia Convention from December 1775 to June 1776, determined to establish a new constitution for the colony.

Bland next returned to Williamsburg, and soon after, on October 26, 1776, he collapsed in the street. He was removed to the house of John Tazewell, a friend, where he died later that night at the age of 66. Bland

Grave of Richard Bland

was buried on the Jordan Point Plantation, on the Jordan Point Manor, next to his father and other relatives. His tombstone reads, "In Memory, Richard Bland, 1710-1776. *Sperate, Fortes, Et Virite.*" A nearby plaque describes him "as [a] political pamphleteer, constitutional historian, scholar, attorney and public servant [who] championed public rights and represented Virginia in the First and Second Continental Congresses and in all five of Virginia's Revolutionary Conventions."

Bland is further described in the *Dictionary of Virginia Biography*: "[He] was a Virginia planter and statesman whose prolific writings on the colonial right to self-governance helped shape Virginia political opinion in the years leading up to the American Revolution."

Richard Bland College, the junior college of the College of William and Mary, and Bland County in Virginia are named in his honor.

Much of Bland's library was acquired by Thomas Jefferson, who later donated it to the Library of Congress in 1815. Thomas Jefferson remembered his cousin when writing to Thomas Leiper that year:

> Your characters are inimitably and justly drawn. I am not certain if more might not be said of Colonel Richard Bland. He was the most learned and logical man of those who took prominent lead in public affairs, profound in constitutional lore, a most ungraceful speaker . . . He would set out on sound principles, pursue them logically till he found them leading to the recipice [sic] which he had to leap, start back alarmed, then resume his ground, go over it in another direction, be led again by the correctness of his reasoning to the same place, and again back about, and try other processes to reconcile right and wrong, but finally left his reader and himself bewildered between the steady index of the compass in their hand, and the phantasm to which it seemed to point. Still there was more sound matter in his pamphlet than in the celebrated Farmer's letters which were really but an *ignis fatuus*, misleading us from true principles.

Elias Boudinot
(1740–1821)

President During the Treaty of Paris

Buried at Saint Mary's Episcopal Churchyard,
Burlington, New Jersey

Military • US Congress • Mint Director

Elias Boudinot was a deeply devout Christian, abolitionist, lawyer, statesman, and soldier who served under George Washington as an intelligence officer and commissary for prisoners of war. Boudinot served in the Continental Congress and was its president at the end of the Revolution. He later served as a member of the US House of Representatives and as the Director of the US Mint. In 1816, he founded the American Bible Society which has since distributed billions of Bibles worldwide. As a Congressman, he proposed a national day of Thanksgiving.

Boudinot was born on May 2, 1740, in Philadelphia, Pennsylvania, to Elias Boudinot III and his wife, Mary Catherine (née Williams) Boudinot. The elder Boudinot was a merchant and silversmith who was a neighbor and friend of Benjamin Franklin. Boudinot's paternal lineage was French Huguenot. His mother's ancestors were Welsh. The couple married in 1729 and had nine children, five of whom reached adulthood. Sister Annis became the first published female poet in the colonies. Brother Elisha later became Chief Justice of the New Jersey Supreme Court.

Boudinot was tutored in the classics at home and then studied law under Richard Stockton in Princeton, New Jersey, who had married his

Elias Boudinot (1740–1821)

Elias Boudinot

sister Annis. In 1760, Boudinot was admitted to the New Jersey bar and set up a prosperous law practice in Elizabeth, New Jersey. On April 21, 1762, he married Hannah Stockton, his brother-in-law's younger sister. The Boudinots had nine children, four of whom survived to adulthood. One daughter, Susan, later married William Bradford, who became the Chief Justice of Pennsylvania and US Attorney General in the Washington administration.

Boudinot largely avoided politics prior to the Revolution. In 1774, he joined the Essex County Committee of Correspondence and chaired the county's Committee of Safety. He was also elected to the Provincial Congress of New Jersey in 1775. During these early months, Boudinot held out for reconciliation with England, even after the first shots were fired at Lexington and Concord. At a meeting in New Brunswick in April 1776, he voted against Dr. John Witherspoon's call for New Jersey's independence, though he hoped the Continental Congress would address the matter. Wrote Boudinot later:

> There appeared a general Approbation of the Measure, and I strongly suspected a universal Acquiescence of both Committees & Audience in approving the doctor's scheme... I never felt myself in a more mortifying Situation... Two of the Committee had delayed the Question by speaking in favor of it, but no one had spoken in Opposition, till I arose and in a Speech of about half an Hour or better, stated my peculiar Situation and endeavored to show the Fallacy of the Doctor's Arguments.

As Congress declared independence, with his brother-in-law's signature, Boudinot assisted the Patriot cause. He promoted enlistments, loaned money for supplies, and was the aide-decamp to William Livingston of the New Jersey militia. He was also involved in spy activities monitoring the British during the occupation of New York City from Staten Island and Long Island.

Impressed with Boudinot's work with Livingston, George Washington appointed him the Commissary General for Prisoners on May 5, 1777. Congress's Board of War agreed, and Boudinot was commissioned as a colonel in the Continental Army, serving until July 1778. In this role, he was responsible for supplying the American prisoners held by the British. Boudinot was soon at odds with the Congress, who were unreasonable regarding prisoner exchanges with the British. Where General Howe had suggested simple officer for officer, soldier for soldier, citizen for citizen exchanges, the Congress demanded hard currency. This made Boudinot's job more difficult and risked the treatment of prisoners. On March 8, 1778, he was summoned to Philadelphia for a meeting with an oversight committee of Congress where he explained his position for the fair treatment of prisoners on both sides as both moral and ethical and reflective of the wishes of General Washington. Boudinot, who had been elected to the Congress months earlier and had not taken his seat, filed his report. He had used his own money to fund the supplies for the prisoners. Wrote Boudinot at the time:

> When I found every application to obtain hard money from Congress for the Cloathing of our Prisoners in vain, I waited on Genl Washington, and proposed my resignation, as my Character was at stake, having (on the promise of the Secret Committee

to yield me every necessary aid) pledged myself to the officers in Confinement that they should be regularly supplied with every necessary, but they now suffered more than ever. In much distress and with Tears in his Eyes, he assured me that if he was deserted by the Gentn of the Country, he should despair. He could not do everything ... He was Gen. Quarter Master and Commissary. Everything fell on him and he was unequal to the task. He gave me the most positive Engagement that if I would contrive any mode for their Support and Comfort he would confirm it as far as was in his Power—On this I told him, I knew of but one way and that was to borrow Money on my own private Security. He assured me that in Case I did, and was not reimbursed by Congress, he would go an equal share with me in the loss. I then formed the plan of obliging Genl. Burgoyne to pay hard money for the support of the British Prisoners whom we supplied with daily rations, and in the meantime proceeded to borrow money or take Goods in New York on my own Credit. Thus I furnished 300 officers with a handsome suit of Cloaths each, and 1100 Men with a plain suit, Found them Blanketts, Shirts etc. and added to their provisions found by the British a full half ration of Bread and Beef p[e]r. day for upwards of 15 Months. Part of this I supplied by sending wheat and flour to New York, and selling them for hard money, under leave from Genl Robertson. Sometime in the beginning of the year 1778, Congress recd from Genl Burgoyne nearly 40,000 Dollars in hard money. In the beginning of 1778, I was chosen a Member of Congress, but continued in the Army till June, when Genl. Washington, knowing that I was near thirty Thousand Dollars in advance for the Prisoners, urged me to go and take my Seat in Congress, where I might get some of the hard money recd from Genl[.] Burgoyne before it was all expended, for if it was once gone, I should be totally ruined. I accordingly left the Army and joined Congress on their return from York Town in Pennsylvania, after the British had evacuated the City of Philadelphia. [10]

In July, he resigned from the commissary role, as General Washington suggested, and took his seat in Congress as a delegate from New Jersey.

In this new role, he continued to advocate for the treatment of prisoners. Boudinot left the Congress in 1779. But was reelected in 1781 and served through 1784. He was involved in the debates over the Articles of Confederation and the peace treaty with Britain. On November 4, 1782, despite his difficulties in the past with the Congress over prisoners, Boudinot was elected the President of the Confederation Congress, succeeding John Hanson. During Boudinot's year in the role, he signed the peace treaty with Great Britain on April 15, 1783. In June 1783, he led Congress's move from Philadelphia to Princeton, where they met at Nassau Hall on the college campus.

Boudinot left Congress at the end of his term and returned to New Jersey to practice law. After the US Constitution was ratified, he ran for office in the House of Representatives and served in the First through Third Congresses (from 1789 to 1795). On September 25, 1789, the day after the House of Representatives voted to recommend the First Amendment of the newly drafted Constitution to the states for ratification, Congressman Boudinot proposed that the House and Senate jointly request President Washington to proclaim a day of thanksgiving for "the many signal favors of Almighty God." Said Boudinot:

> "I cannot think of letting the session pass over without offering an opportunity to all the citizens of the United States of joining, with one voice, in returning to Almighty God their sincere thanks for the many blessings he had poured down upon them."

President Washington officially declared the Thanksgiving Holiday on October 3, 1789, setting the first official date as November 26, 1789.

Boudinot refused to align with political parties and was one of only nine representatives who voted against the Eleventh Amendment of the Constitution, regarding jurisdictional standing in lawsuits.

Following the death of his son-in-law, William Bradford, in 1795, daughter Susan, now a widow, moved in with her parents and began editing her father's papers regarding the Revolutionary era. In October of that year, President Washington named Boudinot to succeed David Rittenhouse as the Director of the US Mint in Philadelphia. He kept this position until resigning in July 1805. When he, Hannah, and Susan moved to a new home in Burlington, New Jersey. Hannah died a few years after the move, leaving Boudinot a widower with his daughter.

In addition to numerous civic, religious, and educational causes, for nearly fifty years, Boudinot was a trustee for Princeton University. He also speculated on large tracts of land in Ohio, owning more of Green Township in what is now the western suburbs of Cincinnati. In response to Thomas Paine's deistic *The Age of Reason* (1794), Boudinot wrote, in 1801, the Christian response, *The Age of Revelation*. He was elected as a member of the American Antiquarian Society in 1814. In 1816, a devout Presbyterian, he founded the American Bible Society and served as its president for the rest of his life.

The grave of Elias Boudinot.

Boudinot was a philanthropist later in life, giving away his fortune to aid freed Blacks and Native Americans. He gave away his Ohio lands to the benefit of the American Board of Commissioners for Foreign Missions. He also sponsored students at the Board School for Indians in Connecticut. A Cherokee student named Gallegina Uwatie, aka Buck Watie, stayed with the Boudinots in Burlington on his way to school. The young man was so impressed with Boudinot that he asked permission to take his name. He was later known as Elias Boudinot and became the editor of the first newspaper in the nation published in Cherokee and English, the *Cherokee Phoenix*.

Boudinot died in Burlington, New Jersey, on October 24, 1821, at 81. He was laid to rest at St. Mary's Episcopal Church Cemetery in Burlington. He willed 13,000 acres to the city of Philadelphia for parks and other uses.

There are many honors for Elias Boudinot, beyond an avenue in Cincinnati. There are also streets in Philadelphia and Princeton, a lane in Franklin Township, New Jersey, and a Place in Elizabeth, New Jersey. Elias Boudinot Elementary School is in Burlington, New Jersey, and the Boudinot-Southard Farmstead is in Bernards Township, New Jersey. Princeton Library holds the Boudinot-Stockton papers and many other family possessions and portraits.

Carter Braxton
(1736–1797)

Most Descendants

Buried at Unknown Location
Chericoke Plantation, King William County, Virginia

Signer of the Declaration of Independence • Continental Congress

Carter Braxton was a conservative Virginia plantation owner and merchant, a grandson of Robert "King" Carter, one of the wealthiest landowners in Virginia's history. Braxton was active in Virginia's legislature for a quarter century and during a brief stint in the Continental Congress, signed the Declaration of Independence. He fathered eighteen children via his two wives and is believed to have more descendants than any other Founding Father.

Braxton, born on September 10, 1736, at Newington Plantation in King and Queen County, Virginia, was the youngest of two sons of George Braxton. His mother, the youngest daughter of Robert "King" Carter, died as a consequence of his birth. Both the mother's and father's families were very wealthy landowners on Virginia's Northern Neck and were active in the colony's legislature.

Braxton's father died when he was 13, leaving him and his siblings orphaned. He and his brother George, the heir to the estate, were raised by neighbors and tutored privately. Braxton entered the College of William and Mary in 1755. That year, he married Judith Robinson of Middlesex County, Virginia, the niece of the Speaker of the House of Burgesses, John Robinson. The marriage lasted only two years when she

Carter Braxton

died in childbirth during the birth of their second daughter. For about four years, Braxton, a widower, traveled to England, with daughters Mary and Judith, where he mixed with high society and gained a reputation for extravagance.

Braxton returned to Virginia in 1760 and moved into Elsing Green, an estate in King William County overlooking the Pamunkey River that his brother had built for him while he was overseas. Braxton then married Elizabeth Corbin in 1761, with whom he had sixteen children, ten of whom survived to adulthood. He also entered the House of Burgesses, serving until 1785, except for a brief time as county sheriff.

On October 3, 1761, Braxton's brother George died in his 28th year, leaving him the entire estate. Unfortunately, it was saddled with significant debts, and the family lost Newington. Apparently, some malfeasance kept up the Braxtons' lifestyle, as it was revealed in the 1766

John Robinson estate scandal that they were the largest beneficiaries of the late speaker's interest-free loans of redeemed paper money supposed to have been destroyed. Ultimately, Braxon still owned over 12,000 acres and approximately 165 slaves. Braxton purchased a small schooner and became engaged in trade between the West Indies and the colonies. In 1767, the Braxtons moved to Chericoke, a new home built a few miles northwest of Elsing Green.

Despite his long affinity for England and high culture, Braxton turned against the motherland in 1769 when he sided with his fellow Virginians in signing the Virginia Resolves against parliamentary meddling, and the First Virginia Association, a nonimportation agreement protesting the Townshend duties. However, Braxton did not sign on to the Second and Third Virginia Associations that would have expanded the boycotts. However, in 1774, he joined the Fourth Virginia Association authorizing committees of safety and local militia and joined the Virginia Committee of Safety.

After Patrick Henry's "Give me liberty or give me death!" speech in Richmond on March 23, 1775, Lord Dunmore, the Royal Governor of Virginia, became very concerned about the potential for armed rebellion. The day after Lexington and Concord, on April 21, 1775, though news had not reached Virginia of the shots fired, Lord Dunmore ordered the Royal Marines to remove the gunpowder and flintlocks from the armory in Williamsburg. This caused outrage among the colonists, who threatened a military uprising. Braxton helped negotiate a settlement between fellow member of the House of Burgesses, Patrick Henry, and his father-in-law, Richard Corbin, who was the Deputy Collector of Royal Revenue. This averted the crisis by paying for the powder taken, but it was only a few weeks until Dunmore fled on June 8, and the royal government collapsed.

On October 22, 1775, Peyton Randolph passed away in Philadelphia while serving as president of the Continental Congress. On December 15, 1775, the Virginia legislature selected Braxton to succeed Randolph. He arrived in Philadelphia in February 1776, critical of the independence movement and worried that France would take over the colonies. Braxton served until August and ultimately warmed to the idea, signing the Declaration of Independence that summer.

Braxton returned home and was thanked, along with Thomas Jefferson, by the House of Burgesses for his services. Just before Christmas 1776, Chericoke burned to the ground, and the family moved to Grove House, West Point, Virginia. Braxton continued his representation in the legislature, opposing the Lee family since their involvement in the Robinson estate scandal, and sparring with Arthur Lee in the press. Braxton was most involved with tax moratoriums and debt relief measures.

Regarding the American Revolution, Braxton loaned money and funded shipping and privateering activities. With a consortium of patriotic planters, he traded tobacco and corned meat abroad to secure arms, ammunition, wheat, salt, cloth, and other trade goods. During this time, the British captured his ships and destroyed his plantations. He was censured by Congress in 1780 for his role in the *Phoenix* affair of 1777 when his privateer seized a neutral Portuguese vessel from Brazil, causing a diplomatic incident.

By the end of the war, Braxton had accumulated considerable debt and had to consolidate his holdings, selling most of his land and slaves. In 1787, he settled into a rented rowhouse in Richmond to clear the debt to the Robinson estate. He was also embroiled in a lengthy lawsuit with Robert Morris, who eventually declared bankruptcy. During this difficult time, Braxton served on the Virginia Council of State from 1786 to 1791 and again from 1794 until his death.

Carter Braxton died in Richmond on October 10, 1797. According to family tradition, the sheriff was at the door trying to collect debts when Braxton expired. His body was buried at Chericoke, which had been rebuilt in 1781 and given to a son. Wrote Dr. Benjamin Rush of Braxton:

> He was not deficient in political information but was suspected of being less detached than he should be from British prejudices.
> He was an agreeable and sensible speaker and in private life, an accomplished gentleman.

Elizabeth Braxton lived until July 5, 1814. Many of the children of Braxton's eighteen offspring fought in the Civil War for the Confederacy, including Majors Carter Moore Braxton, Tomlinson Braxton, and Elliott Muse Braxton. General Braxton Bragg was named for Carter Braxton but was not a relative. Most African Americans with the name Carter Braxton since the end of the Civil War are presumably descendants of slaves from Braxton's plantations.

In 1910, the family graves at Chericoke were exhumed, and the bodies were moved and reinterred at Hollywood Cemetery in Richmond. Unfortunately, Carter Braxton's remains could not be located, so it is assumed he remains at Chericoke, though he is mentioned on the marker in Richmond.

Chericoke remains in private hands. Elsing Green still stands and is open to tourists. Braxton County, West Virginia, was named in his honor, as was the World War II Liberty Ship SS *Carter Braxton*. The Waterman Steamship Company also had a break bulk freighter named the SS *Carter Braxton* in service from the 1960s to the 1980s.

The Newington Archaeological Site was added to the National Register of Historic Places in 2010.

Grave of Carter Braxton

David Brearley
(1745–1790)

Judge and Master Mason

Buried at Saint Michael's Church Cemetery
Trenton, New Jersey

Signer of the US Constitution • Military

David Brearley was the Chief Justice of the New Jersey Supreme Court, a delegate from New Jersey to the Constitutional Convention, a signer of the US Constitution, and a US District Court Judge for New Jersey.

Brearley was born on June 11, 1745, at Spring Grove Farm, in Lawrence Township, Mercer County, New Jersey, to David Brearley Sr. and his wife, Mary.

Brearley attended Princeton University, then the College of New Jersey, but did not graduate. He read law and entered private practice at Allentown, New Jersey through 1775. Circa 1767, Brearley married Elizabeth Mullen.

Upon the outbreak of the war, in late 1775, Brearley's brother, Joseph, was commissioned a captain in the Second New Jersey Continental Regiment and saw service in Canada. Brearley agitated for independence and participated in the creation of a new constitution for independent New Jersey. In June 1776, he joined Colonel Philip Van Cortland's regiment as a lieutenant colonel. Brearley served for five months, fighting in and around New York, and then joined the retreat through New Jersey, when his term expired on November 30. He returned home to his wife in

David Brearley (1745–1790)

David Brearley

Allentown, New Jersey, the next day. Brother Joseph soon arrived home, too, and decided to leave the Continental Army and serve locally with the First Hunterdon County Militia.

Brearley had been made a lieutenant colonel in the Fourth New Jersey Continental Regiment but switched to the First New Jersey Regiment on January 1, 1777. He fought in New Jersey against the British and Hessians who were trying to occupy the colony. He then served through the Philadelphia Campaign of 1777, at the Battles of Brandywine and Germantown. During this year, his wife, Elizabeth died. After winter at Valley Forge, he fought at the Battle of Monmouth in June 1778.

In March 1780. Brearley resigned from the military to become the Chief Justice of the New Jersey Supreme Court, serving until 1789.

He wrote the decision for *Holmes v. Walton*, deciding that the judiciary had the authority to determine the constitutionality of laws. Princeton granted him an honorary M.A. degree afterward. In 1783, he married Elizabeth Higbee.

Brearley was elected a delegate from New Jersey to the Constitutional Convention of 1787. He was a close follower of William Paterson and his New Jersey Plan. He was the Chairman of the Committee of Postponed Parts, which provided many of the final edits of the document, including the presidency, vice presidency, Electoral College,

Grave of David Brearley

method of impeachment, patents and copyrights, the role of the House of Representatives regarding finance, Native American relations, and other matters. Brearley signed the US Constitution.

Brearley presided over the New Jersey convention to adopt the Constitution. Afterward, he was a presidential elector for George Washington. On September 25, 1789, President George Washington nominated Brearley to the US District Court for the District of New Jersey. He was confirmed by the Senate that day and received his commission the following day.

Besides his judicial duties, Brearley was the Grand Master of the Masonic Order in New Jersey and helped found, in 1783, the Society of the Cincinnati in the State of New Jersey. He was that order's vice president for the rest of his life. He also served as a delegate to the Episcopal General Conference of 1786 and helped to write their prayer book. In 1789, he was elected to the American Philosophical Society.

Only 45, Brearley suffered from a long illness that took him on August 16, 1790, in Trenton, New Jersey. He was interred in the churchyard at Saint Michael's Episcopal Church in Trenton, where a cenotaph was erected in 1924 in his honor. It reads:

> Sacred to the memory of the Hon. David Brearley, Lieutenant Colonel in the Army of the United States, a member of the state and federal conventions, nine years Chief Justice of New Jersey. As a soldier, he was cool, determined and brave; as a judge, intelligent and upright; as a citizen, an early, decided, and faithful patriot; in private and social life, irreproachable. He died, much regretted, 16th of August 1790, in the 45th year of his age.

Brearley Lodge Number 2 in Bridgeton, New Jersey is a Masonic Lodge named in his honor. Several streets in Wisconsin and New Jersey are named for him, as is David Brearley High School in Kenilworth, New Jersey.

Pierce Butler
(1744–1822)

The British Soldier Who Became a Founder

Buried at Christ Episcopal Churchyard,
Philadelphia, Pennsylvania.

U.S. Constitution • Military

This founder proudly pointed out that he was a descendant of the Duke of Ormond. Born to the British aristocracy, he chose to pursue a military life. He was a major in the British army when he arrived in America with his majesty's forces to fight in the French and Indian War. Later troops under his command fired the shots at what came to be known as the Boston Massacre. He was, however, among many British soldiers who liked what they saw in the new world: plenty of land, easy access to clean running water, and numerous orchards that appealed to the planter in him. By 1773 he had resigned his commission in the army, married, and moved to Charleston. When the Revolution began, he found himself fighting on the patriot side. He became active in South Carolina politics and represented his state at the Constitutional Convention where he played an active part and signed the finished product. His name was Pierce Butler.

Butler was born on July 11, 1744, in County Carlow, Ireland. He was the third son born to Sir Richard Butler, 5th Baronet of Cloughgrenan, and his wife, Henrietta Percy. As one of the younger sons born to wealthy aristocrats, Butler had little chance of inheriting his father's wealth. He did have the advantage of quality education, including according to the

Pierce Butler (1744–1822)

Pierce Butler

historian Clinton Rossiter "working knowledge of the law." In young Butler's view, he had a choice to either pursue a life in the church or the military, and he decided on the latter. It was the French and Indian War that brought him to the country that would become his home.

In 1771 Butler married Mary Middleton, the daughter of Thomas Middleton and niece of Declaration of Independence signer Arthur Middleton. Shortly after his marriage he resigned his commission in the British army and decided to take up the life of a planter in the Charleston area. It was here he hoped to live the life of a gentleman farmer. The Revolution would interrupt those plans.

In the early years of the American revolt against British rule, military action was centered mainly in the northern and middle colonies. In 1778 the Crown's forces decided to pursue a "southern strategy" in the hope that loyalists in the southern states would rally in support of the British troops. By this time Butler had been elected to the state legislature and at the request of South Carolina Governor John Rutledge assumed the post as the state's adjutant general. This position carried with it the title of brigadier general though Butler preferred being addressed as major, which had been his combat rank.

Butler helped organize the South Carolina militia to prepare for the expected British invasion. He was also active in Georgia where he served under General Lachlan McIntosh. The troops the duo hastily raised and just as quickly trained could not stand against the British regulars and the effort to relieve Savannah ended in failure for the patriot side. In 1780 the British conquered Charleston, South Carolina, and Butler joined a resistance movement that included the "Swamp Fox" Francis Marion. Being a former British officer, Butler represented a special target for his majesty's forces, and he barely avoided capture on multiple occasions. He also aided the American effort by personally donating both money and supplies to the army in which he now served.

The British did confiscate Butler's property, including his slaves. When the Revolution ended in victory, he traveled to the Netherlands and, using his land as collateral, obtained a sizable loan from the Dutch. He used this money to purchase both slaves and equipment to resume his life as a planter. Several bad harvests nearly ruined him, and only a law passed by the South Carolina legislature saved his property from being seized by his creditors. It probably didn't hurt that he was a member of the body that passed the law that brought him relief.

In 1787 Butler joined the South Carolina delegation as a representative to the Constitutional Convention in Philadelphia. He was a very active member of the gathering who attended every meeting and spoke approximately seventy times. He also proposed the secrecy rule that the delegates adopted. Later James Madison would say that "no Constitution would ever have been adopted by the convention if the debates had been public." While Butler came to favor the establishment of the strong federal government proposed by Madison, he tempered that support by opposing any measures that would have limited slavery under the new government. He also joined fellow South Carolinian Charles Pinckney in proposing a requirement that fugitive slaves be returned to their owners. Not a single member of the convention voted against that proposal and many credit Butler with being the man responsible for the Constitution's fugitive slave clause.

As a delegate to the Philadelphia Convention Butler favored requiring only nine states for adoption rather than eleven. Butler "revolted at

Pierce Butler (1744–1822)

Grave of Pierce Butler

the idea that one or two states should restrain the others from consulting their safety." Though Butler strongly supported the ratification of the U.S. Constitution, he did not take part in his state's convention.

He did represent his state in the first Congress serving as a United States Senator for three terms. When political parties began to form Butler first joined the Federalist ranks, but by 1795 he had switched sides and joined the party favoring Thomas Jefferson. In 1804 he declared himself an independent. That same year he hosted Vice President Aaron Burr at one of his plantations. Burr had just killed Alexander Hamilton in a duel and was laying low after having been indicted for murder in both New York and New Jersey.

The years following the Constitutional Convention were also good ones for Butler financially. Bountiful harvests had turned him into one of the wealthiest men in America. When his wife died in 1790, he sold his holdings in South Carolina and invested in Georgia sea island plantations. He also purchased homes in Philadelphia and, during his last years, moved there to be closer to his daughter. He passed away in the City of Brotherly Love in 1822 at the age of 77 and was laid to rest at the Christ Church Episcopal Churchyard.

Charles Carroll of Carrollton
(1737–1832)

The Catholic Signer

Buried at Doughoregan Manor Chapel,
Ellicott City, Maryland

Continental Congress • Declaration of Independence

Though born into one of the wealthiest families in America, this founder had to overcome religious intolerance to take his place among the signers of the document that declared the thirteen colonies independent. Born in Maryland, which was initially founded as a Catholic colony and named after a Catholic queen, by the time this founder entered the world, there were restrictions against Catholics prohibiting those of that faith to practice law, teach or hold public office. Despite these obstacles, this founder, with the aid of the family fortune, received a classical education in France, where he became fluent in that language. A gifted writer, his well-framed arguments against British rule earned him the respect of his fellow patriots. He was instrumental in persuading Maryland to give the colony's delegates to the Continental Convention the instructions to vote for independence. He would later rally the state's support for the Constitution and serve as one of Maryland's first United States senators. When he passed away at the age of 95, he was the last surviving signer of the Declaration of Independence. His name was Charles Carroll, but his signature generally read Charles Carroll of Carrollton.

Carroll was born on September 19, 1737, in the Carroll Mansion located in Annapolis, Maryland. He was the only child of Charles Carroll

Charles Carroll of Carrollton (1737–1832)

Charles Carroll of Carrollton

of Annapolis and Elizabeth Brooke. His father was a wealthy tobacco farmer. Carroll was educated at a Jesuit preparatory school until the age of eleven, when he was sent to France to continue his studies. Among the French schools he attended was the Louis the Great College in Paris, from which he graduated in 1755. For the next decade, he continued his studies in France, becoming fluent in the French language before studying the law in England. He returned to America in 1765 as an intelligent and cultured young gentleman.

Initially, upon returning to the land of his birth, Carroll showed little interest in politics. This lack of interest may have been abetted by a Maryland law passed in 1704 that prohibited Catholics from holding public office to prevent "the growth of Popery in the Province." Also, as detailed by Milton Lomask in his book *Charles Carroll and the American Revolution*, Carroll's father urged him to be cautious in addressing the political issues of the day, especially the increasing tensions between Great Britain and the colonies. He did marry during this period wedding Mary (Molly) Darnell, on June 5, 1768. The couple would have seven children before Mary's death in 1782, but only three would survive infancy.

By 1772 Carroll's reluctance to engage in political debates had vanished. He engaged in what Denise Kieran and Joseph D'Agnese described as "a duel of pens" in their work *Signing Their Lives Away: The Fame and Misfortune of the Men Who Signed the Declaration of Independence*. In this "duel," which began with both participants writing under pseudonyms, Carroll was pitted against a well-known Maryland Attorney and crown loyalist Daniel Dulany the Younger. The subject of their debate was the decision by the proprietary governor to raise taxes so that government officials could receive a pay raise. Dulany supported the governor, while Carroll viewed the move as further taxation without representation. After a series of their arguments were published in a newspaper, word spread as to the true identities of the authors. Dulany began attacking Carroll personally, stressing the fact that he was a Catholic. Carroll's responses to these personal attacks were careful and restrained. He wrote that his opposition had resorted to "virulent and illiberal abuse," adding that "we may fairly presume, that arguments are either wanting, or that ignorance or incapacity know not how to apply them." Dulany's personal attacks backfired, resulting in Carroll being recognized as a strong and leading opponent of British rule.

While Carroll may have risen to patriotic prominence through his pen, he was one of the initial founders who came to believe that the disputes with England would have to be settled by the sword. Legend has it that in a conversation with Samuel Chase, another future signer of the Declaration of Independence, Carroll took the position that it would take more than written arguments if the colonies were to prevail over the British. When Chase asked what else the colonists could resort to, Carroll answered, "The bayonet. Our arguments will only raise the feelings of the people to that pitch when open war will be looked to as the arbiter of the dispute."

On October 19, 1774, Carroll played a prominent role in the event that came to be known as the Annapolis Tea Party. During this time, the colonists were engaged in widespread tea boycotts to protest the British Tea Act of 1773, which permitted only one company, the British East India Company, to sell tea in the colonies without paying tax. These protests had already led to the more famous Boston Tea Party. As a result of the boycotts, most ship captains refused to transport tea. However, in 1774 an English merchant loaded a ton of tea aboard a ship called the *Peggy Stewart*. The ship arrived in Annapolis on October 14, 1774. The co-owner of the ship, Anthony Stewart, was notified of the tax that needed to be paid before any of the ship's cargo could be brought ashore. The cargo included 53 indentured servants who had already endured a harsh crossing and were unlikely to survive a forced return to England. Seeing no other alternative, Stewart guaranteed payment of the tax, got the servants ashore but left the tea on the ship while he met with the local committee that supervised the boycott to resolve the situation.

Stewart met with Carroll, who was chairman of the committee, and an agreement was reached that the tea would be burned and Stewart and his co-owners would publish an apology in the *Maryland Gazette*. On the morning of the 19th, the ship's crew ran her aground. Stewart arrived and, before a large crowd touched a torch to oil-soaked rags in the bow of the *Peggy Stewart*. The ship, tea and all, burned down to the waterline. According to Lomask, after the event, Carroll told his wife, "You must admit that when we hold a tea party here in Annapolis, we do a better job of it than they do in Boston. We do not disguise ourselves as Indians. We do not hide behind war paint and feathers. And we do not lay hands on property that is not ours. We do everything legally and openly - and in a grand manner."

By the time the American Revolution began in 1775, Carroll was one of the colonies' wealthiest men. He inherited enormous agricultural estates, and his personal fortune was 2.1 million pounds sterling, which would amount to over $250 million today. He lived on and ran a ten-thousand-acre estate in Maryland that was worked by approximately 1,000 African slaves.

Carroll became a member of the first Annapolis Committee of Safety in 1775 and served as a delegate to the Annapolis Convention, which ran Maryland's revolutionary government. He was asked to represent his colony in the First Continental Congress but declined, probably believing that his Catholic faith would create problems for the representatives from other colonies. He did accompany Maryland's representatives to Philadelphia as an unofficial member of the delegation.

Though not an official member Congress soon found work for Carroll to do. In 1776 largely due to Benjamin Franklin and Samuel Chase's influence, Carroll was persuaded to head a mission to Canada to convince that country to join the fight against the British. Sending the Catholic French-speaking Carroll to Catholic-heavy Canada seemed a wise choice, but the effort came to naught for several reasons. Most notably, the Americans had invaded Canada less than a year earlier, and in 1774 the British parliament had passed the Quebec Act giving freedom of religion to Canadians and recognizing the Catholic Church. The First Continental Congress, despite Carroll's protests, had criticized the Parliament for passing the act. The Canadians felt they had more to fear from their southern neighbors than from the British crown.

In the summer of 1776, Congress scheduled a vote for July 2 on Richard Henry Lee's resolution calling for American independence. Maryland had yet to advise their delegates on how to vote on the resolution, so Carroll and his old friend Samuel Chase headed back to Maryland to work the Annapolis Convention to support independence. Their arguments proved persuasive, and the convention freed Maryland delegates to support the Lee resolution. On July 4, 1776, Carroll was elected to the Continental Congress, and this time he agreed to serve. He arrived back in Philadelphia too late to vote in favor of independence, but he proudly signed the document that declared the American colonies free of English rule on August 2, 1776. He signed as Charles Carroll of Carrollton. There are stories about this signature, most likely apocryphal. In the 1940s, there was a journalist with a popular syndicated column named John Hix. He wrote in his column "Strange As It Seems" an explanation for Carroll's distinctive signature. Every member of the Continental Congress who signed this document automatically became a criminal, guilty of sedition against King George III. Because of his wealth, Carroll had more to lose than most yet had a very common name. Those signers with common names might hope to avoid being identified by the King. According to Hix's research, when it was Carroll's turn to sign the declaration, he rose, went to John Hancock's desk where the document rested; signed his name "Charles Carroll," and returned to his seat. At this point, another member of the Continental Congress, who was prejudiced against Carroll because of his Catholicism, commented that Carroll risked little in signing the document as there must be many men named Charles Carroll in the colonies so the King would be unlikely to order Carroll's arrest without clear proof that he was the same one who signed. Carroll immediately returned to Hancock's desk, seized the pen again, and added "of Carrollton" to his name. The Society of the Descendants of the Signers of the Declaration of Independence claims that President John Hancock made the comment.

Carroll would represent Maryland in the Continental Congress until 1778. He was a major supporter of George Washington as the two had become friends when the future president made multiple visits to the Carroll estate. He served on the committee that visited Washington and his troops during the harsh winter they spent at Valley Forge. He played a significant role in defeating the Conway Cabal that sought to replace Washington as commander of the new nation's armies. During his final year in Congress, he was asked to serve as President, an honor he declined. He also provided considerable financial support to the Revolutionary War effort throughout these turbulent times.

Carroll returned to Maryland in 1778 to assist in the formation of a state government. Since he had assisted in drafting the state constitution two years prior, he was well prepared for this task. He was elected to the state senate in 1781, where he served for more than a decade. He was elected to represent his state at the Constitutional Convention of 1787 but did not attend the gathering in Philadelphia. He was active in rallying support for ratification of the historical document produced by that convention. In 1789 he was elected to serve as one of Maryland's first two United States Senators. In 1792 the Maryland legislature passed a law prohibiting anyone from serving in the state and national legislature at the same time. Preferring service in the Maryland Senate, he resigned from the United States Senate in November of 1792.

Like many of the nation's founders, Carroll was a slave owner who wrestled with the question of slavery through much of his life. While he supported the gradual abolition of slavery and said, "It is admitted by all to be a great evil," he did not free any of his slaves. He did introduce a bill calling for the gradual abolition of slavery in the Maryland Senate, but it found little support. In 1828, when he was 91 years old, he served as the president of the Auxiliary State Colonization Society of Maryland. This group supported sending black Americans to lead free lives in African states such as Liberia.

When John Adams and Thomas Jefferson both passed away on July 4, 1826, Carroll became the last surviving founder of those who had courageously signed the Declaration of Independence. He lived his final years with a daughter in Baltimore. His last public act, on July 2, 1828, was the laying of the cornerstone of the B&O's Carrollton Viaduct, named in his honor and still in use today. In May 1832, he was asked to appear at the first-ever Democratic Party Convention but did not attend because of poor health. He passed away at the age of 95 on November 14, 1832. He was laid to rest in his Doughoregan Manor Chapel located in Ellicott City, Maryland.

There are numerous cities and counties named in his honor, and his family manors remain standing. The family still owns Doughoregan Manor, although it is closed to the public. There are numerous memorials to Charles Carroll throughout the eastern United States. Counties in twelve states bear his name, as do elementary and middle schools and a residence hall at the University of Notre Dame. His likeness can be found in many paintings depicting the Signers of the Declaration of Independence, and a statue of him resides in Statuary Hall in the US Capitol.

William Clingan
(1721–1790)

Chester County Continental Congressman

Buried at Upper Octorara Church Cemetery,
Parkesburg, Pennsylvania.

Articles of Confederation

William Clingan was a Continental Congressman born circa 1721 who attended the Congress from 1777 to 1779, including the months when it met in Lancaster and then York, Pennsylvania during the British occupation of Philadelphia. During this time, Clingan signed the Articles of Confederation which was later ratified by the states in 1781.

Born near Wagontown in Caln Township, Chester County, Pennsylvania, Clingan was likely the son of immigrants from Northern Ireland or Scotland. His educational details are lost to history, but he did marry twice: first to Catherine (maiden name unknown) with whom he had a son before her death in 1785; and second to Rachel Gilleylen (1756-1843), a widow with six children from her first marriage, who survived him.

Clingan owned hundreds of acres of land in the Wagontown area and resided along the King's Highway from Philadelphia to Lancaster, the current Route 340, just west of Wagontown. The current address for the property is 101 Hatfield Road, Coatesville, Pennsylvania. From 1757 to 1786, he served as a justice of the peace in Chester County and, for the last six years, President of the Chester County Courts.

GRAVES of our FOUNDERS

William Clingan

William Clingan was elected to the Continental Congress as a delegate from Pennsylvania on September 14, 1777. He attended sessions from November 1 to about November 28, 1777; from January 1, 1778 to about March 24, 1778; from about April 25, 1778, to about May 19, 1778; from about June 16, 1778 to about June 27, 1778; and from about September 14, 1778 to about December 2, 1778. He was re-elected on November 20, 1778.

These dates of service put William Clingan in the room for the final debates on the Articles of Confederation and then the adoption on November 15, 1777, in York. Beginning on July 9, 1778, the delegates began signing the document. Along with Clingan, Robert Morris, Daniel Roberdeau, Jonathan Bayard Smith, and Joseph Reed signed for Pennsylvania.

William Clingan's nephew and namesake married Jane Roan, the beautiful daughter of revered pastor John Roan and his wife Anne, on June 11, 1778. Jane's uncle John Cochran was a distinguished surgeon in the Revolutionary army. The wedding was noteworthy enough to receive a lot of coverage in *The Pennsylvania Packet* newspaper:

> Was married, last Thursday, Mr. William Clingan, Jr., of Donegal, to Miss Jenny Roan, of Londonderry, both of the County of Lancaster—a sober, sensible, agreeable young couple and very sincere Whigs. This marriage promises as much happiness as the state of things in this our sinful world will admit.
>
> This was indeed a Whig wedding, as there were present many young men and ladies, and not one of the gentlemen but had been out when called on in the service of his country, and it was well-known that the groom, in particular, had proved his heroism, as well as Whiggism, in several battles and skirmishes. After the marriage was ended, a motion was made, and heartily agreed to by all present, that the young unmarried ladies should form themselves into an association by the name of the "Whig Association of the Unmarried Ladies of America," in which they should pledge their honor that they would never give their hand in marriage to any gentleman until he had first proved himself a patriot, in readily turning out when called to defend his country from slavery, by a spirited and brave conduct, as they would not wish to be the mothers of a race of slaves and cowards.

The younger Clingan was a soldier who participated in the battles at Trenton, Princeton, Brandywine, and Germantown and had served in the army elsewhere. The couple later moved northwest to the Buffalo Valley near Lewisburg, Pennsylvania.

Following his service in Congress, the elder Clingan returned to his duties on the court in Chester County. He was a Justice of the Peace for the district of West Caln, Sadsbury, and West Fallowfield Townships, and Justice of the Court of Common Pleas of Chester County. He also presided in the Court of Quarter Sessions and the Orphans' Court there. Clingan was instrumental in the planning and construction of a new prison and court facilities in Chester County.

GRAVES of our FOUNDERS

Throughout his life, William was a leading member of the Upper Octorara Presbyterian Church, which is along present-day Route 10 near Parkesburg, Pennsylvania. According to an early *History of Chester County, Pennsylvania*, Clingan was robbed of the church collections:

> At one time during the career of the noted robbers, the Doanes, Mr. Clingan was visited by them. In some business transactions, he had received a large amount of money in gold, and the visit of the Doanes had reference to this treasure, which they supposed was in the house. While searching for it, one of them announced that he had found it. Mr. Clingan's desk had been opened, and there stood a large leathern bag full of money, and seizing a violin which was in the house, as they said, to have a jubilation over their good luck, they mounted their horses and were off. The bag, however, which they supposed to contain the gold was simply filled with coppers, the church collections as he had brought them home from Sunday to Sunday, and which, when he had a quantity on hand, he exchanged for larger money. One of the gang, afterward executed, was visited by Mr. Clingan in prison, and he told him of their chagrin when they discovered their mistake.

The grave of William Clingan

William Clingan (1721–1790)

William Clingan died on May 9, 1790, and was laid to rest in the Upper Octorara Burial Grounds. His tombstone reads:

> Here lyeth the Body of WILLIAM CLINGAN, Esq. Who departed this Life, The 9th Day of May 1790. Also CATHERINE, his Wife, Who departed this Life, The 8th Day of Feby 1785.

William Clingan left no descendants.

George Clinton
(1739–1812)

"The Father of the Empire State"

Buried at Old Dutch Churchyard
Kingston, New York

Military • Continental Congress • Governor • Vice President

George Clinton was best known as the first Governor of New York and a two-time Vice President of the United States under Jefferson and Madison. He was also an effective military leader appointed to brigadier general, favored by George Washington. Later, as an Antifederalist, he was a proponent of a Bill of Rights and was at odds with Alexander Hamilton, John Jay, and Aaron Burr in New York.

Clinton, born July 26, 1739, in Little Britain, Ulster County, New York, was one of two sons of Charles Clinton, a wealthy landowner, and his wife, Elizabeth (née Denniston) Clinton. The elder Charles was of Scots-Irish descent, born in County Longford, Ireland. Due to their Catholic heritage and unwillingness to conform to the Anglican Church, the family had been unable to recover their estates in England, so Charles organized seventy people, including relatives and friends and chartered the *George and Anne* to bring them to Philadelphia in 1729. They then established a colony in Ulster County. During the French and Indian War, Colonel Charles commanded a regiment. George's brother James also later served in the American Revolution as a general.

As a lad, young Clinton was tutored privately. In 1757, at age 18, he left home and became a steward's mate on the privateer *Defiance* in

George Clinton (1739–1812)

George Clinton

the Caribbean. He returned to New York in 1758 and joined the colonial forces fighting the French and Indians, enlisting in a militia unit led by his father, the colonel. They participated in the capture of Fort Frontenac, near Lake Ontario, that year, and Clinton rose to the rank of lieutenant. Clinton and his brother James were also instrumental in capturing a French vessel.

In 1759, the governor, a distant relative, appointed Clinton the Clerk of the Ulster County Court of Common Pleas, a position he held for 52 years. For the next four years, Clinton studied law with one of New York's leading legal minds, William Smith Jr., in New York City. He was admitted to the New York Bar on September 12, 1764. He then opened a law practice at Little Britain in Ulster County in 1765 and surveyed New Windsor, New York. He became district attorney for Ulster County in 1766 and was elected to the New York Colonial Assembly in 1768, associating with the Livingston faction, which was anti-British. On February 7, 1770, Clinton married Sarah Tappen, the daughter of Peter Tappen, of Dutch ancestry. The couple had five daughters and one son: Catharine Clinton (1770–1811) married firstly to John Taylor, and secondly Pierre Van Cortlandt, Jr.; Cornelia Tappen Clinton (1774–1810) married Edmond-Charles Genêt; George Washington Clinton (1778–1813) married Anna Floyd, daughter of William Floyd; Elizabeth Clinton (1780–1825) married Matthias B. Tallmadge; Martha Washington Clinton (1783–1795); and Maria Clinton (1785–1829) married Dr. Stephen D. Beekman, a grandson of Pierre Van Cortlandt.

Clinton served in the Colonial Assembly until 1775 as an opponent of British imperialism. He motioned for the approval of the resolutions of the First Continental Congress, but this was rebuffed. Clinton warned the assembly the colonies would soon need to take up arms. Following his motions in March concerning his opposition to taxes imposed by Parliament his stature in the delegation was increased. He joined his brother James at the New York Provincial Convention in New York City on April 20, following the Battles of Lexington and Concord. A member of the New York Committee of Correspondence, Clinton, Philip Livingston, James Duane, John Alsop, John Jay, Simon Boerum, William Floyd, William Wisner, Philip Schuyler, Lewis Morris, Francis Morris, and Robert R. Livingston Jr. were elected to the Second Continental Congress on April 22.

Clinton took his seat in Philadelphia on May 15, 1775. On December 19, he was commissioned as a brigadier general in New York's militia. He was asked to defend the Highlands of the Hudson River, causing him to be absent from Congress. During this time, he saw to the building of two forts and the stretching of the chain across the Hudson.

When the Declaration of Independence was being discussed and ratified on July 4, 1776, New York did not have permission from Albany to vote in the affirmative. Though he was inclined to vote in favor, Clinton missed the opportunity to do so when he was appointed a Brigadier General in the Continental Army on July 8 with a focus on further fortifying the Hudson River region of New York. Clinton remained in the military throughout the Revolutionary War.

When New York adopted its new constitution in April 1777, Clinton ran for lieutenant governor but ended up winning the governor's

George Clinton (1739–1812)

George Clinton

seat, surprising his opponents, Philip Schuyler, John Morin Scott, and John Jay. He was inaugurated as the first governor of New York State in Kingston, Ulster County, on July 30, 1777. George Washington asked Clinton to return to military duty to defend the Highlands forts, Fort Clinton and Fort Montgomery. Though they were overwhelmed by a superior force in October 1777, Clinton and 600 defenders made the British pay a high price in casualties.

As governor, Clinton was known for his poor treatment of Loyalists. He seized their estates and used the funds to pay for the government's expenses, keeping taxes down. During the winter of 1777-1778, in support of his friend, George Washington, Clinton sent food to the troops at Valley Forge. Clinton was also strongly against permitting Vermont to enter the union as a state, siding with those New Yorkers who had land claims.

In 1780, Clinton led militia raids into the Indian territories in western New York to protect settlers against Loyalists, British soldiers, and Iroquois loyal to the British. The latter had been raiding the settlements, and Clinton chased them out, raising the stature of his administration. In 1783, at Dobbs Ferry on the Hudson, Clinton and Washington negotiated with General Carleton for the evacuation of the last British troops from the United States. Clinton then became an original member of the New York Society of the Cincinnati, serving as president from 1794 to 1795. Clinton was re-elected five times as governor, serving until June 1795 and chairing the state's Constitutional Convention in 1788, though he was opposed to it largely regarding federal taxation.

As an Antifederalist, Clinton wrote letters to the newspapers in opposition to the Constitution, signing them as "Cato." Alexander Hamilton responded to these as "Caesar." Ultimately, George Clinton became more popular in New York than Hamilton and was responsible for the rapid expansion of the state and the planning for the canal system therein. Some credit Clinton for making New York "The Great Empire State." His financial management during the Confederation years made New York a net creditor to the United States, thanks to low land prices, which encouraged more sales and settlements.

Clinton's Antifederalist stance during the Constitutional debates made him the most prominent opposition candidate. He garnered less than ten percent of the vote in the 1788 election and only three electoral votes from New York. He finished seventh in the presidential election, losing to Washington and Adams. However, Clinton supported his friend, Washington, by riding to his inauguration with him in New York City. He then threw an elaborate dinner party for the new president.

In 1792, as the leading Antifederalist, Clinton again ran for president, finishing third behind George Washington and John Adams. Though Thomas Jefferson was preferred as a potential vice president, the electors could not vote for two people from the same state, Virginia, thus Clinton was the leading opposition candidate. This time, Clinton won

George Clinton (1739–1812)

50 electoral votes, carrying New York and the South. Adams won the vice presidency again by finishing second with 77 electoral votes from Pennsylvania and New England. George Washington received all 132 votes possible for one candidate, winning re-election unanimously.

In 1796, though not an official candidate, Clinton finished far back in the field with only 7 electoral votes. Thomas Jefferson became the leading Antifederalist in the Democratic-Republican party with 68 votes to become John Adams' vice president. Clinton retired from politics for several years.

In 1800, after the death of his wife, Clinton was coaxed out of retirement to run for the state assembly from New York City, believing that controlling the New York State Assembly would then influence the electoral votes for New York. Clinton won and then half-heartedly threw in for the vice-presidential race, losing to Aaron Burr, who became Thomas Jefferson's vice president. However, when Burr then tried to also win the New York governor's race in 1801, Clinton ran and beat him, though he was but a figurehead for his nephew DeWitt Clinton, who ran the day-to-day activities of the office.

For the 1804 presidential election, the 12th Amendment was, in effect, defining the vice presidency as a distinct office in the electoral process. Thomas Jefferson opted to dump Aaron Burr and nominated Clinton as his running mate. He was the first person elected as Vice President via the modern process, and not as a runner-up for president. Jefferson and Clinton won in a landslide in the electoral college, 162 to 14, defeating Federalists Charles Cotesworth Pinckney and Rufus King. Clinton was sworn in as the fourth Vice President of the United States on March 4, 1805. Toasted the *Albany Register*, "George Clinton: His unwearied zeal and patriotism entitle him to the confidence of the people."

Unfortunately, Jefferson largely ignored the older Clinton, who functioned as a figurehead and struggled in his senatorial role. Jefferson hoped Clinton would be too old in 1808 to run for president at age 69, allowing for his preferred successor, James Madison, to win the office. However, Clinton was not deterred and ran for president himself in 1808. Madison, however, out-maneuvered him and offered him to be his running mate. Madison-Clinton defeated the Federalist ticket of Pinckney-King 122 to

Clinton bronze statue

47 in the electoral college. Clinton became the first of two men to be elected vice president for two separate presidents. John C. Calhoun was the other, serving under John Quincy Adams in 1824 and Andrew Jackson in 1828. Clinton was sworn in for his second term on March 8, 1809.

George Clinton (1739–1812)

Clinton opposed the foreign policies of both Jefferson and Madison, preventing the appointment of Albert Gallatin as Secretary of State. Of note, he cast the tie-breaking vote in the Senate on February 20, 1811, preventing the rechartering of the Bank of the United States.

Clinton did not make it to the end of his term, dying of a heart attack on April 20, 1812, at his home in Washington, D.C., at the age of 72. For a time, his seat in the Senate was shrouded in black. His funeral was described in the *Daily National Intelligencer*:

> The mortal remains of the late vice-president of the U. States were on Tuesday evening interred at the burial ground near the navy-yard in this city, in the presence of a concourse of people greater than ever has been gathered together in this city on any similar occasion. The shops were shot at an early hour; and a general gloom pervaded all ranks of society. The hearse with its escort reached the capitol [sic] about 4 o'clock, and the procession moved thence in about half an hour afterwards, in the order which was immortal in our last. The scene was awful and impressive. The martial parade, the glistening arms and nodding plumes of the military corps which preceded the hearse—the solemn melody of the martial band, which attuned all hearts to melancholy.

The first vice president to die in office, Clinton was initially buried in the Congressional Cemetery in Washington, D.C., but was moved to the Old Dutch Churchyard in Kingston, New York, in 1908. A monument over his grave reads, in part:

> To the memory of George Clinton . . . He was a soldier and statesman of the revolution. Eminent in council and distinguished in war, he filled with unexampled usefulness, purity, and ability, among many other offices, those of governor of his native state and vice-president of the United States. While he lived, his virtue, wisdom, and valor were the pride, ornament, and security of his country, and when he died, he left an illustrious example of a well-spent life worthy of all limitations.

Grave of George Clinton

Nephew DeWitt Clinton, the son of his brother James, ran unsuccessfully for president in 1812, losing to James Madison. He served as the Governor of New York from 1817 to 1823. also served as governor of New York (1817-23); in 1812 he ran unsuccessfully for the presidency of the United States, losing to James Madison.

Bancroft Prize-winning historian Alan Shaw Taylor described Clinton as "The astutest politician in Revolutionary New York, who understood the power of symbolism and the new popularity of a plain style especially when practiced by a man with the means and accomplishments to set himself above the common people."

Many places are named after Clinton including Clinton Counties in New York and Ohio and the town of Clinton, Oneida County, New York, and Clintonville, Columbus, Ohio. Clinton's bronze statue was erected in Statuary Hall at the U.S. Capitol in 1873. He is also depicted in Trumbull's painting *Declaration of Independence* even though he did not sign the document. This same painting has been on the reverse of the two-dollar bill since 1976.

Jonathan Dayton
(1760–1824)
Youngest Constitution Signer

Buried at St. John's Episcopal Church
Elizabeth, New Jersey

United States Constitution

Jonathan Dayton was a leading American political figure who represented New Jersey through most of his political career. He was the youngest person to sign the U. S. Constitution and a member of the U.S. House of Representatives, serving as its fourth Speaker and later in the U.S. Senate. His political career waned after he was arrested in 1807 for alleged treason in connection with Aaron Burr. He was subsequently exonerated by a grand jury.

Dayton was born in Elizabethtown (now Elizabeth), New Jersey, to his father, Elias Dayton, who was a storekeeper and was active in local politics, and his mother, Hannah (née Rolfe) Dayton, on October 16, 1760. Elias served as a militia officer in the French and Indian War, and the family was prominent in the community. Elizabethtown had a good reputation for education because of a local academy led by a famous educator, Tapping Reeve, and his protégé, Francis Barber. Two of Dayton's schoolmates at the academy were Alexander Hamilton and Aaron Burr. He then went on to attend the College of New Jersey (today's Princeton University).

In late 1774, the First Continental Congress called for a boycott of goods imported from England, and both Daytons allied themselves

Jonathan Dayton (1760–1824)

Jonathan Dayton

with the Revolutionary Movement and served on Elizabethtown's enforcement committee. When the war broke out in 1775, Dayton quit college and joined the Continental Army, serving under his father in the 3rd New Jersey Regiment. He was fifteen. Despite missing his final year at Princeton, he still graduated with his class and was later awarded an honorary Doctor of Laws degree.

On January 1, 1777, Dayton was commissioned a lieutenant. He soon found himself engaged in heavy skirmishing with British forces threatening Philadelphia, the American capital. When the British tried a flank attack by sea, Dayton's 3rd New Jersey accompanied Washington in a march to Pennsylvania and saw action in battles at Brandywine Creek and Germantown. He remained with Washington at Valley Forge and received solid training under Frederick von Steuben.

In October 1780, Dayton and his uncle, Lieutenant Colonel Matthias Ogden, were captured by a Loyalist raiding party. They spent the winter as prisoners in New York and were then released. Dayton returned to New Jersey, was promoted to captain and sent to Yorktown, where he fought in the decisive battle. During the siege, he led his company in the crucial nighttime bayonet attack on Redoubt 10 under the command of his old schoolmate, Alexander Hamilton. When the war ended, Dayton remained in the service until the Army was dissolved in 1783.

After the war, Dayton turned to studying law and taking part in the family's merchant business. He opened a law practice and divided his time between land speculation, law, and politics. He was a member of the New Jersey General Assembly in 1786 and 1787. In 1787, his father, Elias, was offered to represent New Jersey at the Constitutional Convention in Philadelphia. He declined in favor of his son. At the convention, he spoke with moderate frequency, and although objecting to some provisions of the Constitution, he signed it. He was the youngest person to sign it at 26 years old.

After the Constitutional Convention, Dayton enjoyed a good reputation in his home state. He was elected to the First Congress but preferred instead to become a member of the New Jersey Council and Speaker of the State Assembly. In 1791, he was again elected to the U.S. House of Representatives, but this time he took office and served four consecutive terms. During the last two terms, he served as Speaker of the House (1796-1799).

Beginning in 1799, he served a single term in the U.S. Senate, part of the moderate segment of the Federalist Party. He was pragmatic in his approach and, for example, crossed party lines to support President Jefferson's purchase of the Louisiana Territory.

Dayton had become wealthy mainly due to his heavy investment in land speculation in the Ohio region. He owned nearly a quarter million acres. The city of Dayton, Ohio, was named after Jonathan Dayton in 1796. His wealth made him attractive to his old classmate, Aaron Burr, who approached Dayton for financial assistance with plans he had for lands west of the Appalachian Mountains. There are multiple theories as to what Burr's plans were. In *The Burr Conspiracy* by James E. Lewis Jr., the author notes that Burr enticed others to join him with plans to liberate Spanish Mexico, with promises of western lands, or with a plan to create a new western empire. President Jefferson, who didn't trust Burr, embraced the latter theory. His administration ordered the arrest of Burr and others, including Dayton. Burr was charged with treason, but the evidence against him was thin and confusing, and he was acquitted. Dayton's case went to a grand jury, where he was exonerated. Although the charges were never proven, his political career was finished on the national level. Except for a one-year term in the New Jersey legislature, he retired from public life.

Shortly before his death on October 9, 1824, Dayton entertained his old comrade-in-arms, Lafayette, in Elizabethtown on his grand tour of the United States. He was interred in an unmarked grave that is reportedly now under the St. John's Episcopal Church in Elizabeth, New Jersey, which replaced an original church in 1860. Our attempts to visit his grave were unsuccessful, as the place seemed abandoned. Our calls went unanswered, and our messages were unreturned. It seems a shame that he is so under-memorialized after contributing so much.

Dayton's grave lost in the weeds in Elizabeth, New Jersey

Eliphalet Dyer
(1721–1807)

"... an honest, worthy man..."

Buried at Windham Cemetery
Windham, Connecticut

**Continental Congress • Signer of the Continental Association
Militiaman**

Eliphalet Dyer had one of the more unusual names among Continental Congressmen. "Eliphalet" was derived from Hebrew, meaning "God who delivers." Congressman Dyer certainly "delivered" for his constituents in Windham, Connecticut, throughout a long political career. Dyer was variously a lawyer, jurist, and statesman who was a delegate to the Continental Congress and signed the Continental Association.

Dyer was born in Windham, Connecticut, on September 14, 1721, the son of Thomas Dyer and his wife, Lydia (née Backus) Dyer. The elder Dyer was a native of Weymouth, Massachusetts, who moved to Connecticut circa 1715. There, he married Lydia, the daughter of John Backus of Windham. Upon settling in Windham, Thomas served in the Connecticut General Assembly and rose to become a major in the Windham County militia.

Young Eliphalet was taught "preparatory studies" prior to enrolling at Yale College (now Yale University) in New Haven in 1740. Dyer was already a town clerk as a teenager and studied law at Yale. In May 1745, he married Huldah Bowen of Providence, Rhode Island, the daughter of

Eliphalet Dyer

Colonel Jacob Bowen. Upon graduating from Yale, Dyer was admitted to the colonial bar in 1746 and practiced law in Windham.

Following in his father's footsteps, Dyer joined the militia and was elected justice of the peace and to the colonial assembly in 1747. He served in sessions in that body in 1747, 1748, 1753, and 1753, and then from 1756 to 1784. During this time, he became directly embroiled in territorial disputes between Connecticut and Pennsylvania. In 1754, the Susquehanna Land Company published in Philadelphia a claim that

Connecticut's grant included the lands westward as "far as the South Sea." This happened to carve off the northern tier of William Penn's colony. The Connecticut General Assembly was lobbied to permit Connecticut's citizens to settle the lands, but the outbreak of the French and Indian War distracted from this.

During the war, Dyer was a lieutenant colonel in the Connecticut militia, participating in the capture of Crown Point in 1755. He was promoted to lieutenant and led a regiment in the 1758 attack on Canada.

After the war, in 1763, Dyer traveled to London representing the Susquehanna River land claim but was turned down due to the just-passed Proclamation Line Act, which established set boundaries for the colonies. Unfortunately, this was unsatisfactory for many Connecticut settlers who had invested in land, leading to conflicts known as the Yankee-Pennamite Wars. Three times, hostilities flared between Pennsylvania and Connecticut. Ultimately, after the Revolution, the region was affixed to Pennsylvania by the Continental Congress, and Pennsylvania permitted the Yankees to stay as Pennsylvania citizens.

In September 1765, Dyer was a representative from Connecticut in the Stamp Act Congress. He was then elected a justice on the superior court in 1766, holding the post until 1793. He was chief justice after 1789.

As the American Revolution began to simmer, Dyer was named to Connecticut's Committee of Safety. In July 1774, when the Committee of Correspondence met regarding a delegate to the First Continental Congress, Dyer was selected to represent the colony in Philadelphia. He served in Congress until 1775, then 1777 to 1779, and finally from 1782 to 1783.

On October 20, 1774, Dyer signed the Continental Association, banning certain British imports, including tea. Dyer was not in Congress when it moved to York following the invasion of Philadelphia, but he did return to Philadelphia to hear the final debates about the Articles of Confederation although he was not a signer. In his diary, John Adams described Dyer as "longwinded and roundabout, obscure and cloudy, very talkative and very tedious, yet an honest, worthy man; means and judges well."

After leaving Congress, Yale conferred a Doctor of Divinity degree to Dyer in 1787. He continued to serve as a judge in Connecticut, retiring in 1793 as the chief justice. Dyer died on May 13, 1807, at age 85, and was buried at Windham Cemetery.

The Litchfield Monitor of Connecticut stated, "Died, at Windham, the Hon. ELIPHALET DYER, in the 87th year of his age. He was distinguished for his useful talents and the faithful and honourable discharge of his important duties."

Grave of Eliphalet Dyer

New York's *The Morning Chronicle* said, "He was one of those illustrious patriots (whose name will live in the annals of our nation to all posterity) who signed and assisted in supporting the Declaration of Independence in 1776, which was the keystone to the 'wide arch of our rais'd empire.'"

Well, contrary to the New York paper declaring so, Dyer never signed the Declaration of Independence and was not in Congress at the time to debate or pass the measure. As Mark Twain once said, "If you don't read the newspaper, you're uninformed. If you read the newspaper, you're misinformed."

Fortunately, you have our series of books to sort out a most accurate account of the accomplishments and contributions of our Founders.

William Floyd
(1734–1821)

Major General in the Congress

Buried at Westernville Cemetery
Oneida County, New York

**Continental Association • Declaration of Independence
Major General**

William Floyd was a wealthy farmer and merchant who was a major general in the New York state militia and a Continental Congressman who signed the Continental Association and Declaration of Independence. He was the first delegate from New York to sign the Declaration of Independence.

Floyd was born on December 17, 1734, in Brookhaven, New York, on Long Island, to Nicholl Floyd and his wife, Tabitha (née Smith) Floyd. The family was of Welsh origin, descended from Richard Floyd, who visited Jamestown, Virginia, in 1620 before settling in New York in 1640 to practice law. Circa 1688, Floyd's grandfather purchased 4400 acres from Tangier Smith's family in the Mastic Neck of the town of Brookhaven, on Long Island. Floyd's father built a house there in 1723, where Floyd was born. Floyd's siblings included sister Ruth, who married Brigadier General Nathaniel Woodhull; sister Charity, who married Continental Congressmen Ezra L'Hommedieu; and brother Charles, who married Margaret Thomas.

Floyd was not formally educated despite his father's wealth. Instead, he learned etiquette and how to run the plantation. Floyd's parents

William Floyd

died months apart in 1755, leaving the farm to young William. In 1760, he married Hannah Jones (1740–1781), the daughter of William Jones from Southampton, Long Island, New York. The couple were the parents of Nicoll Floyd (1762–1852), who married Phoebe Gelston (1770–1836), daughter of David Gelston (collector of the Port of New York); Mary Floyd (1764–1805), who married Colonel Benjamin Tallmadge, who oversaw President George Washington's spy ring; and Catherine Floyd (1767–1832), who married Reverend William Clarkson (1763–1812). Floyd became one of the wealthiest men in New York and was often approached by Governor Johnathan Trumbull of Connecticut for loans.

Floyd was against the economic policies of the British Parliament in the 1760s and 1770s. As tensions increased with Britain, Floyd became directly involved. On August 11, 1774, he was elected a delegate to the First Continental Congress in Philadelphia. There he signed the Continental Association.

On September 5, 1775, he joined the Suffolk County Militia as a colonel. When a small British naval force gathered at Gardiner's Bay to gather supplies, Floyd's unit arrived and chased them off. He rose to the rank of major general in the militia.

Floyd was reelected to the Continental Congress, attending through July 1776, when he signed the Declaration of Independence. Later that summer, on August 17, 1776, Long Island was taken by the British and many estates were plundered. Floyd learned of this while at the Congress and wrote:

> I]s New York to be Evacuated as well as Long Island without fighting, or will our army like the Romans of old Consider the Invaluable prize for which they are Contending and with their fortitude Attack the Enemy were Ever such they can find them[?]

Floyd's family was harassed and forced to flee to Middletown, Connecticut. He left the Congress and joined them there. For seven years, the rest of the war, he was unable to return to his estate. Later in 1777, after the adoption of the new state constitution, Floyd was appointed a state senator. The following October, he again represented New York in the Continental Congress.

Hannah Floyd died in 1781 because of the strain of the estate crisis. After the war was over, in 1784, Floyd married Joanna Strong of Setauket, New York, the daughter of Benajah Strong and Martha (née Mills) Strong. The family estate on Long Island had been ransacked and all papers and records destroyed. While Floyd recovered this property, he also purchased land on the Mohawk River in upstate New York. There he built a farm, and the couple had two daughters: Ann Floyd (1785–1857), who married George Washington Clinton (1771–1809), son of George Clinton, the first Governor of New York and the fourth Vice President

House of William Floyd

of the United States; and Elizabeth Floyd (1789–1820), who married James Platt (1788–1870), youngest son of Continental Congressmen Zephaniah Platt.

On July 4, 1787, Floyd was made a member of the Society of the Cincinnati for New York. He was elected to the First Congress in March 1789, serving until 1791. He was not reelected. He did act as a presidential elector in 1792, voting for George Washington and George Clinton.

In 1795, Floyd ran for lieutenant governor of New York with Robert Yates as a Democratic-Republican, but was defeated by John Jay and Stephen Van Rensselaer. He was again an elector for president in 1800, selecting Thomas Jefferson and Aaron Burr, and in 1804 when he selected Jefferson and George Clinton. Floyd was a member of the New York Senate for the Western District in 1808.

In 1820, Floyd was chosen as a presidential elector but did not attend the Electoral College. Martin Van Buren replaced him. At this point, he was 86, living in Westernville, New York. Floyd died on August 4, 1821, and was buried at the Westernville Cemetery in Oneida County. His widow passed in 1826. The *American Mercury* reported at the time:

> Thus, another patriot of the Revolution is gone! He was one of the remaining four, viz: John Adams, Thomas Jefferson, Charles

William Floyd (1734–1821)

Carroll, and William Floyd, who signed the Declaration of our Independence.

The old William Floyd House at Mastic Beach on Long Island is open to visitors as part of the Fire Island National Seashore. Over 200 years, eight generations of Floyds have lived there, managing the 25-room mansion on over 600 acres. It was listed on the National Register of Historic Places in 1980. Floyd's Westernville, New York, home remains privately owned, known as the General William Floyd House. It was listed on the National Register of Historic Places in 1971.

Several public schools have been named for William Floyd, including elementary, middle, and high schools in the William Floyd School District in Brookhaven Town. There is also the General William Floyd Elementary School in Oneida County and the Floyd Memorial Library in Greenport, New York. The William Floyd Parkway in Brookhaven bears his name as does the town of Floyd in Oneida County.

Grave of William Floyd

Christopher Gadsden
(1724–1805)

"Sam Adams of the South"

Buried at St. Philip's Churchyard
Charleston, South Carolina

Continental Association • Brigadier General

Christopher Gadsden was a Charleston merchant, brigadier general in the South Carolina state militia, lieutenant governor of South Carolina, and Continental Congressman who signed the Continental Association. He designed a flag with a coiled rattlesnake waiting to strike in defense while sitting on a tuft of grass, a yellow field behind it. The flag became known as the Gadsden Flag.

Gadsden was born on February 16, 1724, in Charleston, South Carolina, to Thomas Gadsden and his wife, Elizabeth Gadsden. The elder Gadsden was the customs collector for the Port of Charleston after being a lieutenant in the Royal Navy. The grandfather, Edward Gadsden, had emigrated to South Carolina from England in 1695. Christopher was the only child from Thomas's first marriage to survive to adulthood. Gadsden's mother died when he was a boy. As a teenager, Gadsden was sent to live with relatives in England to attend school and learn the classics.

Gadsden's father died in 1741 when Christopher was only seventeen. In 1741, he was back in America, serving as an apprentice at a Philadelphia counting-house, when his father passed. At that time, he

Christopher Gadsden (1724–1805)

Christopher Gadsden

inherited a large fortune. As a young man, he was also the purser on the British warship HMS *Aldborough* from 1745 to 1746 during King George's War.

Later, in 1746, Gadsden married Jane Godfrey. By 1747, he had compiled enough capital to repurchase lands sold by his father under duress. In 1750, he built Beneventum Plantation House near Georgetown, South Carolina. Gadsden and his wife had one child, a daughter, Elizabeth.

In 1757, Gadsden was elected to the Commons House of Assembly in South Carolina. He was also the captain of a militia company that fought against the Cherokee in 1759. However, tragedy struck that year when his wife, Jane, died at only 29, leaving Christopher with young Elizabeth.

By 1761, Gadsden was well-known as a prosperous merchant and plantation owner in the Charleston area. He dealt in fine goods, indigo, furs, and rice. He added ships to his holdings and began selling slaves. He became known as a "Country Factor," someone who dealt with the local produce, as opposed to a merchant who traded with England. He next married Mary Hasell, with whom he had a daughter and a son.

In 1762, Governor Boone, out of concern for voting irregularities, dissolved the Commons. Gadsden's reelection was one that was questioned as he earned eighty percent of the vote in a three-way race. When the governor held the elections again, Gadsden still won, leading to tension with the royal government that would last for years.

Gadsden reacted harshly to the Sugar Act (1764) and Stamp Act (1765) and was selected to represent South Carolina at the Stamp Act Congress in New York City. He refused to participate in any conciliatory discussions, instead arguing for the colonists' rights. This came to Samuel Adams' attention, and the two began a long friendship. Gadsden was eventually known as the "Sam Adams of the South." After the Stamp Act was repealed, Gadsden was one of three South Carolinians, including Thomas Lynch and John Rutledge, who had their portraits painted at state expense. Thus, he was one of the founding members of the Sons of Liberty in South Carolina.

In 1767, Gadsden completed the wharf in Charleston Harbor that bears his name. Between its erection and 1808, it is believed that nearly 40% of all enslaved Africans who entered the colonies were processed through this wharf.

Tragedy struck the Gadsden house again in 1769 when his wife, Mary, passed away, leaving two young children. Gadsden, now in his mid-forties, married once more, Anne Wragg, with whom he stayed the rest of his life.

As hostilities increased with England, Gadsden rose to the rank of lieutenant colonel in the militia. He was also elected as a delegate to the First Continental Congress in 1774 along with Thomas Heyward, Jr., Thomas Lynch, Henry Middleton, and Edward Rutledge. John Adams recorded some observations about Gadsden:

> Visited Mr. Gadsden, Mr. Deane, Colonel Dyer, etc. at their lodgings. Gadsden is violent against allowing to Parliament any power of regulating trade, or allowing that they have anything to do with

us. 'Power of regulating trade,' he says, 'is power of ruining us; as bad as acknowledging them a supreme legislative in all cases whatsoever; a right of regulating trade is a right of legislation, and a right of legislation in one case is a right in all; this I deny.' Attended the Congress and committee all the forenoon . . .

Silas Deane observed about Gadsden:

(Christopher Gadsden) leaves all New England Sons of Liberty far behind, for he is for taking up his firelock and marching direct to Boston; nay, he affirmed this morning, that were his wife and all his children in Boston, and they were to perish by the sword, it would not alter his sentiment or proceeding for American liberty.

Despite the harm that it did to his trade business, Gadsden signed the Continental Association, boycotting trade with England.

Gadsden was elected to the Second Continental Congress in 1775 and assigned to the Marine Committee, outfitting the country's first naval mission under the direction of George Washington. At the time, the Marines carried drums painted yellow depicting a coiled rattlesnake with thirteen rattles and the motto "Don't Tread on Me." Realizing the new US Navy needed a flag, Gadsden borrowed the design from the drums and utilized it for a yellow rattlesnake flag he gave to Commodore Esek Hopkins, who used it as his personal standard on his flagship, the USS *Alfred* on December 20, 1775 while the ship was near Philadelphia.

On February 9, 1776, before returning to South Carolina to command the 1st South Carolina Regiment of the Continental Army and aid in the defense of Charleston, Gadsden gave President of Congress William Henry Drayton an example of the flag. This flag has since become known as the Gadsden Flag.

Back in South Carolina, in addition to his military duties, Gadsden served in the state house. In 1778, Gadsden participated in the convention to draft a new constitution for South Carolina. He was then named the lieutenant governor of the state, replacing Henry Laurens, who was off to the Continental Congress.

When Charleston fell to the British in 1780, Governor John Rutledge fled the state to North Carolina to be a "government in exile." Meanwhile Gadsden stayed behind and surrendered the city. He was paroled at his house in Charleston. However, when General Cornwallis took over for General Clinton, the British were harsher towards the

Grave of Christopher Gadsden

parolees and sent twenty men, including Gadsden, to the old Spanish fortress, Castillo de San Marcos, in St. Augustine, Florida. There, he stayed for forty-two weeks.

When released in 1781, Gadsden learned of the British defeat at Cowpens and Cornwallis's movement towards Yorktown. He returned to South Carolina to restore the government.

Though elected governor in 1782, Gadsden declined on his health, having suffered in the prison in Florida. Instead, John Mathews became governor. Gadsden remained involved in the state house, however, and was against the confiscation of the property of Loyalists who had fled the state. In 1788, Gadsden was a member of the state convention to ratify the new US Constitution. During the intervening years, Gadsden was a strong supporter of both Presidents Washington and Adams.

Gadsden built a house at 329 East Bay Street in Charleston in 1798. It incorporated the snake motif from the Gadsden flag in the iron works.

Following an accidental fall on August 28, 1805, Gadsden died in Charleston. He was buried in St. Philip's Churchyard in the city alongside his parents. Charleston's *City Gazette* reported at the time:

> The long and meritorious services of this most valuable and lamented citizen are too well known to his countrymen to require a lengthy recital of them here—suffice it to say, that he was one of the earliest patriots of Carolina and the revolution; that as a soldier in the field, as a statesman 0f our councils, and in the private walks of the citizen, his whole life was devoted to the service of his country.

The Gadsden Purchase of Arizona was named for Gadsden's grandson, James. Battery Gadsden on Sullivan's Island at Fort Moultrie is named after him.

Nathan Hale
(1755–1776)

"But One Life"

Buried at Nathan Hale Cemetery (cenotaph)
South Coventry, Connecticut

Hero and Martyr

Nathan Hale was a young Connecticut Patriot who spied for the Continental Army and was captured and executed by the British. Ever since he has been lauded as a hero for his devotion to the Patriot cause despite his young age.

Hale, born June 6, 1755, in Coventry, Connecticut, was the son of Deacon Richard Hale, a minister, and his wife, Elizabeth (née Strong) Hale. The elder Hale was a descendant of the Reverend John Hale of the Salem witch trials of 1692.

From 1769 to 1773, Hale attended Yale College with his older brother Enoch. While there, they befriended fellow student Benjamin Tallmadge, who later became a spy for the Patriot cause. The Hale brothers were members of the Linonian Society of Yale, a debate club that discussed the issues and culture of the day. Hall graduated with honors at age 18 and became a teacher in East Haddam and then New London.

Following the Battles of Lexington and Concord, Hale joined the Connecticut Militia. Possibly concerned about his teaching contract that was set to expire in July 1775, Hale stayed behind when his company was involved in the Siege of Boston. On July 4, 1775, Hale received a letter

Nathan Hale (1755–1776)

Bronze statue of Nathan Hale

from his friend Benjamin Tallmadge, who was in Boston to witness the siege. Wrote Tallmadge:

> Was I in your condition, I think the more extensive service would be my choice. Our holy Religion, the honor of our God, a glorious country, & a happy constitution is what we have to defend.

Hale was so inspired by the letter that he rejoined the 7th Connecticut Regiment led by Colonel Charles Webb and was commissioned as a first lieutenant. As the Siege of Boston ended and the focus shifted to New York City, Hale joined Knowlton's Rangers, the first organized intelligence unit in the Continental Army. Lieutenant Colonel Charles Knowlton and his men helped to defend Manhattan. As the British routed the Continentals on Long Island, General Washington escaped from Brooklyn Heights to Manhattan under cover of darkness. When the commander in chief, via Knowlton, called for a spy to serve behind enemy lines on Long Island, Hale was the only volunteer, the others preferring to risk dying in battle rather than in disguise. Thus, Hale, disguised as a Dutch schoolteacher seeking work, was ferried across the Long Island Sound to Huntington, New York, on September 12, 1776.

Unfortunately, on September 15, the British invaded the southern tip of Manhattan, forcing Washington to Harlem Heights on the north end of the island. On September 21, the Great New York Fire of 1776 blazed through the town. Some thought the Americans sabotaged the city, but Washington and the Congress had rejected the idea. The Americans accused the British of burning and sacking the town. Regardless, after the fire, more than 200 Patriots were detained for questioning, Hale being one of them.

There are conflicting accounts as to how Hale was caught. Consider Tiffany, a Loyalist Connecticut shopkeeper, related that Major Robert Rogers of the Queen's Rangers recognized Hale at a tavern and duped him by pretending to be a Patriot. He then took him into custody in Queens, near Flushing Bay. Another possibility involved a Loyalist cousin, Samuel Hale, who betrayed him.

Regardless, Hale was searched and interrogated. It is said General William Howe questioned him himself. That night, Hale was either held in a greenhouse or one of the bedrooms of Howe's headquarters. His requests for a Bible and clergyman were both denied. He was permitted to write two letters, one to his brother Enoch and the other to his commanding officer. Both were never sent. They were torn up the next morning in front of Hale.

That morning, September 22, 1776, Nathan Hale was marched along the Post Road to the Park of Artillery next to the Dove Tavern (currently 66th Street and 3rd Ave in Manhattan). There, he was hanged

Nathan Hale (1755–1776)

Execution of Captain Hale

by the British as a spy. He was only 21 years old. All accounts state Hale composed himself very well despite the situation. Wrote British officer Frederick McKensie, who was present:

> He behaved with great composure and resolution, saying he thought it the duty of every good Officer, to obey any orders given him by his Commander-in-Chief; and desired the Spectators to be at all times prepared to meet death in whatever shape it might appear.

There were no official records of Hale's final words. According to tradition, based on the account of British Captain John Montresor, a witness, he famously said, "I only regret that I have but one life to lose for my country." Montresor had spoken to American Captain William Hull the next day under a flag of truce. Hull recorded in his memoirs the following related by Montresor:

"On the morning of his execution," continued the officer, "my station was near the fatal spot, and I requested the Provost Marshal [William Cunningham] to permit the prisoner to sit in my marquee, while he was making the necessary preparations. Captain Hale entered: he was calm, and bore himself with gentle dignity, in the consciousness of rectitude and high intentions. He asked for writing materials, which I furnished him: he wrote two letters, one to his mother and one to a brother officer. He was shortly after summoned to the gallows. But a few persons were around him, yet his characteristic dying words were remembered. He said, 'I only regret, that I have but one life to lose for my country.'"

Some scholars believe Hale was paraphrasing or quoting lines from a popular play, *Cato*, which he was likely familiar with:

How beautiful is death, when earn'd by virtue!
Who would not be that youth? What pity is it
That we can die but once to serve our country.

There are varying accounts of what he said or how it was said. Most likely, the British officer was only telling the most prominent line of a much longer speech. Regardless, it was certainly a tragic and profound moment.

Besides the 66th Street and 3rd Avenue location, City Hall Park and Grand Central Terminal both claim to be the hanging site. A plaque hung by the Daughters of the American Revolution at the Yale Club at 44th Street and Vanderbilt Avenue claims the event occurred near the club. Grand Central Terminal is only feet away.

Hale's body was not recovered by the family and has been lost to time. They erected a memorial with an empty grave at the Nathan Hale Cemetery in South Coventry, Connecticut.

Nathan Hale is one of the most memorialized of all Patriots. He has had numerous statues and portraits made, though there are no known paintings of him in life. His name has been assigned to buildings, schools, forts, ships, and towns. He has appeared on several postage stamps. His ancestral home is also a historic site, and there are numerous markers throughout Long Island and Manhattan.

A full-sized statue of Hale was unveiled in Langley, Virginia, at CIA headquarters on June 6, 1973, the bicentennial of his graduation from Yale. In a statement at that time, Hale was said to be "the country's first intelligence officer." According to Agency tradition, an officer who places a Washington quarter at Hale's statue when leaving on an assignment will return safely.

Monument to Nathan Hale

Edward Hand
(1744–1802)
Lancaster's Major General

Buried at St. James Episcopal Church Cemetery,
Lancaster, Pennsylvania.

Military • Continental Congress

Edward Hand was born and raised in Ireland and first came to America as a doctor in the British army. He was sympathetic to the American cause and enlisted in the Continental Army where he had an illustrious career rising to retire as a Major General. He served with George Washington at the battle of Trenton and served as Adjutant General during the Battle of Yorktown. He later was elected to the Continental Congress and the Pennsylvania Assembly and was a delegate to the Pennsylvania Constitutional Convention.

Edward Hand was born December 31, 1744, in Clyduff, Kings County (now County Offaly) in central Ireland. He was educated at Trinity College in Dublin where he studied medicine. He decided to put his medical training to use by joining the British army as a surgeon's mate and was assigned to the 18th Royal Irish Regiment of Foot.

He and his regiment set sail from Cobh, County Cork, on May 20, 1767, and arrived in Philadelphia on July 11, 1767. He was 23 years old when he arrived in the colonies and was assigned to Fort Pitt. Along with his regiment, he marched west from Philadelphia to the fort located where the city of Pittsburgh sits today.

Edward Hand (1744–1802)

Edward Hand

Fort Pitt was, at the time, one of the key defensive positions and one of the most imposing, complex, and elaborate British installations in the Americas.

Hand would remain at Fort Pitt for the remainder of his time in the British army. In 1774, he resigned his commission and moved to Lancaster, Pennsylvania and practiced medicine. There he met Katherine Ewing and married her on March 13, 1775. The couple would have four children, three daughters and a son. Only one of the daughters and the son would survive to adulthood.

In April 1775 Hand had sided with the American cause against England and volunteered for service in the Continental Army. He was commissioned as a Lt. Colonel on the 1st Pennsylvania Regiment of Riflemen, made up of mostly Scots-Irish. He was second in command to Colonel William Thompson from County Meath, which is just north of Dublin. Their first assignment was to support the Continental Army's siege of Boston. They were renamed the 1st Continental Regiment, and after the siege, in March 1776 they were sent to reinforce American troops in Canada. When Colonel Thompson was captured during an attack in Quebec, Hand assumed command. After they withdrew from Canada, the regiment rejoined the Continental Army in New York.

There the regiment was involved in the Battle of Long Island in August 1776. In danger of being destroyed, Washington ordered an evacuation of the army to Manhattan. Hand and his Pennsylvania riflemen made up the rear guard and delayed the British until the rest of the army was safe across the East River in Manhattan.

Hand's regiment made up the rear guard all during the army's retreat across New Jersey to Pennsylvania. Next Hand and his Pennsylvania riflemen took part in the Battles of Trenton in December 1776 and Princeton in January 1777. Hand's men played a significant role in Trenton on January 2 that led to Washington's victory in Princeton on January 3.

The grave of Edward Hand

Edward Hand's home, Rock Ford Plantation

Impressed by Hand's consistently fine conduct and his demonstrating tactical and administrative abilities, Washington prevailed on Congress to appoint Hand Brigadier General on April 1, 1777.

Ironically he was then assigned to Fort Pitt where he improved the effectiveness of the local militia and secured the neutrality of the Delaware and Shawnee Indians.

In 1780, he was recalled from the west and given command of a brigade of light infantry in Lafayette's division. In that capacity, he sat on the court-martial that condemned Major John André to death for spying.

In 1781, Washington appointed Hand as the Adjutant General serving directly under him. He reorganized the army despite scant supplies. He also worked closely with Washington at Mt. Vernon and Williamsburg during the planning for the Siege and Battle of Yorktown which led to the surrender of the British Army in October of 1781.

At the end of the war, Hand resigned his commission from the army but not before he received a promotion to Major General in September 1783 in recognition of his long and distinguished service. He resigned in November 1783 and returned to practice medicine in Lancaster. He purchased several hundred acres of land and built a mansion he named "Rock Ford Plantation."

On November 12, 1783, the Pennsylvania legislature elected Hand to a seat in the Continental Congress. The following year Hand received a letter from Washington expressing his appreciation for the "great zeal, attention and ability manifested by you, in conducting the business of your Department, and how happy I should be in opportunities of demonstrating my sincere regard and esteem for you."

Hand served in the Pennsylvania assembly from 1785-1786 and in 1790 was chosen as a delegate to the Pennsylvania Constitutional Convention.

On September 4, 1802, Edward Hand died at his home in Lancaster. There are some reports about the cause of his death including stroke, typhoid, dysentery, pneumonia, and cholera. He is buried in St. James Episcopal Church Cemetery in Lancaster. His estate Rock Ford is a historic site and open to the public.

John Hanson
(1715–1783)

President of the United States in Congress Assembled

Buried at Addison Burial Ground,
Oxon Hill, Maryland

Articles of Confederation • President of Congress

John Hanson was a merchant and politician from Maryland who was a member of the Continental Congress. He signed the Articles of Confederation and was then elected the first President of Congress Assembled after their ratification.

John Hanson was born on April 3, 1715, at the plantation "Mulberry Grove" in Port Tobacco Parish, Charles County, Maryland, the son of Samuel Hanson (1685-1740), a planter, and his wife, Elizabeth (née Storey) Hanson (1688-1764). Samuel owned more than 1,000 acres and served in various political offices, including the Maryland General Assembly. Hanson's grandfather, also named John, was an indentured servant who came to Charles County, Maryland, circa 1661.

There is no record or mention of Hanson receiving formal schooling, so it is assumed by historians he was tutored privately, as was customary. He followed in his father's footsteps, managing the plantation. Circa 1744, Hanson married Jane Contee of a well-known Maryland family. She was only sixteen at the time, and the couple remained married for Hanson's entire life. The couple had nine children, five of whom lived to adulthood.

John Hanson

Hanson's first political office was sheriff of Charles County in 1750. He then followed his father as the representative of Charles County in the Maryland General Assembly, serving for twelve years starting in 1757. During the 1760s, Hanson was a leading agitator against the Sugar Act of 1764 and the Stamp Act of 1765. In 1769, he signed the nonimportation resolution boycotting British imports in response to the Townshend Acts. At this time, Hanson resigned from the General Assembly, sold his Charles County properties, and moved to Frederick County, Maryland. There, he was elected deputy surveyor, sheriff, and county treasurer.

As tensions increased with Great Britain in 1774, Hanson became a leading patriot in Frederick County. He led the passage of a town resolution opposing the Boston Port Act and sent 200 pounds of his own money to support the citizens. The next year, he was a delegate to the Maryland Convention that replaced the General Assembly and was the Maryland Committee of Correspondence chairman. He signed the Association of Freeman on July 26, 1775, hoping for reconciliation, but calling for military resistance to the enforcement of the Coercive Acts.

Hanson was also highly active in organizing the local military, recruiting and arming soldiers, paying them with his own funds. Frederick County sent the first southern troops to join George Washington. They were led by Michael Cresap and Thomas Price, arriving in Boston on August 9, 1775, after marching twenty-two days. Hanson's son, Lieutenant Peter Contee Hanson, was among them. He was mortally wounded at Fort Washington and died in November 1775.

In June 1776, Hanson and his Frederick County patriots urged Maryland's delegates in the Continental Congress to declare independence from Britain. Meanwhile, Hanson was busy "making gunlocks, storing powder, guarding prisoners, raising money and troops, dealing with Tories, and doing the myriad other tasks which went with being chairman of the committee of observation."

In 1777, Hanson was elected to the new Maryland House of Delegates, serving five annual terms. In December 1779, they named him a delegate to the Second Continental Congress. Hanson began serving in Philadelphia in June 1780, immediately becoming involved in various finance committees. At the time, the ratification of the Articles of Confederation was stalled in Maryland because of concerns about western land claims. After the other states agreed to relinquish their western claims that interfered with Maryland, Hanson and Daniel Carroll signed the Articles on March 1, 1781. At this point, the Articles were officially ratified at the national level and went into effect.

Since its inception, the Continental Congress had a presiding officer titled the President of Congress who oversaw the debates and deliberations. Eight men had played this part in the early days of our nation. With the signing of the Articles of Confederation, the new office of President of the Congress Assembled was created as the first presiding officer of the officially united colonies. At that moment, Samuel Huntington, the incumbent President of Congress, transitioned from the prior role to the new one, but his term was now exceeding a year. On July 9, 1781, Samuel Johnston was the first man elected to the new office, but he declined. Thomas McKean was next elected but served only a few months, resigning after the surrender at Yorktown. On November 5, 1781, Congress elected Hanson as President of Congress Assembled, succeeding Thomas McKean. The role involved moderating discussions, handling official correspondence, and signing documents. Hanson did not enjoy the role out of the gate and discussed resigning after one week, citing his health and family responsibilities. His colleagues urged him to remain due to the lack of a quorum necessary to choose a successor. Hanson carried out his duty through his entire one-year term, ending November 4, 1782.

During his term, Hanson welcomed George Washington back to Philadelphia following his victory at Yorktown. Washington presented Cornwallis's sword to Congress. He also lightened his administrative burden by creating executive departments to deal with the myriad of correspondence and contracts, including the Treasury Department, the first Secretary of War, and the first Foreign Affairs Department. He saw to the removal of all foreign troops from American lands, as well as their flags. He gained agreement on the eventual statehood of the Western Territories. Hanson was also responsible for establishing Thanksgiving Day as the fourth Thursday in November. Elias Boudinot succeeded Hanson on November 5, 1782, but he continued as a delegate in the Congress for one more term.

In 1783, Hanson retired from Congress and returned to his nephew's estate near Oxon Hill in Prince George's County, Maryland. Oddly, word circulated in the papers that he had died in May 1783, but he had not. Retractions followed,

> The account published in the Philadelphia papers, of the death of the Honorable John Hanson, Esq; late President of Congress, we have the pleasure of assuring the public is premature; that worthy patriot being now in perfect health.

However, Hanson did die later in the year, on November 22, 1783. He was entombed on the estate at Oxon Hill, now known as the Addison Burial Ground. Unfortunately, the exact location of his grave has been lost, and the precise location of his remains is unknown. There was substantial development in the area, and the grave may have been vandalized.

According to biographer Seymour Weyss Smith, the American Revolution had two primary leaders: George Washington over the military and John Hanson in politics. However, this biography has been criticized as lacking academic support.

Of Hanson's children, Jane Contee Hanson (1747–1781) married Philip Thomas (1747–1815); Peter Contee Hanson, as mentioned, died at Fort Washington; and Alexander Contee Hanson (1749–1806) was a notable essayist. Alexander's son, by the same name, was a newspaper editor and U.S. senator from Maryland from 1813 to 1819.

John Hanson is one of the two Marylanders honored with a statue in the National Statuary Hall Collection in Washington, D.C. However, some lawmakers have recently lobbied to replace it with Harriet Tubman.

In 1972, Hanson was honored with a U.S. postal card featuring his name and portrait. He was also featured on a postage stamp. Route 50 between Washington, D.C., and Annapolis is named the John Hanson Highway. Middle schools in Oxon Hill and Waldorf, Maryland, are named after him. At one time, there was a bank named in his honor.

Since the 1970s, April 14 is John Hanson Day in Maryland thanks to a measure sponsored by descendent John Hanson Briscoe, who served as Speaker of the Maryland House of Delegates. The Hanson Memorial Association was created in 2009 to erect the John Hanson National Memorial and educate the public about Hanson. The memorial includes a statue at the courthouse in Frederick, Maryland.

George Robert Twelves Hewes
(1742—1840)

"The Shoemaker and the Tea Party"

Buried at Grand Army of the Republic Cemetery
Richfield Springs, New York

Boston Massacre • Boston Tea Party • Privateer • Soldier

George Robert Twelves Hewes is not a household name, but around the time of his death, his memoirs about the American Revolution were very popular and he had become a celebrity. Hewes, who lived nearly 100 years, was a witness or participant in both the Boston Massacre and the Boston Tea Party. He was later a militiaman and privateer. More recently, historian Alfred Young wrote about Hewes in his popular history *The Shoemaker and the Tea Party*.

Hewes was born on August 25, 1742, in the South End of Boston, Massachusetts, to a poor family. He was named after his father, George, his uncle, Robert, and his maternal grandmother, whose maiden name was Twelves. When Hewes was only seven, his father, a failed tanner and soap boiler, died. His widowed mother was hard on Hewes, and at fourteen, she apprenticed him to a shoemaker named Downing, whom he disliked. Scrawny and only 5'1" tall, Hewes ran off in the spring of 1756 and attempted to join the British Army with a friend named Paul Revere but was rejected due to his size. Revere was admitted, and though turned away, Hewes' rebellious nature festered.

According to his memoirs, after 4,000 soldiers occupied Boston in 1768, Hewes was sometimes the victim of British soldiers taking from his

George Robert Twelves Hewes (1742—1840)

George Robert Twelves Hewes

shop without paying, and he resented when challenged by sentries while minding his own business. He protested with other artisans who were also shirked or who had their jobs taken by moonlighting soldiers. Struggling as a shoemaker, Hewes borrowed money for a proper suit so he could court the daughter of the sexton of the First Baptist Church, Sarah "Sally" Sumner. The two married that year and eventually had fifteen children.

Hewes was present on February 22, 1770, when ten-year-old Christopher Seider was shot and killed by a customs official, Ebenezer Richardson, who later received a royal pardon. About two weeks later, on March 5, 1770, Hewes joined a mob of craftsmen in support of Edward Garrick, who was harassing Lieutenant John Goldfinch over a previous debt. The mob threw snowballs and jeered at the British soldiers who were present. In response, a soldier clubbed an apprentice wigmaker with the butt of his musket, increasing the tension. The mob dared the soldiers to fire as Richardson had done. A melee ensued, and Hewes, who was unarmed, was struck in the shoulder by Private Matthew Kilroy's musket. Other soldiers opened fire, killing five men, four of whom were friends of Hewes, including James Caldwell, whom Hewes caught as he fell dead from a wound to the chest. Returning home following what became known as the Boston Massacre, Hewes verbally confronted two British soldiers, per the official deposition he gave the next day.

Noticing Hewes's radicalism and outspokenness, the Loyalist tailor to whom he owed about $300 in modern terms sought payment of the debt. Unable to pay, and with a young bride and a baby at home, Hewes was thrown in debtors' prison in September 1770.

When Britain implemented the Tea Act, the colonists first refused to buy East India Company tea and turned ships away at the docks. After the British Navy arrived to force the unloading of the tea, Hewes was among the sixty disguised protestors at Boston Harbor on the cool moonlit night of December 16, 1773. He joined one third of the rabble, which was boarding the *Dartmouth*. Meanwhile, two other parties boarded the *Eleanor* and *Beaver*. Hewes, on account of his ability to whistle, was made "boatswain" for his party, given the responsibility to demand the keys to the tea chests from the captain. Recalled Thompson Maxwell, who was sent by John Hancock, "I went accordingly, joined the band under one Captain Hewes; we mounted the ships and made tea in a trice. In the heat of conflict, the small man with the large name had been elevated from a poor shoemaker to Captain Hewes."

Hewes described the events in his memoir:

> It was now evening, and I immediately dressed myself in the costume of an Indian, equipped with a small hatchet, which I and my associates denominated the tomahawk, with which, and a club, after having painted my face and hands with coal dust in the shop of a blacksmith, I repaired to Griffin's wharf, where the ships lay that contained the tea. When I first appeared in the street after being thus disguised, I fell in with many who were dressed, equipped, and painted as I was, and who fell in with me and marched in order to the place of our destination.
>
> When we arrived at the wharf, there were three of our number who assumed an authority to direct our operations, to which we readily submitted. They divided us into three parties, for the

purpose of boarding the three ships which contained the tea at the same time. The name of him who commanded the division to which I was assigned was Leonard Pitt. The names of the other commanders I never knew.

We were immediately ordered by the respective commanders to board all the ships at the same time, which we promptly obeyed. The commander of the division to which I belonged as soon as we were on board the ship appointed me boatswain and ordered me to go to the captain and demand of him the keys to the hatches and a dozen candles. I made the demand accordingly, and the captain promptly replied, and delivered the articles; but requested me at the same time to do no damage to the ship or rigging.

We then were ordered by our commander to open the hatches and take out all the chests of tea and throw them overboard, and we immediately proceeded to execute his orders, first cutting and splitting the chests with our tomahawks, so as thoroughly to expose them to the effects of the water.

In about three hours from the time we went on board, we had thus broken and thrown overboard every tea chest to be found in the ship, while those in the other ships were disposing of the tea in the same way, at the same time. We were surrounded by British armed ships, but no attempt was made to resist us.

We then quietly retired to our several places of residence, without having any conversation with each other, or taking any measures to discover who were our associates; nor do I recollect of our having had the knowledge of the name of a single individual concerned in that affair, except that of Leonard Pitt, the commander of my division, whom I have mentioned. There appeared to be an understanding that each individual should volunteer his services, keep his own secret, and risk the consequence for himself. No disorder took place during that transaction, and it was observed at that time that the stillest night ensued that Boston had enjoyed for many months.

During the time we were throwing the tea overboard, there were several attempts made by some of the citizens of Boston and its vicinity to carry off small quantities of it for their family use. To effect that object, they would watch their opportunity to snatch up a handful from the deck, where it became plentifully scattered, and put it into their pockets.

One Captain O'Connor, whom I well knew, came on board for that purpose, and when he supposed he was not noticed, filled his pockets, and also the lining of his coat. But I had detected him and gave information to the captain of what he was doing. We were ordered to take him into custody, and just as he was stepping from the vessel, I seized him by the skirt of his coat, and in attempting to pull him back, I tore it off; but, springing forward, by a rapid effort he made his escape. He had, however, to run a gauntlet through the crowd upon the wharf nine each one, as he passed, giving him a kick or a stroke.

Another attempt was made to save a little tea from the ruins of the cargo by a tall, aged man who wore a large, cocked hat and white wig, which was fashionable at that time. He had sleightly slipped a little into his pocket, but being detected, they seized him and, taking his hat and wig from his head, threw them, together with the tea, of which they had emptied his pockets, into the water. In consideration of his advanced age, he was permitted to escape, with now and then a slight kick.

The following morning, the harbor was awash in tea. Hewes further described:

> The next morning, after we had cleared the ships of the tea, it was discovered that very considerable quantities of it were floating upon the surface of the water, and to prevent the possibility of any of its being saved for use, a number of small boats were manned by sailors and citizens, who rowed them into those parts of the harbor wherever the tea was visible, and by beating it with oars and paddles so thoroughly drenched it as to render its entire destruction inevitable.

The following month, the scrappy Hewes was involved in another incident that made the *Massachusetts Gazette*. He came upon Loyalist customs official John Malcolm, who was now in Boston after being tarred and feathered in Portsmouth, New Hampshire, the previous November.

The zealous Malcolm, whom Hewes often harassed, was seen taking his cane to an insolent child. Hewes intervened, and the two argued. Malcolm told the lower-class Hewes to stay out of the business of gentlemen. Hewes quipped that at least he had not been tarred and feathered like Malcolm, who whirled with his cane and struck Hewes so hard on the forehead that it split open, and he was knocked unconscious. Some of the witnesses who were present carried Hewes off to be treated by Dr. Joseph Warren. Meanwhile, others who remained thought Hewes was dead. Dr. Warren was able to revive Hewes, but he bore the mark on his forehead for the rest of his life.

The following morning, Hewes went to a magistrate's office to place charges against Malcolm. Later that night, January 25, 1774, an angry mob, thinking Hewes dead, descended on Malcom's home and seized him. They dragged him onto King Street and stripped him to the waist. They covered Malcolm in tar and feathers and hauled him to the Liberty Tree, where they threatened to hang him or remove his ears if he did not apologize. Hewes showed up and attempted to stop the crowd from killing Malcolm, who complied and was released.

As Britain implemented martial law in Boston, Hewes and many other Patriots fled the city. He sent his family to his father's hometown of Wrentham and then tried to escape Boston by boat, posing as a fisherman. For nine weeks, Hewes continued a ruse that he was a fisherman, and was permitted to use his boat provided the British soldiers had first pick of the fish. When he was finally ready to escape, he applied for his fishing permit. According to his memoir, *Traits of the Tea Party, Being A Memoir of George R. T. Hewes* by Thatcher:

> Hewes was a civil man, and he made his bow to the Admiral and asked for his pass. The old gentleman, for some reason or other, looked more inquisitive than his wont.
>
> "How many are going, Hewes?" he enquired, looking him sharp in the eye.
>
> "Three, your honor," said Hewes.
>
> "And who will be skipper?"
>
> "Your humble servant, Sir—for want of a better."

"Very well, Mr. Skipper Hewes!"—and here he went on to remind him of the rules and closed his discourse with warning him of all deserters, which, to be sure, had in several cases proved to be no joke, as Hewes well knew; "and now," he added, with a profound emphasis, "I know what you want—I see it in the twinkling of your eye, Skipper; but mark what I tell you—if we catch you running off—look out! Skipper—that's all—look out!"

Of course, Hewes and his comrades "ran off" after heading out into the harbor to fish. In choppy seas, they had one more guard boat to pass. The two companions hid below while Hewes addressed the captain, promising to stop there first with any fish. The captain waved him on. The companions returned atop, and no one pursued them as they landed in Lynn and headed for Newhall's Tavern, where they were taken into custody by the guards.

The following morning, Hewes and his escapees were taken before the Committee of Safety, who then sent them on to meet with General Washington, who was headquartered nearby. In the yard of the general's quarters, Washington came out and inspected them. The men removed their hats in respect, but Washington quietly told them to return them to their heads.

"I am only a man," said George, referring to his lack of nobility.

As Washington interrogated them, one of the persons present, Parson Thatcher, recognized Hewes and mentioned his uncle was a "Great liberty man." Washington then pulled Hewes aside and took him into the parlor where Hewes related his entire story to the general and answered all his questions. Satisfied and intrigued, Washington invited the rest of the men inside and treated them to lunch, with Mrs. Washington helping to serve the guests. She had just recently arrived at the camp to be with George.

After dinner, Washington offered them some money, but they declined. However, the offer for a new pair of shoes for one of the party, who had very poor shoes, was graciously accepted. Washington provided passes for the men to get through the lines and head inland to join their families. Hewes then spent the rest of the Revolution with the family in Wrentham but left for service periodically. Of his former business in Boston, he later said, "The shop which I had built in Boston, I lost; it was pulled down and burned by British troops."

In the fall of 1776, Hewes was a privateer aboard the *Diamond*, capturing three enemy vessels in the first three months. When the captain tried to extend the voyage longer without any additional prizes, Hewes joined in a threatened mutiny if the ship did not return to Providence, Rhode Island.

In 1777, Hewes served in the militia for a few months and saw action at the Battle of Rhode Island in 1778.

In 1779, Hewes was back aboard ship, sailing on the *Defence* under Captain Samuel Smedley for seven and a half months. Despite capturing four ships and thousands of dollars, the captain refused to give Hewes his share.

Hewes served on land in the militia in 1780 and 1781. The following year, he hired a substitute to avoid the draft, the pressures of family weighed too heavily.

The Hewes family continued to live in Wrentham through the beginning of the War of 1812. It is believed eleven of the fifteen Hughes children survived. Two of his sons volunteered for the militia in 1812.

After the war, Hewes and his wife moved to Richland Springs in Otsego County, New York, close to some of their children. Hewes continued his shoemaking business, even in old age. As the fiftieth anniversary of the Revolution occurred in 1826, organizers began looking for the few remaining veterans in the community. Hewes was one.

Wife Sarah Hewes died in 1828 at age 77. Hewes, now a widower, continued to be recognized for his long-ago service in the Revolution. Soon, he was the oldest surviving member of the community who had direct involvement. He would appear at festivities in his militia uniform every July 4th.

One day, in the 1830s, writer James Hawkes "discovered" Hewes and wrote a biography titled *A Retrospect of the Boston Tea-Party*. The book sold very well, and Hewes toured New England in 1835, achieving celebrity status. He was a guest of honor at a celebration with the last surviving members of the Tea Party. He sat for a portrait by Joseph

Cole called *The Centenarian* which still hangs in the Old State House in Boston. A second biography, *Traits of the Tea Party* by attorney Benjamin Bussey Thatcher, followed.

Unfortunately, on July 4, 1840, while boarding a carriage to attend the annual festivities, Hewes was injured in an accident. He died November 5, 1840, at 98, though some believed him to be 109. He was buried without any commemoration at Richland Springs. In 1896, Hewes was reburied with a proper ceremony at the Grand Army of the Republic Cemetery among other veterans.

Historians have been amazed at how connected Hewes appeared to have been, interacting with some of the most famous people of his age. Many have challenged his veracity, but the stories and records available have been checked out, and no one has been able to disprove his eyewitness accounts.

Historian and biographer Alfred Young summed up Hewes: "He was a nobody who briefly became a somebody in the Revolution and, for a moment near the end of his life, a hero."

Grave of George Robert Twelves Hewes

Stephen Hopkins
(1707–1785)

"Greatest Statesman of Rhode Island"

Buried at North Burial Ground
Providence, Rhode Island

**Continental Congress • Continental Association
Declaration of Independence**

Stephen Hopkins was a Quaker colonial governor of Rhode Island and Providence Plantations who sided with the Patriots and signed the Continental Association and Declaration of Independence as a member of the Continental Congress. In John Trumbull's famous painting, *The Declaration of Independence*, Hopkins is seen standing in the back with his distinctive hat. Hopkins was also a judge, educator, merchant ship owner, and surveyor.

Hopkins was born March 7, 1707, in Cranston, Rhode Island. He was the first son and second of nine children of the itinerant farmer William Hopkins and his wife, Ruth (née Wilkinson) Hopkins. The elder Hopkins was the son of William Hopkins, a prominent Rhode Island politician, and the grandson of Thomas Hopkins, one of the original settlers of the Providence Plantations, sailing from England with his cousin, Benedict Arnold, in 1635. Arnold was the first governor of Rhode Island following its charter in 1663 and was an ancestor to the famous general and traitor of the American Revolution. The family tradition, in some genealogies, linking Hopkins to Stephen Hopkins of the *Mayflower* is unfounded.

Stephen Hopkins

Hopkins' mother was the granddaughter of Lieutenant Lawrence Wilkinson of Charles I's army, who was taken prisoner by the Scots at the surrender of Newcastle-on-Tyne on October 22, 1644. He lost his lands and thus emigrated to New England circa 1646 as an indentured servant and was in Providence by 1652. He was a freeman by 1658 and became a deputy of the General Court, a soldier in the Indian wars, and a member of the Colonial Assembly in 1659.

Hopkins grew up on a modest farm in Scituate, Rhode Island. His mother started his education by teaching him to read and write. His uncle and grandfather taught him mathematics and surveying, and he read the English classics in his grandfather's library. He learned farming from his father, who gave him his first farmland at 19.

Also at age 19, on October 9, 1726, Hopkins married Sarah Scott, a relation of Anne Hutchinson and Joseph Jenks, with whom he had seven children before she developed a debilitating illness in the 1750s. She committed suicide at age 47 in 1753. Hopkins married Ann Smith, a widow, in 1755.

At age 23 in 1730, Hopkins began his public career as a justice of the peace in Scituate, Rhode Island. In 1732, he was elected the town clerk, a post he held until 1741, and to a seat in the General Assembly, where he served until 1752, for his first tenure. He was Speaker of the Assembly from 1738 to 1744 and in 1749. Despite not having a law degree, Hopkins was named Chief Justice of the Court of Common Pleas for Rhode Island, and in 1747, was appointed as a Justice on the Rhode Island Supreme Court, serving until May 1749. From May 1751 to May 1755, Hopkins became the Chief Justice of this court. During these years, he became President of the Scituate Town Council.

Hopkins sold his farm in Scituate in 1742 and moved to Providence. Here, he became a merchant and outfitted ships with his brother, Esek Hopkins. They traded in wool and cloth. He was part owner, with Sheriff John Mawney and his son, Colonel Peter Mawney, of the privateering vessel *Reprisal* in 1745. The painter John Greenwood included Hopkins (drunk and dozing at the table) in his satirical 1750s painting *Sea Captains Carousing in Surinam*. Later, Hopkins became involved in manufacturing and was partners with brothers Moses and John Brown in establishing the Hope Furnace. They made pig iron, which was used in the Revolutionary War. Son Rufus Hopkins managed the foundry for four decades.

Following the death of his first wife, Hopkins became more interested in colonial politics, supporting the colonies in developing their own voice in matters affecting them. He helped establish a public subscription library and was the first chancellor of Rhode Island College, which became Brown University. He became a member of the American Philosophical Society of Newport.

In 1754, he served as a delegate to the Colonial Congress meeting in Albany, New York, with 150 members of the Iroquois Nations. The meeting aimed to prevent the natives from joining with the French and to create an alliance with the colonies that granted them additional rights. Unfortunately, the colonies did not approve the agreement, but it was a precursor to later attempts at unified action. Hopkins penned a history of the proceedings in *A True Representation of the Plan formed at Albany, in 1754, for Uniting all the British Northern Colonies*. He also met Ben Franklin in Albany, and the two remained friends for the rest of their lives.

In 1755, Hopkins was elected Governor of Rhode Island, serving for nine of the next fifteen years. During this time, he became embroiled in political intrigue with rival governor Samuel Ward, who served when Hopkins was not. The two engaged in what became known as the Ward-Hopkins War or Ward-Hopkins Controversy between Hopkins' "Providence faction" and Ward's "Newport faction." In 1757, Ward accused Hopkins of using his office for personal gain. Enraged, Hopkins brought countercharges, resulting in a court case that had to be held in Massachusetts due to the fractious nature of Rhode Island. James Otis represented Hopkins, and the two became friends, but Otis lost this case, and Hopkins had to pay all the court costs. Hopkins bitterly threatened to "blow Ward's brains out" and subsequently lost the next election to William Greene, a leader of the Ward Faction. However, when Ward died suddenly in 1758, the General Assembly selected Hopkins as his successor, bypassing Ward.

Hopkins started two very successful newspapers, the *Providence Gazette* and *Country Journal*, in 1762. He used them to his political advantage, especially concerning the Stamp Act and the controversy regarding currency; Ward supported hard currency, and Hopkins supported paper, and the two continued to tangle. Hopkins, meanwhile, was the only colonial governor not to take an oath in support of the Stamp Act. In 1766, he penned a pamphlet, *The Grievances of the American Colonies*, calling for the basic human rights of the colonists. Ten years before the Declaration of Independence, Hopkins wrote:

> Liberty is the greatest blessing that men enjoy, and slavery is the greatest curse that human nature is capable of. Hence it is a matter of the utmost importance to men, which of the two shall be their Portion. Absolute liberty is perhaps incompatible with any kind of government. The safety resulting from society and the advantage of just and equal laws hath caused men to forego some part of

their natural liberty and submit to government. This appears to be the most rational account of its beginning; although it must be confessed, mankind has by no means agreed about it: some have found its original in the divine appointment; others have thought it took its rise from power . . .

Finally, in 1768, the two rivals agreed not to run against each other, and Josias Lyndon was elected governor as a compromise candidate.

In 1769, Hopkins coordinated the construction of a telescope in Providence and personally took measurements of Venus's transit across the Sun in 1769.

In 1770, Hopkins returned as the Chief Justice of the Supreme Court of Rhode Island. This put him in the middle of the *Gaspée* Affair beginning in June 1772. The HMS *Gaspée*, led by Lieutenant William Duddingston, was a customs enforcement vessel sent by the British to monitor the Navigation Acts long set by the British Parliament to control trade in the colonies. Captain Abraham Whipple, sailing a vessel owned by Hopkins' business associates, John and Moses Brown, did not appreciate the incursion in Narragansett Bay on the colonies' sovereignty and lured the British vessel into a chase. The British captain did not immediately realize the ruse and soon ran aground on a shallow point near Warwick, Rhode Island, now known as Gaspée Point. The Sons of Liberty, led by John Brown, alerted to the opportunity, sailed out to the customs ship, arrested the crew, and set it afire, burning it to the waterline on the night of June 9 to 10. Lieutenant Duddingston was wounded in the raid, and he and his men were taken ashore as booty.

Throughout the colonies, fellow Patriots saw this as a heroic effort. The Rhode Island court issued arrest warrants for Duddingston and his crew for attempting to seize goods in violation of Rhode Island law. Meanwhile, the British in London were outraged and sent orders to the Supreme Court in Rhode Island to prosecute the perpetrators. Chief Justice Stephen Hopkins refused to sign any court orders sent by the British. Using his influence, he told the commissioners sent from London who investigated the incident that, though he shared their outrage, none of the men could be identified and "neither apprehend by my own order nor suffer any executive officer in the colony to do it, for the purpose of transportation to England for trial." Realizing the effort would be fruitless, the British gave up, never charging anyone. Unknown to them, one of Hopkins' relatives was among the raiders and Hopkins, his subordinates, and others coordinated to lose evidence, threaten witnesses, and discredit those who testified. Meanwhile, the British inquiry spurred the creation of Committees of Correspondence in the colonies.

Hopkins, who owned six slaves, including a man, a woman, and three boys, freed the man, named Saint Jago, on October 28, 1772. He wrote on the manumission document:

> But, principally, and most of all, finding that the merciful and beneficent goodness of Almighty God; by the blessed Gospel of Jesus Christ our Lord: hath by the blessed Spirit taught all, who honestly obey its Divine Dictates, that, the keeping any of his rational Creatures in Bondage, who are capable of taking care of, and providing for themselves in a State of Freedom: is, altogether inconsistent with his Holy and Righteous Will.

However, he did not free the woman, Fibbo, even though it cost him membership in the Quaker meeting. He felt she and her children required care and could not live independently. Early in 1774, at a meeting of the General Assembly of Rhode Island, Hopkins introduced a bill prohibiting the importation of slaves. It was one of the first anti-slave trade laws in the colonies.

He and his former enemy, Samuel Ward, were sent as delegates to the First Continental Congress. There, he declared: ". . . powder and ball will decide this question. The gun and bayonet alone will finish the contest in which we are engaged, and any of you who cannot bring your minds to this mode of adjusting this question had better retire in time." He and Ward both signed the Continental Association on October 20, 1774.

Speaking of the 100th anniversary of this First Congress, orator Henry Armitt Brown described Hopkins, who had developed palsy in his old age:

Stephen Hopkins (1707–1785)

... yonder sits the oldest of them all. His form is bent, his thin locks, fringing a forehead bowed with age and honorable service, and his hands shake tremulously as he folds them in his lap. It is Stephen Hopkins.

John Adams wrote in his diary at that time about Hopkins:

Mr. [Francis Lightfoot] Lee [of Virginia], Mr. [Christopher] Gadsden [of South Carolina], were sensible men, and very cheerful, but Governor Hopkins of Rhode Island, above seventy years of age, kept us all alive. Upon business, his experience and judgment were very useful. But when the business of the evening was over, he kept us in conversation till eleven, and sometimes twelve o'clock. His custom was to drink nothing all day, nor till eight o'clock in the evening, and then his beverage was Jamaica spirit and water. It gave him wit, humor, anecdotes, science and learning. He had read Greek, Roman, and British history, and was familiar with English poetry, particularly Pope, Thomson, and Milton, and the flow of his soul made all his reading our own, and seemed to bring to recollection in all of us, all we had ever read ... Hopkins never drank to excess, but all he drank was immediately not only converted into wit, sense, knowledge, and good humor, but inspired us with similar qualities.

After the Battles of Lexington and Concord in April 1775, the Second Continental Congress convened. Hopkins signed the Olive Branch Petition that summer. In February 1776, he arranged for his younger brother, Esek, to be named the first commander-in-chief of the Continental Navy. On March 26, 1776, while in Philadelphia, Samuel Ward died suddenly, leaving a vacancy in the Second Continental Congress. He was replaced by William Ellery.

Rhode Island declared independence from Great Britain on May 4, 1776. Hopkins and Ellery, at the Congress, knew this and participated in the debates. At one point on July 1, a thunderstorm gathered outside the hall while John Dickinson rambled into his second hour of speaking.

Suddenly, there was a thunderclap, and Hopkins dropped the cane on which his head had been perched, snapping it up quickly.

John Penn of North Carolina, believing the man was frightened, whispered to Hopkins reassuringly, "There is a rod atop the State House—one of Dr. Franklin's inventions—the celebrated lightning rod. If by chance a bolt of lightning should strike the belfry, that same rod would run the bolt into the ground."

Hopkins turned to Penn and roared, "I don't give a damn about any rod or lightning bolt. I'm just tired of Dickinson's long-winded harangue!"

Ellery and Hopkins signed the Declaration of Independence. Hopkins was the second oldest to sign, only one year younger than Ben Franklin, who was 70. Though his body shook from palsy, making it difficult to walk, Hopkins held his shaking right hand with his left as he signed, saying, "My hand trembles, but my heart does not." Thus ended his stint in Congress.

For the next three years, Hopkins occasionally participated in the Rhode Island Council of War and at conventions of the New England States, serving as president of the 1777 convention. He was elected to participate in the discussions about the Articles of Confederation but soon returned to Rhode Island due to his health. Hopkins died in Providence, Rhode Island, on July 13, 1785, at age 78. He was interred in the North Burial Ground, accompanied by a large, distinguished funeral procession. One side of his obelisk reads:

> Sacred to the Memory of the Illustrious Stephen Hopkins. Of Revolutionary Fame. Attested by his Signature to the Declaration of Our National Independence. Great in Council, From Sagacity of Mind: Magnanimous in Sentiment: Firm in Purpose: and Good, As Great, from Benevolent Heart.

Hopkins is remembered in many ways. Hopkinton, Rhode Island, was named after him. The SS *Stephen Hopkins* was a liberty ship that was the first US ship to sink a German surface vessel in World War II. His home, originally at the corner of Hopkins and South Main Streets in

Providence, was moved twice to different locations on Hopkins Street, now at number 15, on the edge of the Brown University campus.

Many have written well of Hopkins over the years. In his diary, Reverend Ezra Stiles called him "... a man of penetrating astucious Genius, full of Subtlety, deep Cunning, intriguing & enterprising ... a man of a Noble fortitude & resolution" and "a glorious Patriot!"

The historian Irving Berdine Richman dubbed Hopkins "the greatest statesman of Rhode Island."

Grave of Stephen Hopkins

James Armistead Lafayette
(1748 or 1760 – circa 1830)

Lafayette's Double Agent

Buried at Unknown Location
New Kent County, Virginia

Spy

James, later known as James Armistead Lafayette or just James Lafayette, was a slave of African descent in Kent County, Virginia, who served in the Continental Army under the Marquis de Lafayette in the latter years of the American Revolution. Gaining the trust of Benedict Arnold and Lord Charles Cornwallis, James was a double agent, feeding false information to the British and intelligence reports to the Americans leading up to the decisive Battle of Yorktown.

James was born in either 1748 or 1760 in Kent County, Virginia, on the plantation owned by Colonel John Armistead. Unlike most slaves, James was taught to read and write. Sometime before Colonel Armistead's death in 1779, James was given to the colonel's son, William Armistead, the local commissary of military supplies, to be his personal manservant. James was the first slave owned by William.

During the American Revolution, between 5,000 and 8,000 free and enslaved Black men fought for the Patriots, amounting to about three percent of the estimated 230,000 soldiers who served. Early in the war, General Washington, a slaveowner, was uncomfortable with permitting armed Blacks in the armed forces. On July 10, 1775, he barred any additional Blacks from joining them. However, by 1778, at

James Armistead Lafayette (1748 or 1760 – circa 1830)

James Armistead Lafayette

the urgings of others, Washington gradually changed his position. The Marquise de Lafayette, an ardent abolitionist, was one officer who supported permitting enslaved and freed Africans to take up arms and did so openly in his corps.

Upon hearing of Lafayette's openness to Blacks, James requested and was granted permission by his master, a supporter of the Patriot cause, to serve in the Continental Army. In 1781, still enslaved, James joined Lafayette's division and was initially ordered to carry information between the French units. Soon, though, Lafayette realized James's potential to be a spy. Lafayette suggested that James pose as a runaway and seek to infiltrate the British Army.

In November 1775, Lord Dunmore, the colonial Governor of Virginia, issued a proclamation that any slave who fought in the British Army would be emancipated. In the subsequent years, it is estimated that over 100,000 slaves escaped bondage by fleeing to British lines. With this apparent desire and his knowledge of the local roads and terrain in Virginia, Lord Cornwallis was quick to trust James, permitting him in the headquarters. Cornwallis assigned James to spy for Brigadier General Benedict Arnold, himself a recent turncoat. Arnold asked James to spy on the Americans, especially the Marquise de Lafayette! Thus, James shuttled back and forth between the camps, providing Arnold and Cornwallis with false information about the Americans while sharing true information about his adversaries with Lafayette.

In the summer of 1781, General Washington asked Lafayette for any intelligence he had on the positions, equipment, and potential strategies of the British troops. Lafayette sent James to gather this information. James reported back on July 31, 1781, about Cornwallis's movement of 10,000 troops from Portsmouth, Virginia, to Yorktown, Virginia. Washington and French General Rochambeau were then able to devise a blockade and bombardment of Cornwallis, leading to his defeat on October 19, 1781. When Lord Cornwallis surrendered at Lafayette's headquarters, he was stunned to see James, whom he considered his trusted personal slave, among the Americans.

After the war, despite Virginia's manumission act in 1782 granting freedom to slaves who fought in the Revolution, James remained the property of William Armistead. He was restricted by a 1783 law regarding only freeing enslaved service members who had been issued firearms and had served as substitutes for their masters. Because James had been a spy and not a soldier, he did not carry a gun, and was thus not eligible.

Unfairly overlooked, James petitioned the Virginia Assembly for his freedom. In 1784, the Marquise de Lafayette wrote a letter on his behalf detailing James's service to the cause, saying that James had rendered "services to me while I had the honor to command in this state. His intelligence from the enemy's camp were industriously collected and more faithfully delivered. He properly acquitted himself with some important commissions I gave him and appears to me entitled to every reward his situation can admit of." However, despite his master, William Armistead, a member of the House of Delegates, promoting the measure, it took until January 9, 1787, for the governor and both houses to grant his

James Armistead Lafayette (1748 or 1760 – circa 1830)

manumission. For the rest of his life, James appended Lafayette to his name in honor of his friend who had vouched for him. Note that others later appended Armistead to him, a name he never used in his lifetime.

James Lafayette, now a freeman, purchased a forty-acre farm in New Kent County, Virginia, in 1816. He was twice married, raised a family, and became relatively wealthy. He also owned slaves. In 1819, after years of petitioning for it, James began receiving a pension as a Revolutionary War veteran from Virginia.

While touring all twenty-four of the United States in 1824 on the invitation of President James Monroe, Lafayette visited Virginia, stopping at Yorktown, Washington's tomb at Mount Vernon, and gave a speech to the General Assembly at the capital of Richmond. While in Richmond, Lafayette saw James in the crowd and ordered his carriage to stop. He exited the coach and called out to James. The two warmly embraced in front of an astonished crowd. It was unusual behavior in Antebellum Virginia.

James returned to his farm afterward. He lived until either 1830 or 1832, dying in Baltimore, Maryland, or New Kent County, Virginia. His burial location is lost.

James Lafayette is honored in several, mostly nondescript, ways. A Black servant depicted in a portrait of Lafayette by Jean-Baptiste Le Paon in 1785 might be James. He was mentioned in James E. Heath's two-volume historical novel *Edge Hill: or the Family of the Fitz Royals*, published in 1828. A portrait of him was painted by John Blennerhassett Martin at the time of the book. The Lafayette memorial at Prospect Park in Brooklyn, New York, might include a figure of James. A Virginia historical marker was erected in 1997 at the New Kent County courthouse honoring him.

Henry Laurens
(1724–1792)

First President of the Recognized USA

Laurens Family Cemetery
Moncks Corner, Berkeley County, South Carolina

Articles of Confederation

Henry Laurens was a South Carolina plantation owner, merchant, and partner in the largest slave-trading house in North America. Laurens was active in state and national politics as the Vice President of South Carolina, Continental Congressman, and President of Congress. He signed the Articles of Confederation, presiding over its adoption. He was also the Minister to the Hague during the Revolution but was captured by the British on his return and imprisoned in the Tower of London for fifteen months.

Laurens, born on March 6, 1724, in Charleston, South Carolina, was the eldest son and third child of Jean Samuel Laurens and Hester (née Grasset) Laurens. His father was of French Huguenot descent, arriving with his parents in New York in the late 1600s. About 1715 or 1716, the elder Laurens married a French Huguenot wife from Staten Island; the young couple moved to Charleston, South Carolina, where Henry was born a decade later. Mother Hester Laurens died in 1741, and her husband remarried Elizabeth Wickling. Jean Samuel Laurens then passed in 1747, leaving his estate to his eldest son, Henry.

Laurens was initially educated in Charleston. In 1744, at age 19, he went to England to study business with Richard Oswald, the principal

Henry Laurens (1724–1792)

Henry Laurens

owner of Bunce Island, a slave-trading island base in the Sierra Leone River of Africa. He stayed there until his father's death three years later.

Leveraging his inheritance, Laurens quickly rose as a leader of the merchant class in Charleston, trading with England and the West Indies. His plantation on the Cooper River employed over 300 slaves, and he was an active importer and trader of slaves throughout the colonies.

On June 25, 1750, Laurens married Eleanor Ball, the daughter of a South Carolina rice planter. The couple had thirteen children, most of them dying in childhood. During the 1750s, Laurens held local offices and, in 1757, was elected to the Commons House of Assembly, staying there through the beginning of the Revolution in 1775, except for 1773, when he arranged his sons' education in England.

From 1757 to 1761, Laurens was also a lieutenant colonel in the militia, fighting a campaign against the Cherokee during the French and

Indian War. During the spring of 1760, smallpox raged throughout the low country of South Carolina. Lauren's infant daughter, Martha, apparently succumbed to the disease. As was customary, her little body was laid on a bed by an open window. The family then gathered around for a wake for the deceased. Outside, a light rain began to fall, and a cool breeze blew a few droplets on the young girl's head. She began to stir, clearly not dead. The child had narrowly avoided being buried alive! Little Martha recovered, married Dr. David Ramsay, and lived a full life.

In 1764 and 1768, Laurens was named to the King's Council of South Carolina but declined. Wife Eleanor died in 1770 of complications from the childbirth of their last child. Laurens left his local offices to care for his children and then, realizing the harsh impacts of British trade policies, traveled to London to attempt to unsuccessfully negotiate a resolution.

In 1772, Laurens joined the American Philosophical Society of Philadelphia and became well-acquainted with the other members. In 1773, on the eve of the Revolution, Laurens took his three sons to England to be educated. John, the oldest, studied law. However, he returned to America in 1776 and served in the Revolution.

Meanwhile, in South Carolina, Laurens, who initially hoped for reconciliation with England, was elected to the Provincial Congress on January 9, 1775. As he became convinced of the need for independence, he became the President of the Committee of Safety and presided over the Congress from June until March 1776. He was then appointed the Vice President of South Carolina through June 27, 1777.

Laurens was elected to the Continental Congress on January 10, 1777, serving until 1780. From November 1, 1777, until December 9, 1778, he was the President of Congress, succeeding John Hancock. During this time, he oversaw the debate and creation of the Articles of Confederation while the Congress was in York, Pennsylvania. Laurens signed the document as President. He then led the transfer of the Congress back to Philadelphia on July 2, 1778.

Congress named Laurens the Minister to the Hague (Netherlands) in the fall of 1779. In early 1780, he traveled to Amsterdam and gained Dutch support for the colonies. However, on his return trip, while aboard the packet *Mercury* off the coast of Newfoundland, Laurens was captured by the HMS *Vestal*. Laurens tossed his dispatches in the water, but they were recovered. Among them was the draft of a treaty with the Dutch that prompted the British to declare war on the Dutch Republic, triggering the Fourth Anglo-Dutch War. Laurens, charged with treason, was examined by British officials. Some of the interrogation by Lord Hillsborough was published in newspapers in England and the colonies:

> "Is your name Henry Laurens?"
>
> "It is."
>
> "Are you the same Henry Laurens who was the President of the Congress in America?"
>
> "I am."
>
> "We are ordered by the King and Council to examine you and have certain questions to propose."
>
> "Your Lordships may save yourselves the trouble of an examination, as I think it my place to answer no questions you may put."
>
> "Sir, we are directed to commit you [as a] prisoner to the Tower."
>
> "I am ready to attend."

Thus, former President Henry Laurens became the only American held prisoner in the Tower of London. Fortunately, his former business mentor, Richard Oswald, still thought fondly of him and lobbied for his release. This finally occurred on December 31, 1781, when he was exchanged for General Lord Cornwallis, who was captured at Yorktown. He came home to find his plantation home, Mepkin, had been burned by the British, and the family lived in an outbuilding while they recovered.

Tragically, Colonel John Laurens, Henry's eldest son, was killed in 1782 at the Battle of the Combahee River before the Treaty of Paris ended the war. Father and son had argued over the years about the evils of slavery. John had urged his father to free his slaves and had offered the 40 he was to inherit to the cause, but Laurens did not relent and never manumitted his slaves.

In 1783, Laurens was sent to Paris to assist in negotiating peace with Britain, whose principal negotiator was Richard Oswald. Laurens, though not a signer of the Treaty of Paris, helped to negotiate settlements for the Netherlands and Spain.

Following the Revolution, Laurens retired from public life, declining to continue service in the Continental Congress or the Constitutional Convention. However, he served briefly in the state convention in South Carolina in 1788 for the ratification of the US Constitution.

Laurens died from complications of gout on December 8, 1792, at Mepkin. Due to his fear of being accidentally buried alive, the family waited three days before proceeding with his funeral. Laurens' will ordered the following:

> I come to the disposal of my own person. I solemnly enjoin it on my son (Henry Jr.) as an indispensable duty, that as soon as he conveniently can after my decease, he cause my Body to be wrapped in twelve yards of tow cloth, and burnt until it be entirely and totally consumed. And then collecting my bones, deposit them where ever he shall think proper.

Laurens is believed to be the first Caucasian to be cremated in the United States. However, it did not go well. The pyre was built along the banks of the Cooper River, and his remains were burned as wished. Accounts vary, but due to the amount of fluid in the body, the liquid poured forth and extinguished most of the flames prematurely. Then, the head broke from the corpse, hair aflame, and rolled down the bank into reeds by the water. A slave was sent into the mud to perform the gruesome task of retrieving it. His remaining bones, ashes, and charred head were then buried in the family plot at Moncks Corner, now on the grounds of Mepkin Abbey.

Some in the press did not approve of Laurens' method of disposal. There was a sonnet by someone using the penname Amicus titled "Lines written on reading the singular manner in which Henry Laurens, Esq. ordered his corpse to be disposed of." It read:

> The Pagans oft their funeral piles have made,
> To offer victims, or consume their dead;
> But who in Christian lands, e'er built a fire
> To expatiate their crimes, or burn a Sire!

Henry Laurens (1724–1792)

The gravestone of Henry Laurens, who was cremated.

Will Christian people dread the worms of earth,
Since they expect to rise to second birth?
When Jesus bids the grave its prey resign,
In his blest likeness they may hope to shine.

The city and county of Laurens, South Carolina, are named for Laurens. The village of Laurens in New York is also named for him. Laurens County, Georgia, is named for his son John. Fort Laurens in Ohio was named for Henry by his friend, General Lachlan McIntosh. Historian C. James Taylor summarized Laurens as follows:

> In both his public and private life, Henry Laurens' commitment to duty and hard work were recognized and admired. Unfortunately, his impatience and criticism of individuals who did not meet his

standards made him appear petty and inflexible. As the strongest political figure in South Carolina during the transition from provincial to state government, he worked to protect the rights of Loyalists and moderate the zeal of the radicals. In Congress, his constancy during the British occupation of Philadelphia and the trying exile at York may have been his most significant contribution to the national cause. The poor health he endured after confinement in the tower and the emotional shock of his son John's death in August 1782 robbed him of the vigor that had marked his career to that time.

Warning of the dangers near the grave of
Henry Laurens.

Benjamin Lincoln
(1733–1810)

Received the Surrender at Yorktown

Buried at Old Ship Burying Ground
Hingham, Massachusetts

Major General • Secretary of War

Benjamin Lincoln was a Major General during the American Revolution who participated in and was present at three major surrenders: Saratoga, Charleston, and Yorktown. As the war was ending, Lincoln became the first Secretary of War for the new nation. He also led the suppression of Shay's Rebellion in Connecticut. Lincoln was not related to the future sixteenth President of the United States, Abraham Lincoln.

Lincoln, born January 24, 1733, in Hingham, Suffolk County, Massachusetts, was the first son and sixth child of Colonel Benjamin Lincoln and his second wife, Elizabeth (née Thaxter) Lincoln. The elder Lincoln was descended from Thomas Lincoln, a cooper who was one of the community's first settlers. He was also one of the wealthiest men in Suffolk County, owning vast amounts of land, and served on the governor's council from 1753 to 1770. Colonel Samuel Thaxter, Lincoln's maternal grandfather, was also an influential citizen and helped to settle the boundary with Rhode Island in 1719.

Young Lincoln attended local schools and worked on the family farm and then established his own farm. At age 21, in 1754, he became the town constable. The following year, he joined the 3rd Regiment of

Benjamin Lincoln

the Suffolk County Militia under his father, the colonel. At age 23, in 1756, Lincoln married Mary Cushing, the daughter of Elijah Cushing of Pembroke, Massachusetts, who was also from an old Hingham family. Over the years, the couple had eleven children, seven of whom survived to adulthood.

In 1757, Lincoln was elected the town clerk of Hingham and held the post for twenty years. He also remained in the militia throughout the French and Indian War but saw no action. In 1763, he was promoted to major.

After the war, in 1765, Lincoln was elected town selectman in Hingham. He held this post for six years. During this time, he protested the new taxes imposed by Parliament and the Boston Massacre, making

Benjamin Lincoln (1733–1810)

him a leading force among the Patriots in Hingham. In 1772, Lincoln was elected to represent the town in the provincial assembly. He was also promoted to Lieutenant Colonel of the 3rd Regiment of the Suffolk Militia.

In 1774, General Thomas Gage arrived as the Governor of Massachusetts. He officially dissolved the assembly, but it reconstituted itself as the Massachusetts Provincial Congress. Lincoln was elected to this body and oversaw militia organization and supply. Following the nearby Battles of Lexington and Concord in April 1775, Lincoln was appointed to the Congress's Committee of Safety and was elected to the executive council, governing Massachusetts outside occupied Boston. As the Continental Army was forming, Lincoln was involved in securing supplies, ammunition, and gunpowder, reinforcing the siege and buying time until Gage and the British left Boston upon the arrival of Henry Knox's cannons.

Lincoln was promoted to Major General of the Massachusetts Militia in January 1776. He was responsible for defending Massachusetts following the British evacuation. He and General Artemas Ward of the Continental Army led the defense of the state and improved fortifications. That May, the last Royal Navy ships were expelled from Boston Harbor.

With the aging of Artemas Ward, Lincoln saw an opportunity for promotion and lobbied for a Continental Army position. While this was not forthcoming, he was sent with some militia to assist General George Washington in his defense of New York in August 1776. While in Connecticut, Lincoln was ordered to prepare an expedition across Long Island Sound to raid British forces on Long Island. However, Washington retreated, and the mission was aborted. Lincoln was then ordered to assist in securing the retreat of the Continental Army at White Plains, New York. There, his regiments joined the main Continental Army during the Battle of White Plains in October.

With enlistments expiring, Lincoln returned to Massachusetts to gather new recruits. Obviously, Washington was impressed with Lincoln because, on February 14, 1777, he was promoted to Major General in the Continental Army. Washington described him in his letter to Congress as "a gentleman well worthy of notice in the Military Line."

Two months later, on April 13, 1777, Lincoln led an engagement against the British and Hessians at Bound Brook, New Jersey. The enemy attempted a surprise attack on Lincoln's headquarters, which was only three miles from British sentries. Outnumbered 5,000 to 400, Lincoln barely escaped without being captured.

That summer, in July, British General John Burgoyne threatened northern New York from Quebec, via the Hudson River. Washington sent Generals Lincoln and Arnold and Colonel Morgan to assist General Philip Schuyler, who was subsequently replaced by Horatio Gates. Lincoln and his 2,000 troops were ordered to harass the British supply lines as they moved south. Unfortunately, the leader of the New Hampshire Militia, John Stark, would not cooperate, refusing to be under the control of the Continental Army due to a previous promotion snub. Instead, Stark, in mid-August, led his troops to victory at the Battle of Bennington, capturing or killing 1,000 Hessians from Burgoyne's army.

Next, in September, General Gates ordered Lincoln and his men to join him and assigned him to hold the eastern side of the Hudson River. Lincoln arrived on September 22, following Colonel Morgan's decisive victory at Freeman's Farm, where his sharpshooters killed most of the offices and three-fourths of the artillerymen. They captured six of ten British cannons.

During the Battle of Bemis Heights on October 7, which occurred on the west side of the Hudson, Lincoln's troops saw no action. During the battle, General Arnold was struck in the leg during a charge, even though General Gates had relieved Arnold of command due to insubordination.

Afterward, Lincoln's forces pushed the British back further. He recommended heading off the British at the ford at Fort Edward before they could return to Fort Ticonderoga. Gates agreed, and while enacting the plan, Lincoln's forces engaged in a skirmish and Lincoln was struck in the ankle by a musket ball. He was transported to Albany and treated. There, he learned of Burgoyne's surrender on October 17. Lincoln was bedridden for months, returning to Hingham with his son's help in February 1778. Lincoln's right leg was shorter for the rest of his life. When Arnold's seniority was restored, Lincoln was the lowest-ranking major general, but he decided not to resign over the slight.

Lincoln was back in the saddle in September 1778 when Washington made him the Commander of the Southern Department, replacing Major General Robert Howe. This was a very large and independent command. Lafayette and "Light Horse Harry" Lee were also assigned to Lincoln, opposing Clinton and Cornwallis on the British side.

The following year, in the spring, Lincoln led an attack on the British at Augusta, Georgia, but this left Charleston open to attack. In October, the French under Lincoln, including 500 free Black Haitian soldiers, led a siege of Savannah, Georgia, which failed, resulting in over 1,000 American and French casualties. Lincoln's forces retreated to Charleston, South Carolina, where they garrisoned. The British seized this opportunity in March 1780, devastating Patriot properties in the low country and laying siege to Charleston. Morale was low in South Carolina, but Governor Rutledge convinced Lincoln to fight on. However, when Lincoln requested 1,000 enslaved African Americans to be armed to help fend off the British, the South Carolina legislature declined and permitted the British to pass through South Carolina. Without any Continental Navy support and against superior forces, Lincoln was soon forced to surrender over 5,000 men to General Sir Henry Clinton on May 12, 1780, but some Continental forces and the South Carolina Militia escaped. Lincoln was captured but denied the honors of war in surrender. He was then paroled and sent back to General Washington.

Washington did not give up on Lincoln. Next, he made him second-in-command for the Yorktown Campaign. He led a large portion of the army from Head of Elk, Maryland, to Hampton, Virginia, and then west to Yorktown. After the French helped trap the British on October 19, 1781, General Lord Charles Cornwallis surrendered but feigned illness rather than appear at the surrender ceremony. He sent Irish General Charles O'Hara to do the deed. Washington, insulted by Cornwallis's behavior, had O'Hara surrender to General Lincoln instead, avenging his previous mistreatment.

As the Revolution was ending, under the new Articles of Confederation, Lincoln was made the nation's first Secretary of War, serving from 1781 to 1783. He was succeeded by Major General Henry Knox. Lincoln was also elected to the American Academy of Arts and Sciences in 1781 and was one of the original members of the Massachusetts Society of Cincinnati, selected as its president on June 9, 1783. Ten days later, he supported the election of George Washington as the President General of the order.

In rebellion against tough economic policies following the war, some angry citizens in western Massachusetts, led by Daniel Shays, attempted to seize an armory and overthrow the state in 1787. Benjamin Lincoln, leading 3,000 privately funded militia, led the suppression of the revolt. Known as Shay's Rebellion, this action was one the leading events to trigger the need for a new federal constitution. Lincoln was a strong supporter for the creation of this reform and voted in support of it as a delegate from Suffolk County, Massachusetts. The state ratified the Constitution on February 6, 1788.

During the first presidential election, on February 4, 1789, Lincoln was one of twelve men who received electoral votes, receiving the vote of one elector from Georgia.

Later in life, Lincoln was active in public affairs, serving as Massachusetts's Lieutenant Governor for a term and the lucrative position of Boston's Port Collector for many years. In 1806, when the elderly Lincoln tried to resign as the Collector, President Thomas Jefferson requested that he stay until a successor was found. Representative Josiah Quincy III then tried to have Jefferson impeached in January 1809, even though he was set to leave office in only two more months. Lincoln finally retired in 1809 and passed in Hingham on May 9, 1810.

During Lincoln's funeral, the bells in Boston and other nearby towns were tolled for an hour, and the flags of vessels and at forts and navy yards were flown at half-mast. Pallbearers at his funeral included John Adams, Cotton Tufts, Robert Treat Paine, Richard Cranch, and Thomas Melvill. Lincoln was buried in the Old Ship Burying Ground behind the Old Ship Church in Hingham, Massachusetts.

Lincoln was largely forgotten in the years after the Revolution despite being part of the victories at Saratoga and Yorktown and the defeat at Charleston, though he is shown in the famous painting *The Surrender of Cornwallis* by John Trumball that hangs in the US Capitol.

Typically, towns named Lincoln in the South are named for him as opposed to Abrahan Lincoln. Examples include counties and or towns in

Grave of Benjamin Lincoln

Alabama, Georgia, Kentucky, Missouri, North Carolina, and Tennessee. Lincoln in Vermont and Lincolnville in Maine are also named for him, as are streets in Columbia, South Carolina, and Savannah, Georgia. Lincoln Hall at the U.S. Coast Guard Training Center in Yorktown, Virginia, bears his name.

In 1972, Benjamin Lincoln's lifelong home in Hingham, Massachusetts, was declared a National Historic Landmark.

James Lovell
(1737–1814)

Teacher, Orator, Signer, Spy

Buried at Unknown Location
Windham, Maine

Continental Congress • Signer of the Articles of Confederation

James Lovell was a teacher from a Loyalist Boston family who was imprisoned by the British for spying. Upon his release, he was immediately elected to the Continental Congress, representing Massachusetts. Lovell signed the Articles of Confederation. Despite participating in the Conway Cabal and believing George Washington to be "overrated," President Washington appointed him to a lucrative Customs House position in Boston after the Revolution.

Lovell was born in Boston, Massachusetts, on October 31, 1737. He was the son of John Lovell, headmaster of the Boston Latin School, and his wife, Abigail (née Green). The elder Lovell graduated from Harvard in 1728. Ten years later, he succeeded Dr. Nathaniel Williams as the headmaster of the school where young James, Samuel Adams, and John Hancock received their preparatory education.

James also attended Harvard, graduating in 1756. He then worked with his father at the Latin School. In 1759, James earned a Master of Arts from Harvard, continuing with his father until the school closed in April 1775, as the Siege of Boston was underway.

James and his father were close during these early years. In 1760, James married Mary Middleton, with whom he had more than ten

James Lovell (1737–1814)

James Lovell

children, nine of whom survived to adulthood. Lovell also became a noted orator. One such speech was delivered at Boston's Old Faneuil Hall to a massive crowd following the Boston Massacre in April 1771. Lovell's father was not pleased with the speech. Said James, "The horrid bloody scene we here commemorate, whatever were the causes which concurred to bring it on that dreadful night, must lead the pious and humane of every order to some suitable reflections. The pious will adore the conduct of that Being who is unsearchable in all his ways, and without whose knowledge not a single sparrow falls, in permitting an immortal soul to be hurried by the flying ball, the messenger of death, in the twinkling of an eye, to meet the awful Judge of all its secret actions."

Lovell continued to deviate from his father's Loyalist leanings and joined with patriots James Warren, Josiah Quincy, and the Adams cousins, Samuel and John, in demanding increased freedoms from England.

However, Lovell did not openly participate in the Boston Tea Party or the First Continental Congress. He wrote from Boston on May 3, 1775:

> Mrs. Lovell has suffered extremely in the Head, fears a fixed Disorder there, but is I hope only suffering thus thro Weakness. My Family is yet w[ith] me. Children are prepared to go away, and Mrs. Lovell w[ith] the rest will follow when able, if I so judge proper. I am not yet ripe to determine, I shall tarry if 10 Seiges [sic] take place. I have determined it to be a Duty which I owe the Cause & the Friends of it, and am perfectly fearless of the Consequences. An ill Turn, of a most violent Diarhea [sic], from being too long in a damp place, has contirm'd Doctr Gardners [sic] advice to me not to go into the Trenches, where my whole Soul lodges nightly. How then can I be more actively serviceable to the Friends who think with me, than by keeping disagreeable post among a Set of Villains who would willingly destroy what those Friends leave behind them.

When the body of James Warren was searched by the British after the Battle of Bunker Hill on June 17, 1775, documents were found written in James Lovell's hand showing British troop movements. Ten days later, Lovell's home was searched, and additional documents were found confirming he was a spy for the rebels. He was taken into custody and jailed in Boston. Lovell spent nine months in Boston's stone jail until the British left, at which point he was taken to Halifax, Nova Scotia, where he was imprisoned with Ethan Allen for another nine months. While Lovell could have been executed for spying, he was only imprisoned. Curiously, his father, the Loyalist, followed him to Nova Scotia and later died there in 1778. There is no record of the elder Lovell appealing to the British to spare his son, but the scenario is very likely.

Lovell must have made an impression on his friends in Boston who were in Congress and also with the new commander of Continental forces, George Washington, to whom he had written about his imprisonment. Wrote Washington on December 19, 1775:

Inclosed [*sic*] is a letter I lately received from Mr. James Lovell. His case is truly pitiable. I wish some mode could be fallen upon to relieve him from the cruel situation he is now in. I am sensible of the impropriety of exchanging a soldier for a citizen: but there is something so cruelly distressing in regard to this gentleman, that I dare say you will take it under your consideration.

While the letter from Lovell no longer survives, it also made an impression upon Congress, noting Lovell maintained "under the severest trials the warmest attachment to public liberty, and an inflexible fidelity to his country." Congress agreed to an exchange of Major Andrew Skene, a British prisoner, for Lovell. Washington noted it in a letter to Jonathan Trumbull on September 23, 1776.

Months after being freed, Lovell was elected to a seat in the Continental Congress on December 10, 1776, joining John Hancock, Samuel Adams, John Adams, Robert Treat Paine, Elbridge Gerry, and Francis Dana as representatives from Massachusetts. Lovell was the only Continental Congressman to be "continuously present" for five contiguous years through 1781. Lovell served on the Committees of Foreign Correspondence and Secret Correspondence. He was known for his ciphers, which were impossible to crack without the key, though Ben Franklin tried.

During the summer of 1777, following the loss of Fort Ticonderoga to the British, Lovell was a supporter, along with Dr. Benjamin Rush, of General Horatio Gates to take command of the army. Gates had just taken over the Northern Department from Philip Schuyler. Washington managed to survive the intrigue known as the "Conway Cabal" to remain as the commander-in-chief.

Lovell seems to have been closest to John and Abigail Adams, frequently corresponding with them. He especially seemed close to Abigail when John was in France. He wrote Abigail, whom he called by a pet name, "Portia," wondering what John was doing with his private time in France. The letters were flirtatious in nature.

Lovell signed the Articles of Confederation on July 9, 1778. During this time, Lovell was part of a group known as the anti-Gallicans, who feared a subordinate relationship with France and desired a more open relationship with all of Europe. Among them were Francis Dana, the Adams cousins, and the Lees of Virginia. They were suspicious of Ben Frankin's actions at Versailles. They were also behind sending Dana as Minister to Russia in 1780.

During the Revolution, Lovell's oldest son, James, served as a low-level officer in the Continental Army. He saw action at the Battle of Monmouth and served under "Lighthorse Harry" Lee in the Southern Campaign. He was wounded several times.

Following his service in Congress, Lovell returned to teaching. He also was a tax collector in Massachusetts in the 1780s. Despite their prior differences, President Washington appointed Lowell to a customs position in Boson in 1789, holding the position for the rest of his life.

On July 14, 1814, while visiting his friend, Reverend Peter T. Smith, at Windham, Maine, James Lovell died. He was 86. His burial location remains lost.

Lovell's grandson, Joseph Lovell, was the first Surgeon General of the USA, serving from 1818 to 1836. A connection to *Apollo 13* commander James Lovell has not been proven.

George Mason
(1725–1792)

"The Father of the Bill of Rights"

Buried at Mason Family Cemetery
Lorton, Virginia

U.S. Constitution • U.S. Bill of Rights

A recent biographer described this man as America's most unappreciated and underestimated Founding Father. His writings influenced both American political thinking and events including the American Revolution itself. He was the principal author of the Virginia Declaration of Rights upon which the United States Bill of Rights was based. He was a delegate to the 1787 Constitutional Convention in Philadelphia and one of the three men who refused to sign the finished product put forth by that gathering. His opposition to the Constitution cost him his long friendship with his Virginia neighbor, George Washington. His name was George Mason.

Mason was born on December 11, 1725, at his father's Dogue's Head plantation in Stafford County, Virginia. Both his father (George Mason III) and his mother, Ann, came from well-off families whose forefathers had been among Virginia's oldest settlers. In 1735, Mason's father drowned at the age of forty-nine when his boat capsized as he was crossing the Potomac River. His mother proved to be a major force in his coming of age. She would wake him at dawn and send him to begin his chores on the plantation. Since he was the first-born son, it was assumed

George Mason

that Mason would eventually run the plantation operations. With his father's death, he assumed burdens that normally he would not have had to shoulder at such a youthful age. It is not an exaggeration to say he became an adult sooner than most his age at the time.

According to his biographer, William G. Hyland Jr., in *George Mason: The Founding Father Who Gave Us the Bill of Rights,* Mason developed a toughness because of the responsibilities he had to assume. He also turned to older men to act as his mentors. One of these was his uncle, John Mercer. It was Mercer who took on the responsibility for Mason's formal education. The foundations for Mason's career in politics were instilled by Mercer. Mercer was a lawyer who owned a private library that contained at least fifteen hundred volumes. These works contained books by Pope Milton, Swift, and Voltaire. Reading these authors and others resulted in Mason developing a passion for individual freedom. In addition, the influence of Mercer's library would be seen in Mason's contributions to the Constitution and the Declaration of Independence.

When Mason reached the age of twenty-one, he inherited his father's lands which included a large estate as well as thousands of acres of farmland located in Maryland and Virginia. His inheritance also included lands yet to be cleared in the western part of the country and his father's slaves, which numbered approximately three hundred. Material things were not all he inherited; as his biographer notes, "Mason inherited one quality from both of his parents that became his most important character trait: perseverance. Mason was also taught by his mother and father and later by his tutors and mentors that a Virginia gentleman owed service to his family, to his country, and to his colony—in that order."

After taking possession of his inheritance, Mason returned to his childhood home at Dogue's Neck, where he built Gunston Hall, the home he would live in for the next forty years. In 1750 he married Ann Eilbeck, described as beautiful and charming. Her earlier suitors included George Washington, though all he found was disappointment. The Mason marriage would last twenty-three years and produce nine children that would live to adulthood. At the end of her final pregnancy, she gave birth to twin boys prematurely. Both died the day after they entered this world. She never recovered her health, and she passed away three months later. Mason's grief over her death was evidenced by the fact that he stayed in his room or his study for the next week. Though he would remarry in 1780, he would wear black mourning clothes for the rest of his life.

Even prior to his marriage, Mason had begun his public career. He was one of the largest local landowners, and that came with duties and obligations. In 1747, he was named to the Fairfax County Court. He also served as a vestryman from 1749 to 1785. In addition, he was a colonel in the local militia and in 1758, he was elected to the House of Burgesses.

Even though he had a large family to raise, a plantation to run and his public service, Mason suffered from ill health for much of his adult life. He himself attributed his many ailments to the "gout," which at the time was a catch-all phrase. In Mason's case, his gout affected his feet, hands, and stomach. At times he was only able to walk with the aid of crutches. His ailments also made it difficult for him to travel. As a result, he spent many hours in his study pouring over political philosophy. The conclusions he drew from these studies would make themselves evident in his later writings.

Despite his ailments, Mason found that he had to continue in the public arena to aid in the protest of British taxes. He edited the Nonimportation Association Agreement for Virginia in 1769. Next, he wrote the twenty-four articles protesting the English government that became the Fairfax Resolves. Here he took on the British Parliament's authority over the colony of Virginia. He was also elected to represent Fairfax County in the House of Burgesses. It was as a member of this body that Mason was the main author of both the Virginia Declaration of Rights and the Constitution of Virginia. In 1776. Thomas Jefferson would paraphrase some of Mason's work in the Declaration of Independence. Mason wrote, "That all men are created equally born free and independent and have certain inherent natural rights among which are the enjoyment of life and liberty with the means of acquiring and possessing property and pursuing and obtaining happiness and safety." His Declaration of Rights was approved on June 12, 1776, and appeared in the *Virginia Gazette* and the *Philadelphia Gazette*. This was a full month prior to Jefferson's draft of the Declaration of Independence. According to his biographer "the case can be made that George Mason should be credited with an original draft of what ultimately became the famed Declaration of Independence."

In his Mason biography, William G. Hyland Jr. notes that John Locke's *Second Treatise on Civil Government*, written in 1690, was a major influence on Mason's own works. Locke took the position that the purpose of government was to protect the natural rights, liberty, and property of the people. That a contract existed between the government and the people, and if that contract was broken, the people had every right to rebel. This view resulted in Mason's own conclusion that the colonies deserved independence and a new government. Mason's fellow revolutionaries, especially Washington, admired his literary talent and his constitutional expertise. Thomas Jefferson remarked that Mason "was learned in the lore of our former Constitution," referring to the

George Mason (1725–1792)

Bronze of George Mason at his homestead

British government. Indeed, Mason had made it a point to study every Constitution that had ever existed.

By 1776, Mason was wealthy, had political experience, and had demonstrated his intellectual abilities. He was a perfect choice to represent Virginia in the Continental Congress. Two-thirds of the members of the Virginia legislature appealed to him to serve in the second Continental Congress. Both Patrick Henry and Thomas Jefferson told Mason that the cause needed him. However, Mason declined to serve, saying it would be a full-time job that would take precedence over his motherless children.

The appeal to his family duty succeeded, and Mason avoided the trip to Philadelphia. Still, he himself noted that "my getting clear of this Appointment has avail'd me little." During the Revolution, he served as a member of the House of Delegates from 1776 to 1781, his longest continuous service outside Fairfax County, which he represented in Richmond. Due to an illness brought on by a botched smallpox inoculation, Mason missed a portion of the legislature's spring 1777 session. During his absence, the delegates elected him to the Continental Congress. Once again, he declined, arguing that he was needed at home and that without the permission of his constituents, he could not resign from the General Assembly.

Mason was appointed to the Annapolis Convention of 1786, but like most of the delegates, he decided not to attend. The most crucial decision made at the sparsely attended meeting was a call for a conference to consider amendments to the Articles of Confederation. This conference became the 1787 Constitutional Convention held in Philadelphia. Virginia decided that George Washington, James Madison, George Wythe, James Blair, and Mason would represent that state at the convention. Mason had never traveled outside Virginia or Maryland in his life; however, in this instance, despite his chronic ill health, he decided to make what would prove to be a difficult journey. His decision to attend surprised many as he said he "would not, upon pecuniary motives, serve in this convention for a thousand pounds per day." According to the historian Jeff Broadwater, "Mason went to Philadelphia because he believed the convention would do important work because a near consensus existed among America's political elite that Congress needed new powers and because he saw a stronger central government as a potential check on state legislatures." In *1787: The Grand Convention* by the historian Clinton Rossiter the author speculates that Mason saw the meeting as the last hope for the preservation of property-owning republicanism in the United States.

Mason impressed many of his fellow delegates. William Pierce said, "Mr. Mason is a gentleman of remarkable strong powers, and possesses a clear and copious understanding. He is able and convincing in debate and firm in his principles, and undoubtedly one of the best politicians in America," Virginia Governor Edmund Randolph observes, "Among the numbers who in their small circles were propagating with activity the American doctrines was George Mason in the shade of retirement. He extended their grasp upon the opinions and affections of those with whom he conversed. He was behind none of the sons of Virginia in knowledge of her history and interest. At a glance, he saw to the bottom of every proposition which affected her. His elocution was manly sometimes but not wantonly sarcastic.

Mason favored a more powerful central government, but not at the expense of local interests. He also worried that northern states would dominate the union and pass trade restrictions that would harm Virginia. He supported a balance of powers he viewed as necessary for a durable government. Early in the convention, Mason favored the Virginia plan, which proposed a popularly elected lower house whose members would choose the members of the upper house from lists provided by the states. The plan also called for representation in both houses to be based on population. This part of the plan was opposed by the smaller states. Mason served on a committee to address the conflict. The committee put forward what was known as the Great Compromise, whereby the House of Representatives members would be based on population in which money bills must originate. The upper house, the Senate, would have equal representation from each state.

The convention had opened in late May, and it was in the middle of July that the delegates began to move past their deadlock relative to representation relying on the framework of the Great Compromise. During these debates, Mason exerted considerable influence. He was successful in proposing a minimum age requirement of twenty-five to serve in Congress after expressing his view that younger men lacked the necessary maturity. He also put forth the proposal that the federal government not be in any state capital. On August 6, 1787, the convention received a draft of a constitution written by the Committee of Detail. Mason viewed the draft as acceptable as a starting point for debate.

In the debates that followed, Mason was successful in some of his arguments, including banning Congress from imposing an export tax and placing state militias under federal control. However, he was unsuccessful in obtaining a consensus for certain proposals he deemed necessary, such as the failure of the Constitution to include a Bill of Rights. Despite being the owner of a large number of slaves, Mason also proposed that the Constitution ban the importation of slaves. He failed to prevail as the convention allowed for the importation of slaves to continue until at least 1800. On August 31, 1787, Elbridge Gerry, a delegate from Massachusetts, moved to postpone consideration of the final document, and Mason seconded the motion, stating that "he would sooner chop off his right hand than put it to the Constitution as it now stands."

On September 12th, the Committee on Style submitted its final draft. On September 15th, as the convention was considering each clause contained in the draft, three delegates, Edmund Randolph, Gerry, and Mason, announced that they would not sign the Constitution. Gouverneur Morris, a Pennsylvania delegate who is the principal author of the Constitution, developed a plan to secure those last signatures. Morris drafted the following to appear above the signatures, "Done in Convention, by the unanimous consent of the state's present . . . In witness whereof, we have hereunto subscribed our names." The language reflected that the signers agreed that the states had voted for the Constitution not that every signer agreed with it. The ploy failed. In Mason's view, the Constitution failed to protect the rights of the people, put excessive power in the hands of the federal government and would lead to some form of tyranny. He refused to put his signature on the document. In a letter to his son, John, Mason noted that his action had cost him at least one important friendship, writing, "I believe there were few men in whom (Washington) placed greater confidence; but it is possible my opposition to the new government, both as a member of the national and of the Virginia Convention, may have altered the case."

There are many who view James Madison as the "Father of the Bill of Rights" because he guided the first ten amendments to the Constitution through Congress. Those who hold this view ignore the fact that Madison opposed a Bill of Rights at both the Philadelphia convention and at the Virginia ratifying convention. At both gatherings, it was Mason who championed the need for the Constitution to include a Bill of Rights. Even after failing to prevail, Mason continued to push for amendments

Grave of George Mason

to the Constitution, keeping the issue alive before the American public. Finally, the amendments that make up our Bill of Rights came, according to Mason's biographer, "almost verbatim from the amendments Mason wrote at the Virginia Ratifying Convention and his previous 1776 Virginia Declaration of Rights." These facts certainly support the view that it is Mason who should be regarded as the "Father of the Bill of Rights."

After losing his fight against ratification in Richmond, Mason returned to his home, where he often wrote to political figures regarding his views on the new government. In 1790, United States Senator William Grayson's death left a vacancy, and Mason was offered the position. He declined, citing health reasons, but it is worth noting that Congress required its members to take an oath to support the Constitution. The seat went to future President James Monroe.

In early October 1792, Thomas Jefferson visited Mason at Gunston Hall. He noted that while Mason remained sharp in mind, he needed a crutch to walk. Less than a week after Jefferson's visit, Mason passed away on October 7, 1792. He was laid to rest on the grounds of his estate.

George Mason's vault

John Mathews
(1744–1802)

"The Disagreeable One"

Buried at Circular Congregational Church Burying Ground
Charleston, South Carolina

**Signer of Articles of Confederation • Continental Congress
Governor • Militia**

John Mathews was a lawyer from Charleston, South Carolina, who was involved in politics. He served in local positions and was elected to the Continental Congress in time for the Articles of Confederation, which he signed. Near the end of the American Revolution, he was elected governor of South Carolina for one term. For the remainder of his life, he served in state judicial positions.

Mathews was born in 1744 in Charleston, South Carolina, the son of John Mathews and his wife, Sarah (née Gibbes). His paternal lineage was from Captain Anthony Mathewes (1661-1734), who emigrated to South Carolina from London in 1680.

Early in the 1760s, Mathews fought the Cherokee in South Carolina as an ensign in the South Carolina Provincial Regiment. He was promoted to lieutenant in the process.

Mathews next studied law and went to England, where he entered the Middle Temple in 1764. He graduated in 1766 and returned to South Carolina, where he initially clerked for Colonel Charles Pinckney before he was admitted to the colonial bar. However, Mathews did not

John Mathews

practice law in South Carolina. Rather, he became a politician, speaking against the various actions of the British Parliament following the French and Indian War.

In December 1766, Mathews married Mary Wragg, the half-sister of Charlotte Wragg, who married William Loughton Smith, a fellow delegate to the Continental Congress from South Carolina. The couple had no children. Mathew's sister, Elizabeth, was married to another Continental Congressman, Thomas Heyward Jr.

In 1772, Mathews was elected to the South Carolina Commons House of Assembly. There, he called for a boycott of British goods. From June 1774 until June 1775, Mathews was a member of the Committee of Ninety-Nine, which formed a rebel government in the colony. Mathews also returned to the military as a lieutenant in the provincial militia, guarding Fort Charlotte on the Savannah and Fort Moore near present-day Augusta.

During 1775 and 1776, following the hostilities commencing at Lexington and Concord, Mathews was appointed an associate judge on the state circuit court and a member of the First and Second Provincial Congresses in South Carolina. From 1776 to 1780, Mathews served in the South Carolina House of Representatives, serving as speaker in 1777 and 1778. He also continued his military service as a captain in the Colleton County regiment.

On January 22, 1778, after Christopher Gadsden and Henry Middleton declined to continue serving, Mathews was elected to the Continental Congress. He immediately found himself embroiled in the debates about the Articles of Confederation following the meetings in York, Pennsylvania. Mathews was unhappy from the start, describing the trip from South Carolina to York, Pennsylvania, "A most disagreeable journey, indeed." He followed this with a complaint about the indecision in Congress to John Rutledge on July 7, 1778:

> We are thrown into a good deal of confusion with regard to the Confederation. Before we left York-Town, Congress proceeded to the consideration of the amendments offered by the different States to the Confederation, every one of which have been rejected. It was then ordered to be engroced [sic] to [be] ready for ratification when we came to Philadelphia. Now, that it is so, Mr. Laurens, Mr. Drayton, and Mr. Hutson say they will not sign it because they do not think themselves authorized by our instructions to do so unless the other twelve states will agree to sign it likewise. Maryland has refused to ratify. Mr. Heyward and my self [sic] are of a different opinion, and think we are authorized, not withstanding [sic] one or even two States were to refuse, nor do I apprehend that inconsistancy [sic] will arise in the Confederation, from the Defection of one or two States which these three Gentlemen seem to imagine, however they mean, I believe, to write to the Prest. or to you, to be laid before the Assembly. I do not think it necessary for Heyward

and myself to write on the subject, in our public Characters, as we think we are authorised [sic] to sign it, but as Three are necessary to a final Ratification, we must wait for your decision. This I am clear in, from what I have seen, and know, since I have been in Congress, that if we are to have no Confederation until the Legislatures of the Thirteen States agree to one, that we shall never have one, and if we have not one, we shall be literally a rope of sand, and I shall tremble for the consequences that will follow at the end of this War.

Mathews quickly developed a reputation as a complainer in Congress. He did not enjoy his time in the sessions, complaining about his fellow Congressmen, "Those who have dispositions for jangling and are fond of displaying their Rhetorical abilities, let them come. I never was so sick of anything in my life." He wrote to others about his frustrations with the slow pace of things. Regardless of his mood, Mathews signed the Articles of Confederation on July 21, 1778. His complaints about his fellow members continued, and they also described his temperament as hot, "like the country of his nativity."

Mathews was reelected to the Congress in 1779 and 1780, joining Henry Laurens, Francis Kinloch, Arthur Middleton, and Thomas Bee as delegates from South Carolina. During his tenure, he served on the Committee of Congress, which dealt with military matters. When Mathews got word of Charleston's fall in 1780, he wished to return from Congress. Only John Rutledge, the governor, remained, now in exile in North Carolina. Britain was trying to pry away the Southern states from the rest, but the patriots would not hear it. Rutledge urged Mathews to stay in Congress to help manage affairs there.

After Nathanael Greene's victory at Eutaw Springs on September 9, 1781, the tide turned against the British, who now fell back to Charleston. Rutledge prepared for the re-establishment of South Carolina's government in late 1781. On January 24, 1782, the South Carolina House met and announced the return of John Mathews from Philadelphia. After both Christopher Gadsden and Richard Hutson were elected and declined the post of governor, Mathews was elected. The house voted that

Mathews could not refuse the post! Mathews then retired from Congress and became the governor. He was sworn in on January 31, 1782, and served until February 4, 1783. During this time, the British evacuated Charleston in December 1782, and Mathews threatened the nonpayment of British merchants if the soldiers carried off any goods from the citizens of the city. The negotiation worked.

After his governorship, Mathews was a judge on the state Court of Chancery in 1784 and again served in the South Carolina House. He remained involved in Charleston's affairs and sold off his merchant sloop. He also advertised for a fugitive slave in August 1790, seeking the recovery of Jemmy "of the African country." Mathews was a judge on the state Court of Equity in 1791. He was also a founding trustee of the College of Charleston.

After Mary's passing, Mathews married Sarah Rutledge in May 1799. She was the sister of John and Edward Rutledge, both Continental Congressmen. The couple had no children.

Mathews followed his wife to the grave on October 30, 1802, in Charleston. He was buried at the Circular Congregational Church Burying Ground in Charleston.

Frederick Augustus Conrad Muhlenberg
(1750–1801)

The First Speaker

Buried at Woodward Hill Cemetery,
Lancaster, Pennsylvania.

1st Speaker of the House

Frederick Augustus Conrad Muhlenberg was a Lutheran minister who was the son of Henry Melchior Muhlenberg, the founder of the Lutheran church in America. Frederick was also the grandson of Conrad Weiser, the colonial Indian agent, and interpreter. He was also the brother of Major General Peter Muhlenberg. During the American Revolution, Frederick Muhlenberg served in the Continental Congress representing Pennsylvania. He later served in Pennsylvania's Constitutional Convention and was subsequently elected to the First Congress of the U.S. House of Representatives. There he was elected the first Speaker of the House of the United States.

Frederick Muhlenberg was born January 2, 1750, in Trappe, Philadelphia (now Montgomery) County, Pennsylvania to the Reverend Henry Melchior Muhlenberg and his wife Anna Maria (née Weiser) Muhlenberg. Henry's father, Claus Nicholas Melchior Muhlenberg, hailed from Einbeck, in Hanover (Germany) where Prince George Louis was born. Prince George ascended the English throne as King George I. Henry was a shoemaker, lay deacon, and town councilor. Henry studied

Frederick Augustus Conrad Muhlenberg (1750–1801)

Frederick Muhlenberg

theology and was ordained as a minister in the Lutheran Church. He answered a call from three congregations in Pennsylvania—at Philadelphia, Trappe, and New Hanover. He arrived in Philadelphia on November 25, 1742, and soon settled at Trappe. On April 22, 1745, Henry married Anna Maria Weiser, the daughter of Pennsylvania's colonial Indian agent and interpreter Conrad Weiser (1696-1760), who lived in Womelsdorf, Pennsylvania. The couple had three sons and four daughters.

Reverend Henry was busy with his calling and devoted little time to his sons. When Henry left his family behind in Trappe in 1761 to relocate to Philadelphia, the three sons were sent to be educated at the University of Halle in Germany under the tutelage of Dr. Francke. Frederick studied theology and foreign languages. In September 1770, Frederick returned to Philadelphia with his brother Gotthilf where he was ordained a minister in the Lutheran Church. Soon after, on

October 15, 1771, Frederick married Catharine Schafer, the daughter of a Philadelphia sugar refiner.

Frederick's first assignment was assisting his brother-in-law, the Reverend Christian Emanuel Schulze, at the congregation in Tulpehocken (Womelsdorf), Pennsylvania. He also helped at congregations at Schaefferstown, Brickerville, White Oak, and Manheim until 1774. He then worked in Stouchsburg and Lebanon, Pennsylvania. Regarding the life of a traveling preacher, a descendant, Henry Melchior Muhlenberg Richards, wrote in 1902:

> We, of this age and comfort and conveniences, can hardly realize what the godly men of that day were called upon to endure in the performance of their ordinary duties. Some faint idea of their sacrifices may be gained by a perusal of the account left by Frederick of his trip from the Tulpehocken Valley to Shamokin, in the summer of 1771, to visit a little flock of German Lutherans there located, who were without pastor or church. He tells of his lonely ride through the wilds of the Blue Mountains, and beyond, with his one companion, young Conrad Weiser, the son of his Uncle Frederick; how he passed Fort Henry, already in a dilapidated condition . . . of the beautiful view which stretched before him from the top of the ridge: of the steep and dangerous paths, in one instance a mere shelf of the mountain . . .

The next two years, as the American Revolution unfolded, Frederick transferred to Christ Church in New York City. There he assisted Reverend Bernhard Michael Hausihl, who preached only in English. Frederick delivered prayers in German, which pleased the immigrant community.

By 1776, many in the congregation and Hausihl sided with the British while Muhlenberg sympathized with the Americans. They asked that Muhlenberg leave the church and return when the difficulties were concluded. In May 1776, with the British about to take New York City, the Muhlenbergs fled southward. His family went ahead to Philadelphia where Catharine had their third child. Frederick joined them on July 2, two days before the Declaration of Independence.

While brother Peter had become a colonel in the Continental Army, Frederick moved his family to Trappe where he delivered a sermon to a gathering of Continental troops saying, "Be not ye afraid of them; remember the Lord, which is great and terrible, and fight for your brethren, your sons, and your daughters, your wives, and your houses."

As the British next invaded Philadelphia, Frederick witnessed the defeats at Brandywine and Germantown. In early 1777, he took over the congregation at New Hanover (Falkner's Swamp) and continued for two more years in addition to serving at New Goshenhoppen and Oley.

During this time, Muhlenberg came to support the American Revolution more openly. On March 2, 1779, he was elected to the Continental Congress along with John McClene and Henry Wynkoop, joining Edward Biddle, Daniel Roberdeau, and William Clingan to represent Pennsylvania.

In 1780, Muhlenberg left the Continental Congress when he was elected to a seat in the Pennsylvania Assembly. He served as the Speaker of the Assembly from 1780 to 1783.

In 1787, Muhlenberg was a delegate at the Pennsylvania state constitutional convention which ratified the U.S. Constitution. He was then elected to the U.S. House of Representatives. On his first day in office, he was overwhelmingly elected by the members as the first Speaker of the House. This was arranged as a prize for Pennsylvania due to Virginia having the presidency (George Washington) and Massachusetts having the vice presidency (John Adams).

Muhlenberg served as the Speaker for the first Congress from 1789 to 1791. During this period, the Bill of Rights was passed and sent to the states for ratification. As Speaker, Muhlenberg was the first to sign it. During these formative times, there was a debate about how to address the president. John Adams, as vice president and president of the Senate, suggested such sobriquets as "His High Mightiness" and "His Elected Majesty." According to legend, it was Muhlenberg who suggested, "Mr. President."

For the Second Congress, Jonathan Trumbull of Connecticut was elected to the position but only held it for one term. During this time, on December 15, 1792, Muhlenberg, along with Senator James Monroe and Congressman Abraham Venable, confronted Secretary of the Treasury Alexander Hamilton about the Reynold's Affair, a sex and bribery scandal in which he was embroiled. Hamilton admitted the sordid details of the affair with Mrs. Reynolds but denied any financial impropriety and the three men agreed to keep the matter private. However, James Monroe later shared the letters with Hamilton's rival, Thomas Jefferson, who, five years later, exposed them to embarrass Hamilton. This nearly led to a duel between Hamilton and Monroe, ironically stopped by Aaron Burr's intervention.

Muhlenberg was reelected as Speaker for the third Congress from 1793 to 1795. In 1794, Muhlenberg abstained as the House voted 42-41 against a proposal to translate some of the national laws into German. Said Muhlenberg later, "the faster the Germans become Americans, the better it will be." He was subsequently tagged with the Muhlenberg Legend which claimed he was responsible for preventing German from becoming the official language of the United States.

During the fourth Congress, Muhlenberg yielded the speakership to Jonathan Dayton of New Jersey while retaining chairmanship of the

The grave of Frederick Muhlenberg

Frederick Augustus Conrad Muhlenberg (1750–1801)

Detail of Frederick's grave

Committee of the Whole. There, he cast the deciding vote on April 29, 1796, in support of the Jay Treaty with England, which was unpopular with the Jeffersonians. Muhlenberg was not reelected to the house and left on March 3, 1797.

His national political career over, Muhlenberg returned to Trappe where he served as president of the Council of Censors in Pennsylvania, a government oversight body with the power to suggest amendments to the state constitution and to censure government officials. In 1800, Muhlenberg was appointed as the receiver-general of the Pennsylvania Land Office.

Frederick Muhlenberg died suddenly on June 4, 1801, while attending to his duties in Lancaster, then the state capital. Said the *Lancaster Intelligencer* soon after, "At 11 o'clock on the Tuesday preceding his death, he repaired from his own house to the office of the surveyor-Gen., to attend a meeting of the board of property. He was then in his usual state of high health; but in less than an hour from that time, he was suddenly seized with a violent apoplectic fit; to which his plethorick [sic] habit and extreme corpulence had, perhaps, predisposed him. This stroke was soon succeeded by two others, of greater severity; and within 50 hours from the first attack, his dissolution took place." The article followed with a glowing obituary of his contributions to the commonwealth and the nation.

The Speaker's house in Trappe, Pennsylvania, during the restoration

Frederick Muhlenberg was first buried at Trinity Lutheran Church in Lancaster, where Thomas Mifflin and Thomas Wharton had been recently buried. Muhlenberg was later reinterred at Woodward Hill Cemetery in Lancaster after its founding in 1850. His gravestone makes no mention of his national service. Muhlenberg's house in Trappe, known as the Speaker's House, is a museum administered by the local historical society.

Wrote John Adams about the Muhlenberg brothers, Frederick and Peter, "These two Germans, who had been long in public affairs and in high offices, were the great leaders and oracles of the whole German interest in Pennsylvania and the neighboring States . . . The Muhlenbergs turned the whole body of the Germans, great numbers of the Irish, and many of the English, and in this manner introduced the total change that followed in both Houses of the Legislature, and in all the executive departments of the national government. Upon such slender threads did our elections then depend!"

Muhlenberg Township in Berks County, Pennsylvania, is named after Frederick Muhlenberg as was the World War II liberty ship S.S. F.A.C. Muhlenberg.

John Peter Gabriel Muhlenberg
(1746–1807)

Major General Who Was a Minister

Buried at Augustus Lutheran Church Cemetery,
Trappe, Pennsylvania.

Major General

John Peter Gabriel Muhlenberg was a Lutheran minister who was the son of Henry Melchior Muhlenberg, the founder of the Lutheran church in America. He was also the grandson of Conrad Weiser, the colonial Indian agent, and interpreter. In addition, he was the brother of the first Speaker of the House of Representatives, Frederick Muhlenberg. During the American Revolution, Peter Muhlenberg served in the Continental Army, rising to the level of Major General at the war's end. He later served in the U.S. House of Representatives for four terms and briefly in the U.S. Senate.

Peter Muhlenberg was born October 1, 1746, in Trappe, Philadelphia (now Montgomery) County, Pennsylvania to the Reverend Henry Melchior Muhlenberg and his wife, Anna Maria (née Weiser) Muhlenberg. (Further details of Peter's siblings, parents, and grandparents can be found in the preceding chapter about his brother, Frederick Muhlenberg.)

While Peter's younger brothers, Frederick and Gotthilf, continued their studies in Germany, by 1767 the elder Peter tired of academics and ran off to join the British 60th Regiment of Foot. He also served briefly in a military unit of German dragoons earning the nickname "Teufel

Peter Muhlenberg

Piet" (Devil Pete) and worked as a sales assistant for a grocer in Lübeck. Peter rose to the secretary of the German regiment, but his parents disapproved and recalled him to Philadelphia.

Back home in 1767, he received a classical education at the Academy of Philadelphia, now the University of Pennsylvania. He became an ordained minister in the Lutheran church in 1768 and moved to Bedminster, New Jersey to lead the congregation there as well as the one in New Germantown. Soon after, he transferred to Woodstock, Virginia. There, in 1770, he married the daughter of a successful potter, Anna Barbara "Hannah" Meyer. The two ultimately had six children.

Due to the Anglican Church being the state church of Virginia, Peter was also required to be ordained in that church. On a visit to England in

1772, he achieved that goal, though he served a Lutheran congregation of German immigrants.

By 1774, as the rumblings of the Revolution were in the air, Muhlenberg was elected to the House of Burgesses, was a delegate to the First Virginia Convention, and led his local Committee of Safety and Correspondence in Dunmore County.

Late in 1775, though discouraged by his brother Frederick, upon the personal urging of George Washington, Muhlenberg raised the 8th Virginia Regiment of the Continental Army and served as its colonel. Many of the soldiers in the regiment were German immigrants. At only 29, Muhlenberg was the youngest of the eight Virginia colonels and had more military experience than only Patrick Henry.

According to a biographer in the mid-1800s who was related to Muhlenberg, on January 21, 1776, he gave a sermon to his congregation in Woodstock, Virginia, quoting from Ecclesiastes, "To everything, there is a season . . . a time of war, and a time of peace." He then declared, "And this is the time of war," while removing his clerical robe to reveal his officer's uniform beneath. Immediately, over 162 men were moved to enroll in the regiment, kissed their wives, and enlisted. By the next day, 300 had joined. While historians accept that Muhlenberg formed and led the regiment, they doubt the account of the sermon given its provenance and the lack of reports of such an event before the biography.

The 8th Virginia Regiment was initially sent to Charleston, South Carolina. They first saw combat on June 28, 1776, at the defense of Sullivan Island, off the coast of Charleston. Charles Lee, the American commander, reported concerning the Virginia troops, they were "brave to the last degree," and later added "I know not which corps I have the greatest reason to be pleased with Muhlenberg's Virginians, or the North Carolina troops—they are both equally alert, zealous, and spirited."

On February 1, 1777, the Continental Congress promoted Muhlenberg to brigadier general and ordered him to join the army of George Washington near Philadelphia serving under Nathanael Greene's division at Valley Forge. He was given command of all the Virginia regiments, known as the Virginia Line on May 26, 1777.

Muhlenberg's units were known to be well-disciplined. Washington chose Muhlenberg that August to lead the troops through Philadelphia to confront Howe's invasion force because he felt Muhlenberg's units would make the best impression on the local citizenry.

On September 11, 1777, serving under Nathanael Greene at the Battle of Brandywine, Muhlenberg's troops were not in a position to engage and did not see any action in the American defeat. However, the next month, on October 3 at Germantown, Muhlenberg's forces were among those on the frontlines. One general remembered them "advancing with spirit . . ." Another Continental officer recorded, "Muhlenberg and Scott, pressing forward with eagerness, encountered and broke a part of the British right-wing, entered the village, and made a considerable number of prisoners." Unfortunately, this did not last long. A fog fell upon the field, causing confusion among the units, especially near the Chew House. Muhlenberg's troops held their ground firing their muskets but began to run out of ammunition requiring them to withdraw. William Johnson, Nathanael Greene's biographer, later wrote of the bravery shown by Muhlenberg's Virginia Line saying it was "the only part of the American army that had the good fortune to effect the service allotted it that day."

During the retreat from Germantown, Muhlenberg's brigade was the rearguard and was among the last to leave the field. According to a later biography, Muhlenberg was with the rearguard and was weary from battle. He fell asleep on his horse only to be awakened by the whistle of a British musket ball. He awoke to see a British officer directing his men toward him, drew his pistol and fired, hitting the enemy leader.

The next spring, on March 2, 1778, Muhlenberg was irritated by a decision of a board of his fellow generals when they recognized William Woodford, who had left for a time and returned, as his senior among the Virginia Line officers. Muhlenberg threatened to resign and received support from Washington in the matter. Congress smoothed things over by stating, "the change in seniority was not intended to reflect upon the personal characters or comparative merits of those officers."

During the remainder of 1778 and 1779, Muhlenberg's brigades saw no action though they were present for the attack at Stony Point and were likely at the Battle of Monmouth. During the winter of 1780, most of the Virginia Line was sent south to defend Charleston, but Muhlenberg was given command of all forces in Virginia. However, the state treasury was bare, and there were few troops. Muhlenberg was tasked with raising and training militia units to resist the pending British incursions into the state.

In October 1780, near Portsmouth, Muhlenberg led a small brigade of only 800 raw militia to challenge a much larger British force who fell back and dug in. Muhlenberg was then reinforced by 5000 militia who surrounded the British. By the end of the month, the invaders decided to return to their ships.

Washington next sent Major General Baron von Steuben to Virginia in December 1780 given the increase in enemy activity. Muhlenberg now reported to him, and the two developed a rapport.

Not long after von Steuben arrived, British Brigadier General Benedict Arnold landed at Portsmouth with 2,000 soldiers and began marching inland. Muhlenberg again rallied his militia and once again cornered the enemy at Portsmouth. Rather than attack directly with his inferior force, Muhlenberg continued to harass the enemy until more aid came.

In response, Washington sent Marquis de Lafayette and 1,200 men as reinforcements to attack from land while the French navy attempted to cut off escape by sea. This plot was foiled when the French fleet was defeated by the British. The British then reinforced their position with more troops from New York.

As the pressure mounted from the increasing number of invaders, von Steuben ordered Muhlenberg further inland. On April 24, 1781, the 1,000 American troops encountered 2,500 British soldiers outside of Petersburg. Von Steuben ordered Muhlenberg to establish a defensive position to delay the enemy. These militia units were not as disciplined as the regular units of the Virginia Line, but the men fought well as they retreated. Von Steuben later reported, "General Muhlenberg merits my particular acknowledgments for the good disposition which he made and the great gallantry with which he executed it."

As 1781 proceeded, more attention was focused on the coastal area of Virginia. Washington and his French ally Rochambeau marched to Virginia to attack British General Cornwallis. Muhlenberg was assigned to a brigade of Continentals in Lafayette's Light Division. On September 29, 1781, the allies began their siege of Yorktown.

Over two weeks later, on October 14, Major Alexander Hamilton led a battalion of Muhlenberg's and two from Moses Hazen's brigade to the climactic attack on the British defenses. The rest of Muhlenberg's and Hazen's forces then followed the successful attack, arriving as Hamilton went over the works. The American and French victory at Yorktown marked the end of the major fighting in the Revolutionary War. It was the last military action for Muhlenberg. He continued in Virginia for a time, organizing the local militias. On September 30, 1783, Congress promoted him to major general. The army was then disbanded that November.

Now a civilian, Muhlenberg moved back to Trappe and became an original member of the Pennsylvania Society of the Cincinnati. In 1784, he was elected to the Supreme Executive Council of the Commonwealth of Pennsylvania. From 1785 to 1788, he was made Vice President of the Council (comparable to Lieutenant Governor). Muhlenberg resigned from this position on October 14, 1788.

Next, Muhlenberg was elected to the First Congress along with his brother Frederick who became the first Speaker of the House. In 1793, Muhlenberg founded the Democratic-Republican Societies and won seats as a Republican in the Third and Sixth Congresses.

Muhlenberg was elected by the Pennsylvania legislature to the U.S. Senate in February 1801, defeating George Logan. However, he resigned in June 1801 when President Thomas Jefferson appointed him as the supervisor for revenue in Pennsylvania. He was made customs collector for Philadelphia in 1802, a post he held until his death.

On August 3, 1805, Muhlenberg wrote a letter appealing to the mostly German residents of Berks and Northampton counties to convince them to vote for Governor Thomas McKean rather than the German Simon Snyder who was backed by a radical Democratic faction keen to upset the Constitution. McKean won, and the margin of victory could be found in those counties.

Peter Muhlenberg died on October 1, 1807, his 61st birthday, at Gray's Ferry, Pennsylvania. He was buried at the Augustus Lutheran Church in Trappe next to his father.

John Peter Gabriel Muhlenberg (1746–1807)

The grave of Peter Muhlenberg

There is a memorial to Peter Muhlenberg on Connecticut Avenue in Washington, D.C. The inscription reads, "John Peter Gabriel Muhlenberg 1746–1807 Serving His Church, His Country, His State." Another memorial stands at the Philadelphia Museum of Art. Muhlenberg County, Kentucky is named after him.

Woodstock, Virginia is the home of two statues of Muhlenberg; one in front of the Shenandoah County Courthouse; the other at the Emmanuel Lutheran Church.

A statue of Peter Muhlenberg is located in front of the Shenandoah County Courthouse in Woodstock, Virginia. That town's Emmanuel Lutheran congregation preserves his communion vessels, a baptismal font, and an altar cloth.

Detail of Peter's grave

Another statue of Peter Muhlenberg is located at Muhlenberg College in Allentown, Pennsylvania in front of the Haas College Center on Chew Street.

U.S. Congressman Francis Swaine Muhlenberg, a son of Peter Muhlenberg, represented Ohio for a term. A nephew, Henry Augustus Philip Muhlenberg, had a much longer career in the Congress and was the first United States Minister to the Austrian Empire. A great-great-grandson, Frederick Augustus Muhlenberg was a Representative and Senator from Pennsylvania.

Historian Jerome Greene recently wrote about Muhlenberg, "Outside his home state, he is not well known, but Muhlenberg was one of the many steady unsung heroes of the war."

James Otis Jr.
(1725–1783)

"Founding Firebrand"

Buried at Granary Burying Ground
Boston, Massachusetts

Pamphleteer • Thought Leader

James Otis Jr. was an attorney, legislator, political activist, and pamphleteer from Boston who was an early thought leader in the ultimate pursuit of independence from Great Britain. A mentor of Sam Adams and inspiration for John Adams, Otis is credited with coining the phrase "taxation without representation is tyranny." A Freemason, Otis was also an abolitionist who lobbied for freedoms and rights for all regardless of race. Otis was unable to participate more actively in the Revolution due to his declining mental health and alcoholism.

Otis was born on February 5, 1725, in West Barnstable, Massachusetts, the second of thirteen children of Colonel James Otis Sr. and his wife, Mary (née Allyne) Otis. The elder Otis was a militia officer and attorney. Brothers Joseph and Samuel and nephew Harrison Gray Otis were leading Patriots in the Revolution. Otis's sister, Mercy, married James Warren, and the two were active in the Patriot cause. Mercy was also a satirist and historian.

Throughout his youth, Otis disappointed his father, who expressed this in letters and urged his son to find religion to better himself. Instead, Otis attended Harvard to study law, beginning at age 14. He graduated in

James Otis Jr.

1743 and quickly rose to prominence in Boston as a defense lawyer, successfully defending pirates in Nova Scotia and young men in Plymouth accused of rioting on Guy Fawkes' Day.

In 1755, Otis married a wealthy merchant's daughter, Ruth Cunningham. She had inherited over £10,000, so Otis tolerated their political differences, complaining she was a "High Tory." According to John Adams, Otis said, "She was a good Wife, and too good for him."

Despite the tensions, the couple had three children: James, who lived to age 18; Elizabeth, a Loyalist like her mother who married a British Army captain; and Mary, who married Major General Benjamin Lincoln of the Continental Army.

Otis's first controversy in court occurred in 1760 when Governor Francis Bernard appointed him the Advocate General of the Admiralty Court. However, Otis resigned when the governor reneged on appointing his father as the Chief Justice of the Massachusetts Superior Court and instead appointed Thomas Hutchinson, a longtime rival.

Soon after, Otis represented several Boston businessmen who challenged the Massachusetts Writs of Assistance, permitting local officials to search and confiscate property without cause. In the Superior Court, during *Paxton v. Gray* in 1761, Otis argued against the writs, stating "An Act against the constitution is void . . . and if an act of Parliament should be made . . . the executive courts must pass such acts into disuse."

In a five-hour oration before the State House in February 1761, he continued the fight before five red-robed judges while a young John Adams listened. Said Otis of the Writs of Assistance, "It appears to me the worst instrument of arbitrary power, the most destructive of English liberty . . . that was ever found in an English law book." Otis was unsuccessful in changing the law. However, he did gain the notice of those present and became known as an early revolutionary, especially for labeling the King and Parliament as oppressors of the colonists. Bostonians elected him to the Massachusetts House of Representatives, where he was a member of the Stamp Act Congress.

Recalled John Adams, years later, "Otis was a flame of fire; with a promptitude of classical allusions, a depth of research, a rapid summary of historical events and dates, a profusion of legal authorities . . . Then and there was the first scene of the first Act of opposition to the Arbitrary claims of Great Britain. Then and there, the Child Independence was born. . . . The seeds of Patriots & Heroes . . . were then & there sown." Sections of Otis's 1761 speech were used and enhanced by John Adams over the years.

In 1762, Otis published his first political pamphlet, *A Vindication of the Conduct of the House of Representatives*, where he first uses an example of unsanctioned expenditures by the legislature.

In 1764, Otis published a pamphlet, *The Rights of the British Colonies Asserted and Proved*, that expanded upon his earlier arguments, stating that rights are granted from nature and God rather than from the government and that the purpose of government was for the good of society and not the pleasure of monarchs. He added that the colonies lacked representation in Parliament, and thus, it was unconstitutional for Parliament to tax them, stating: "The very act of taxing, exercised over those who are not represented, appears to me to be depriving them of one of their most essential rights." He also argued for racial equality, stating, "The colonists are by the law of nature freeborn, as indeed all men are, white or black."

By this time, Otis was seen as a firebrand. Lord Mansfield said of his pamphlet, "It is said the man is mad. The book is full of wildness." Friends referred to him as *Furio*, Latin for "in a rage." Rival Hutchinson called him "The Great Incendiary." Wrote John Adams in his diary, "his imagination flames, his passions blaze; he is liable to great inequalities of temper; sometimes in despondency, sometimes in a rage."

Otis's beliefs regarding Natural Law were further described in his 1765 pamphlets, *Considerations on Behalf of the Colonists* and *Vindication of the British Colonies*, espousing equal representation in the government. However, he mysteriously reversed himself in the pamphlet "*Brief Remarks on the Defence of the Halifax Libel*," in which he admitted Parliament had complete authority over the colonies. Some believe this erratic behavior was either to set a potential defense against treason or he had become mentally ill. Regardless, it was Otis's last pamphlet.

Contemporaries noted the mental decline of Otis in the 1760s, and his relationship with his wife was strained. Wrote John Adams in his diary about Mrs. Otis, "She gave him certain lectures."

In 1769, as tensions rose in Boston, Otis worried that "The times are dark and trying. We may soon be called on in turn to act or to suffer." That summer, outraged at a slanderous article about him, Otis threatened to "break the head" of tax commissioner John Robinson. He tracked him down on Boston's Long Wharf at the British Coffee House. The two got into a melee. Robinson grabbed Otis's nose, and the two threw punches and whacked each other with their canes. Loyalists jostled Otis and called for his death while British offices stood by, watching. Ultimately, Otis was cudgeled on the head by Robinson and collapsed, dazed and bleeding. Months later, Otis still had a deep scar on his head that John Adams wrote "You could lay a finger in it."

Otis became a recluse. He began drinking heavily, wandering the taverns and streets, lamenting his opposition of the British. He was apparently suffering a mental break. He could not continue his work and was limited in his legal practice to brief periods of mental clarity. Wrote John Adams in January 1770, "He rambles like a ship without a helm . . .

James Otis Jr. (1725–1783)

Grave of James Otis Jr.

I fear, I tremble, I mourn for the man, and for his country." Later, in February 1771, Adams wrote that Otis was "raving mad, raving against father, wife, brother, sister, friend."

Otis was elected to the House again that year but was unable to contribute, propped up socially by John and Sam Adams. That December, Thomas Hutchinson, in a letter to Governor Bernard, said, "Otis was carried off today in a postchaise, bound hand and foot. He has been as good as his word—set the Province in a flame and perished in the attempt."

Otis was passed between family and friends as he battled mental illness, living in the countryside. After the Revolution in 1783, Governor John Hancock held a dinner in Otis's honor, but he could not handle the speeches and toasts, and had to leave, returning home to the countryside.

In his unsteady state, Otis burned most of his papers, leaving historians with only the published correspondence with others.

On May 23, 1783, while standing in the doorway of a friend's home, watching a thunderstorm, Otis was struck and killed by lightning. He was buried in the Granary Burying Ground in Boston.

GRAVES of our FOUNDERS

It must be noted that Otis did not literally invent the phrase "Taxation without representation is tyranny" but rather formed an idea that John Adams later paraphrased.

Adams eulogized Otis "as extraordinary in death as in life. He has left a character that will never die while the memory of the American Revolution remains."

Thomas Paine
(1737–1809)

"The Mouthpiece of the American Revolution"

Buried at The Thomas Paine Gravesite (now empty)
New Rochelle, New York

Thought Leader

Thomas Paine was a brilliant writer, political thinker, and opportunist. He became famous in the American colonies for his work *Common Sense*, which solidified public resolve regarding the American Revolution. He may have assisted in the drafting of the Declaration of Independence and later was involved in diplomatic efforts. His involvement in the French Revolution following his authorship of *Rights of Man* made him a man without a country despite its profound influences. Also, the architect of a single-span bridge, Paine burned the bridges of all his acquaintances and friendships throughout his later years, especially with his Deist work *The Age of Reason*. Always struggling with finances, Paine died a poor alcoholic in New Rochelle, New York. In later years, his bones were exhumed and subsequently taken to England and lost.

Paine, born January 28, 1737, in Thetford, Norfolk, England, was one of two children of Joseph Pain, a tenant farmer, and his wife, Frances (née Cocke) Pain. The elder Pain was also a staymaker (corset maker) who struggled with finances and an unhappy marriage. Mrs. Pain was the daughter of an attorney and town clerk who, according to an early Paine biographer, had a "sour temper and eccentric character." Paine's younger sister, Elizabeth, born a year later, died in infancy.

Thomas Paine

Paine attended Thetford Grammar School until he was 13, at which point he became a tailor's apprentice assisting his father. At 19, during the Seven Years War, he served aboard the British privateer *King of Prussia*. Afterward, he settled in Sandwich, County Kent, where he established a shop as a staymaker. He married Mary Lambert on September 27, 1759, but his business soon failed. The struggling couple, now expecting, moved to Margate. Sadly, Mary went into early labor, and both mother and child died.

Paine returned to Thetford and worked in temporary roles while also continuing his staymaking. In December 1762, he became an excise officer in Grantham, Lincolnshire, transferring to Alford in August 1764. On August 27, 1765, he was dismissed for "claiming to have inspected goods he did not inspect." A year later, he requested reinstatement, which was granted. In 1767, he transferred to Grampound, Cornwall, and then asked to leave the post, pending a vacancy, and became a schoolteacher in London. Next, on February 19, 1768, he was assigned to Lewes, Sussex, where he lived above the tobacco shop of Samuel and Esther Ollive. Paine became involved in civic matters and the church vestry. On March

26, 1771, he married Elizabeth Ollive, the daughter of the late tobacconist. Paine subsequently took over the shop.

During 1772 and 1773, Paine lobbied Parliament on behalf of fellow excise officers for better pay and working conditions. In the summer of 1772, he published *The Case of the Officers of Excise*, and spent the following winter distributing 4,000 copies around London. In the spring of 1774, he was dismissed from the excise service due to his absence. Around this time, the tobacco shop also failed, and on April 14, he sold his household possessions to avoid debtors' prison. On June 4, 1774, he separated from his wife and moved to London. That September, the Commissioner of the Excise, George Lewis Scott, who was also a mathematician and Fellow of the Royal Society, introduced Paine to Benjamin Franklin. Franklin, the publisher of *The Pennsylvania Gazette*, the largest newspaper in America, suggested that Paine emigrate to America and gave him a letter of recommendation to his son-in-law, Richard Bache. Paine left the next month, but the voyage was difficult. The drinking water on the ship was bad, and five passengers died from typhus. When Paine arrived in Philadelphia on November 30, 1774, he was too sick to disembark. Benjamin Franklin's doctor carried him from the ship and cared for him for six weeks until he recovered. Back on his feet, Paine took an oath to become a citizen of Pennsylvania.

He soon began writing for Robert Aitken's *Pennsylvania Magazine* and was elevated to editor in March 1775. On March 8, 1775, the magazine published an unsigned abolitionist essay describing slavery as "execrable commerce" and an "outrage against Humanity and Justice." Benjamin Rush later assigned the authorship to Paine, who had reacted to seeing black slaves for the first time.

Though Aitken had intended the magazine to be apolitical, Paine brought a revolutionary perspective, writing in his first issue: "Every heart and hand seem to be engaged in the interesting struggle for American Liberty." Readership soared, especially among the working class.

In January 1776, Paine penned his seminal work *Common Sense*, which he signed anonymously 'by an Englishman.' In it, he made the case for American independence in strong prose and easy-to-understand language. Historian Danae Brack described it as "Perhaps the most significant example of protest rhetoric in American history." Word of the pamphlet spread rapidly, and soon, it was being printed, sold, and read in taverns everywhere. Some estimate over 100,000 copies were sold initially, and over the course of the Revolution, nearly a half million, including unauthorized copies. Unlike earlier works which criticized Parliament and remained respectful of the crown, Paine attacked the king and the monarchy.

Loyalists mounted a counterattack on *Common Sense*. James Chalmers of Maryland, in *Plain Truth* (1776), called Paine a "political quack." John Adams disagreed with Paine, publishing his *Thoughts on Government* (1776), where he argued for a more conservative approach to republicanism than radical democracy. Adams did not want the landless rabble to vote or hold office. Later in life, he referred to Paine's work as a "crapulous mass." Regardless, the public was motivated, and many enlisted in the cause. Historian Robert Middlekauff recognized that Paine successfully played on the religious sentiments of the public following the First Great Awakening by pointing out all the debauchery and tyranny associated with the various kings in the Old Testament. These feelings crossed denominations and brought unity in purpose.

Later that spring, the Second Continental Congress was in Philadelphia, deciding upon the course to be taken. Paine was definitely in town at the time and may have been consulted regarding the text of the Declaration of Independence, which was being conceived by the Committee of Five, including Thomas Jefferson, Ben Franklin, John Adams, Roger Sherman, and Robert R. Livingston. One of the early working drafts known as the Sherman Copy contained a statement on the back "A beginning perhaps—Original with Jefferson—Copied from Original with T.P.'s permission." Adams had hastily made this copy and noted the provenance. Some scholars, including the Thomas Paine National Historical Association, believe T.P. referred to Thomas Paine, though there is no official record of his involvement.

During July 1776, Paine served as a secretary for General Daniel Roberdeau in the militia known as the "flying camp" from Maryland, New Jersey, and Pennsylvania. At Fort Lee, New Jersey, Paine became the aide-de-camp for General Nathanael Greene, who then wintered at Brunswick, New Jersey. Faced with desertions and declining morale,

Paine wrote *The American Crisis* to try to improve morale. The first article appeared in *The Pennsylvania Journal* on December 23, 1776:

> These are the times that try men's souls. The summer soldier and the sunshine patriot will, in this crisis, shrink from the service of their country; but he that stands by it now, deserves the love and thanks of man and woman. Tyranny, like hell, is not easily conquered; yet we have this consolation with us, that the harder the conflict, the more glorious the triumph. What we obtain too cheap, we esteem too lightly: it is dearness only that gives every thing [*sic*] its value . . .

Paine continued to write articles updating *The Crisis* until the end of the war.

In 1777, the Continental Congress, with Henry Laurens as President, named Paine the secretary to the Committee for Foreign Affairs, even though he was not a member. During this time, he became embroiled in a scandal involving Silas Deane, who was Congress's commercial agent in Europe, and the family of Robert Morris, the financier. Paine had letters printed in the newspapers accusing Deane of war profiteering. Upon further investigation by Congress, Deane was exonerated, and Paine was removed from his role as secretary in January 1779.

Out of work, Paine struggled to make ends meet. He worked as a clerk in a merchant office and as an auditor of the financial affairs of Robert Morris. In late 1779, he was named a clerk in the Pennsylvania Assembly. The next year, he had an idea for a national bank and put in $500 of his own money. This later became the Bank of North America. Paine wrote about the benefits of banking in *Public Good* (1780). He also criticized the land speculation in the West, saying the additional lands won should be under the control of the government rather than in private hands. This rankled land speculators such as George Washington and other Virginians. Later, the Northwest Territory largely followed Paine's model.

After Henry Laurens was President of Congress, he became involved in diplomacy and was imprisoned in the Tower of London by the British. Laurens' son, Colonel John Laurens, hired Paine to serve as his secretary while he was a special envoy to France. They departed in early 1781 and were successful in securing additional funds in Europe and also the release of the elder Laurens. During this time, Paine wrote about possibly bringing the American Revolution to England.

At the end of the war, Paine was again out of work and needed money despite his books selling well. He was granted $3000 from the Continental Congress, $500 from Pennsylvania, and New York gave him a small farm in New Rochelle that had been seized from Loyalists. Paine was not asked to play any role in the new government and instead investigated the viability of smokeless candles and a single-span bridge across the Schuylkill River. He was admitted to the American Philosophical Society in 1785.

In 1787, nearly destitute and disillusioned, Paine returned to England to try to raise funds for his bridge idea and to apply for a patent. Meanwhile, the French Revolution was underway and drew his attention. He began to write in favor of it, countering the writings of Edmund Burke. In 1792, Paine wrote *Rights of Man*, a rant against monarchy. The English decided to crack down on Paine for his revolutionary rhetoric, fearing the French Revolution could come to England. They sued Paine for seditious libel and tried to arrest him, but he had already fled to France. Said Paine at the time:

> If, to expose the fraud and imposition of monarchy... to promote universal peace, civilization, and commerce, and to break the chains of political superstition, and raise degraded man to his proper rank; if these things be libellous... let the name of libeller be engraved on my tomb."

He was tried in absentia, and lost.

In August 1792, despite not speaking the language, Paine became a citizen of France and was elected to the National Convention. However, Paine soon fell into disfavor when he argued against the execution of King Louis XVI, instead suggesting he should exiled to America. Robespierre, the head of the Committee of Public Safety, called for Paine's arrest, which happened on December 27, 1793. While imprisoned, Paine was to be executed. One night, the guard came through, marking with chalk the doors of those to be decapitated. Paine's door was marked, but because it was open while he was accepting visitors, the inside was marked rather than the outside. Thus, when the executioner later walked past Paine's closed cell, he was spared.

Paine remained in prison in Luxembourg until November 4, 1794, when James Monroe, the new minister to France, vouched for Paine. During his time in prison, Paine had written *The Age of Reason*, his treatise against religion, which was published in two parts in 1794 and 1795. He also penned, in 1795, his *Dissertation on First-Principles of Government*, in which he imagined a more just society, including concepts such as old-age pensions similar to modern Social Security.

In 1796, Paine penned a bitter letter to George Washington, who did not respond because Monroe diverted it. Paine felt Washington had allowed him to be imprisoned in France unjustly. So, Paine published the letter in the newspapers. He called Washington an incompetent general and a hypocrite.

Also, in 1796, Paine finally received a patent in England for his single-span bridge.

In 1798, Paine further explained his personal Deism in *Atheism Refuted; In a Discourse to Prove the Existence of a God*. However, Paine found more critics and fewer fans as time passed.

In 1800, Paine met Napolean, who claimed he had a copy of *Rights of Man* under his pillow. However, when Napolean moved towards monarchy, Paine called him "the completest charlatan that ever existed."

In 1802, at the invitation of Thomas Jefferson, Paine returned from France to his estate in New Rochelle, New York. Unfortunately, he turned to drink, having alienated nearly everyone who had supported him. Paine died in Manhattan on June 8, 1809. Only six people attended his funeral, as he was buried under a walnut tree on his farm after the Quakers refused to accept him in their cemetery. A rhyme from the period went:

> Poor Tom Paine! There he lies:
> Nobody laughs and nobody cries
> Where he has gone or how he fares
> Nobody knows and nobody cares!

GRAVES of our FOUNDERS

In 1819, William Corbett, who intended to give Paine a heroic reburial in his native England, came to New Rochelle and exhumed Paine's bones. Unfortunately, when Corbett returned to England, he did not follow through and still had the bones among his effects when he died in 1834. There is no certainty about what happened to his remains after that. People have variously claimed to have his skull, jaw, right hand, and other bones.

The Thomas Paine Monument remains in New Rochelle, marking the site where he was originally buried. Nearby is his homestead, though the original house was replaced long ago. It is the site of the Thomas Paine Memorial Museum.

Statues of Paine can be found at Parc Montsouris, Paris; Morristown, New Jersey; and Thetford, England. He has been honored in many ways worldwide, and his writings are still studied as classics of political thought.

Monument of Thomas Paine

William Paterson
(1745–1806)

Author of the New Jersey Plan

Buried at Albany Rural Cemetery
Menands, New York

Signer of US Constitution • Governor • Senator • Supreme Court

William Paterson, born in Ireland, was a lawyer from New Jersey who was one of the most respected jurists of his era. Paterson was a signer of the US Constitution, a US Senator, Governor of New Jersey, and an Associate Justice on the US Supreme Court.

Paterson was born December 24, 1745, in County Antrim, Ireland, the son of Richard Paterson and his wife, Mary, both Ulster Protestants. The elder Paterson was a tin plate worker and traveling peddler of household goods. The family immigrated to New Castle, Pennsylvania, in 1747 but moved to New York and Connecticut before settling in Princeton, New Jersey. Here, Richard Paterson established a general store on the main road between New York and Philadelphia, across from Nassau Hall, later the site of Princeton University.

Young William grew up watching the university grow and expand across the street. The family's store catered to this increasing opportunity. But William wanted to be more than just a store clerk, and at age 14, in 1759, he was tested for his proficiency in Greek and Latin. He scored well enough to be admitted and studied the classics, history, political theory, and moral philosophy. Seeking to improve his character and gain proficiency in eloquence and oratorial skill, he took additional classes

William Paterson

towards a Master's degree, awarded in 1766. After he graduated, he next read law with Richard Stockton, one of the best-known attorneys in colonial America, and earned admission to the bar in 1768.

Paterson then moved to New Bromley, in Hunterdon County, New Jersey, and opened a law practice. However, he struggled mightily, and after moving around a few times, found himself keeping store with his brother at his mercantile business in Princeton. Then, his father went bankrupt in 1775. It could not have been timelier.

As hostilities increased with England, Paterson became involved in the Patriot cause. Starting in May 1775, he served as a delegate to the First Provisional Congress of New Jersey. As the assistant secretary of the convention, he assisted in the drafting of the New Jersey constitution.

After independence was declared in 1776, Paterson was appointed New Jersey's first attorney general, serving until 1783. During his tenure, he punished Loyalists. He also settled down at this time, purchasing a farm on the Raritan River in 1779. He constructed a home he dubbed "The Raritan" and married Cornelia Bell, the daughter of a wealthy landowner. A daughter, Cornelia Bell Paterson, was born in 1780.

On November 24, 1780, Paterson was elected to the Continental Congress by the New Jersey legislature, but he declined to take the seat and never served. He was concerned about being away from his wife and young children. A daughter, Frances, was born in 1782 but fell in and died in June 1783. That November, Cornelia gave birth to their son, William Bell Paterson, but she did not survive, dying four days later, on November 13, 1783. Paterson next married Euphemia White in 1784.

In 1787, Paterson, four years removed from his role as attorney general, was selected with Governor William Livingston, David Brearly, and Jonathan Dayton to represent New Jersey at the Constitutional Convention in Philadelphia. At five feet, two inches, Paterson was the smallest member of the convention, but that did not stop him from speaking out about the rights of the smaller states. He proposed what became known as the New Jersey Plan, calling for a unicameral legislative body with equal representation from each state. Said delegate William Pierce of Georgia:

> Mr. Patterson [sic] one of those kind of Men whose powers break in upon you, and create wonder and astonishment. He is a Man of great modesty, with looks that bespeak of no great extent—but he is a Classic, a Lawyer, and an Orator;—and of a disposition so favorable to his advancement that every one [sic] seemed ready to exalt him with their praises. He is very happy in the choice of time and manner of engaging in a debate, and never speaks but when he understands his subject well. This Gentleman is about 34 yrs of age, of a very low stature.

Paterson's notes from the convention were published in 1904 and show the evolution of some of the basic concepts of the Constitution from his perspective:

- Govr Randolph- Propositions founded upon republican Principles.
- The Articles of the Confdn should be so enlarged and corrected as to answer the Purposes of the Instn.
- That the Rights of Suffrage shall be ascertained by the Quantum of Property or Number of Souls—This the Basis upon which the larger States can assent to any Reform. Objn - Sovereignty is an integral Thing— We ought to be one Nation.
- That the national Legr should consist of two Branches.
- That the Members of the first Branch should be elected by the People, etc. This the democratick [sic] Branch—Perhaps, if inconvenient, may be elected by the several Legrs.
- Members of the 2nd Branch to be elected out of the first—to continue for a certain Length of Time, etc. To be elected by Electors appointed for that Purpose.
- The Powers to be vested in the national Legr—A negative upon particular acts, etc. contravening the Articles of the Union—Force.
- A national Executive to be elected by the national Legr.

Of course, following the Great Compromise, the Constitution included both the House of Representatives and the Senate. Following Paterson from his New Jersey Plan and then his notes indicate his creative and compromising nature. Paterson was one of the delegates to sign the Constitution from New Jersey.

In 1789, Paterson, along with Jonathan Elmer, was one of the first senators from New Jersey, serving until 1790. As a member of the Senate Judiciary Committee, he helped draft the Judiciary Act of 1789, which established the federal court system. The first nine sections of this law are in his handwriting.

On November 13, 1790, following the death of his friend, Governor William Livingston of New Jersey, Paterson resigned from the Senate and succeeded him. He remained in the role until 1793, during which he helped review, organize, and codify English laws that were in use in New Jersey.

William Paterson (1745–1806)

Grave of William Paterson

On February 27, 1793, President George Washington chose Paterson to be an associate justice of the United States Supreme Court in the seat vacated by Thomas Johnson. Paterson accepted and resigned as governor of New Jersey. He then spent the last 13 years of his life devoted to building a stable and powerful federal judiciary. Several of the cases he decided laid important foundations for the doctrine of judicial review. He also presided over trials of several of the Whiskey Rebellion conspirators.

In 1795, Paterson declined to accept an appointment to succeed Edmund Randolph as Secretary of State. Instead, Timothy Pickering was selected, serving through the Adams administration. Paterson stayed on at the Supreme Court. He was the heir apparent when Chief Justice Oliver Ellsworth resigned in 1800, but John Adams, out of concern for his close ties to Alexander Hamilton, did not offer the position.

Paterson stayed connected to Princeton, helping to found, with Aaron Burr, the Cliosophic Society. He was elected to the American Philosophical Society in 1789 and as a Fellow of the American Academy of Arts and Sciences in 1801.

In 1803, Paterson was injured when his coach crashed. Following this, his health began to fail. He left New York City and headed to Albany to live with his daughter, Cornelia Paterson Van Rensselaer, the wife of Stephen Van Rensselaer. There, he died, on September 9, 1806, at 61.

Paterson was interred in the vault at the Van Rensselaer Manor House. However, when the home was demolished in 1900, his remains were exhumed and reburied at the Van Rensselaer plot at Albany Rural Cemetery in Menands, New York. There is also a cenotaph in his honor at the Van Liew Cemetery in New Brunswick, Middlesex County, New Jersey.

William Paterson University and the city of Paterson, New Jersey, are named after him.

Timothy Pickering
(1745–1829)

Radical Federalist

Buried at Broad Street Cemetery
Salem, Massachusetts

**Military • Postmaster General • Secretary of War
Secretary of State**

Timothy Pickering was first a soldier and had events happened differently; his unit would have fired the "Shot Heard Round the World" months before Lexington and Concord. Pickering rose in the Continental Army and was appointed Quartermaster General, in charge of all supplies and logistics. During the Washington Administration, Pickering was Postmaster General, then Secretary of War, and then Secretary of State. He was also a US Senator from Massachusetts and served in the US House of Representatives.

Pickering, born July 17, 1745, in Salem, Massachusetts, was one of nine children of Deacon Timothy Pickering and his wife, Mary (née Wingate) Pickering. Pickering's older brother, John, later became the Speaker of the Massachusetts House of Representatives.

Pickering was educated in the local grammar school before studying law at Harvard College, where he graduated in 1763 at age 18. A local minister said of Pickering, "From his youth, his townsmen proclaim him assuming, turbulent, & headstrong." Pickering applied his aggressiveness to public service, where he worked with the Essex County Register of Deeds, John Higginson.

Timothy Pickering

Pickering received his first military commission in January 1766 as a lieutenant in the Essex County Militia. That Spring, on April 8, Pickering married Rebecca White of Salem, and he received a Master of Arts degree from Harvard.

The Massachusetts Bar admitted Pickering in 1768, and in 1769, he was promoted to captain in the militia. Around this time, he published in the local *Essex Gazette* his ideas about drilling soldiers. In 1775, these articles were published as *An Easy Plan for a Militia* and became the drill book used by the Continental Army before the arrival of Baron von Steuben and his *Regulations for the Order and Discipline of the Troops of the United States*.

In 1774, Pickering succeeded Higginson as the Register of Deeds. He was then elected as Salem's representative to the Massachusetts General

Court and served in the Essex County Court of Common Pleas as a justice.

On Sunday, February 26, 1775, two months before Lexington and Concord, British Army Lieutenant Colonel Alexander Leslie was sent from Boston to search North Salem for contraband. Leslie chose Sunday morning, assuming Pickering and his militia would be in church. Unknown to Leslie, a fast rider had noticed the British troop movement at Marblehead and galloped off to North Salem. There, he warned the minister, Reverend Thomas Barnard Jr. of North Church, who left his pulpit and met the British troops at the nearby North River Bridge. Reverend Barnard warned Leslie that the militia was at the ready and that he should peacefully withdraw from the area. In what became known as "Leslie's Retreat," the British commander heeded the warning and returned to Boston, avoiding what would likely have been the opening battle of the American Revolution, postponing the "Shot Heard Round the World" for two more months.

Somewhat ironically, upon hearing of the action at Lexington and Concord that April, Pickering and his militia marched to take part but arrived too late to have an impact, though they did block the British retreat from Concord. They then joined the Siege of Boston.

In December 1776, Pickering moved his militia to New York with General Washington. The Commander in Chief noticed Pickering's abilities and offered the role of Adjutant General of the Continental Army with the rank of colonel. Said Washington of Pickering, he was "a great Military genius, cultivated by an industrious attention to the Study of War, and as a Gentleman of liberal education, distinguished zeal and great method and activity in Business." Pickering was also made a member of the Board of War. In this role, Pickering oversaw at the Sterling Iron Works the forging and building of the great chain across the Hudson River below West Point that thwarted British naval attack for the duration of the war. He was also praised by Congress for his work in supplying the troops. In reward for this, Congress appointed Pickering Quartermaster General in August 1780 until 1784.

In 1783, after the Revolution, Pickering moved to Philadelphia and engaged in a trading operation with friend Samuel Hodgdon, a merchant. At this time, lands along the northern tier of Pennsylvania were still in dispute with Connecticut, and the Third Pennamite-Yankee War was underway. Pickering was held hostage for nineteen days by Connecticut claimants after trying to mediate a settlement on behalf of the Pennsylvania State Assembly. Pickering purchased land in the region and then moved to the Wyoming Valley in 1786. He helped to form Luzerne County, holding a series of offices. As a representative from Luzerne County in 1787, Pickering participated in the Pennsylvania convention to ratify the US Constitution and, from 1789 to 1790, the creation of a new state constitution.

In November 1790, President Washington, via Secretary of War Henry Knox, asked Pickering to negotiate several treaties with the Native Americans. He led the negotiations with the Six Nations at Tioga and then at Newtown Point in July 1791. Washington then appointed Pickering Postmaster General of the United States in 1791, following the resignation of Charles Osgood. Pickering also continued in his role negotiating treaties and completed the Treaty of Canandaigua with the Iroquois Confederacy in 1794, which recognized the Confederacy's sovereignty over a sizable territory within New York State and offered payments, including an annual allowance, in exchange for a peace agreement and the right of passage through Iroquois Territory for U.S. citizens.

In 1795, President Washington appointed Pickering Secretary of War following Henry Knox's resignation amid scandal. Pickering oversaw General Anthony Wayne's negotiations for the Treaty of Greenville with the Wyandots and the completion of the new frigates, *United States*, *Constitution*, and *Constellation*. He was also elected a member of the American Philosophical Society.

In Europe, the French Revolution was underway, as was war between England and France. The Washington Administration, though officially neutral, was split on who to support, with Secretary of State Thomas Jefferson friendly to France and Alexander Hamilton favoring England. As President Washington bent to Hamilton and his Federalists, Thomas Jefferson resigned his post in December 1793. Edmund Randolph, Jefferson's second cousin, was appointed Secretary of State, and former Secretary of State John Jay began negotiations with England. Suspicious of Randolph's intentions as someone favorable to France, like his cousin, Pickering helped to expose Randolph's objections to Jay's efforts. He produced a slanted translation of French documents that had been intercepted by the British Navy and informed President Washington that they proved Randolph's traitorous behavior. As the only cabinet member opposed to the Jay Treaty, Randolph resigned on August 19, 1795, following its narrow passage in the Senate. On August 20, President Washington appointed the loyal Federalist Pickering to the post on an interim basis. He was later confirmed by the Senate on December 10.

During his tenure as Secretary of State, Pickering maintained a pro-England posture, believing obligations to Revolutionary France were negated when the monarchy was overthrown. He also supported the Alien and Sedition Acts, permitting the arrest and deportation of non-citizens and clamping down on dissent in the press. During these years, a Quasi-War with France smoldered, with the French threatening American ships that were trading with England. Against Pickering's objections, President Adams sent a delegation, including Charles Cotesworth Pinckney, Elbridge Gerry, and John Marshall, to France to negotiate a peace, but when the French attempted to bribe them, outrage ensued in what became known as the XYZ Affair. Following the publication of the related papers to the affair, Pickering endorsed open war with France.

In 1799, Pickering sailed to England on the merchant ship *Washington*. On October 24, the French privateer *Bellona* attacked *Washington*, but the Americans repelled the attack despite inferior guns and crew.

Ultimately, President Adams desired peace with France, to which Pickering and Alexander Hamilton were opposed. Adams asked for Pickering's resignation, but he refused. Adams then dismissed Pickering on May 12, 1800.

John Adams failed to win a second term, yielding to Thomas Jefferson as the new President of the United States. In 1802, Pickering led a Federalist New England secessionist movement that sought to join the New England states with Pennsylvania and Virginia and make him president. Pickering sought to be "exempt from the corrupt and corrupting influence and oppression of the aristocratic democrats of the South." Failing that, Pickering was named to the US Senate from Massachusetts in 1803, serving until 1811. He opposed the Louisiana Purchase of 1803 and the annexation of Spanish West Florida in 1810 as unconstitutional, fearing they would increase the South's power.

In 1807, Pickering opposed President Jefferson's Embargo Act, which sought to restrict foreign trade during the Napoleonic Wars. He conferenced with British envoy George Rose, persuading British Foreign Secretary George Canning to maintain a hard line against America, hoping that Jefferson would act more severely and, therefore, weaken the Democratic-Republicans.

When Pickering published harsh criticism of the Embargo Act, he was charged with reading confidential documents in an open Senate session before an injunction of secrecy was removed. For this, the Senate censured Pickering on January 2, 1811, 20 to 7. He was the first US Senator to be censured. He lost his reelection bid and returned to his farm in Salem for a year.

In 1812, Pickering was elected to the US House of Representatives, serving for two terms until 1817. During this time, he renewed his call for Northern secession as part of the Essex Junto at the Hartford

Grave of Timothy Pickering

Convention in 1814. The remaining Federalists were unhappy with the concentration of power in the South and the Madison Administration's prosecution of the War of 1812.

During his time in Congress, Pickering was elected a Fellow of the American Academy of Arts and Sciences in 1815. However, he lost his re-election bid in 1816 and retired from politics to his farm in Salem.

Pickering died on his farm on January 29, 1829, at age 83. He was buried at the Broad Street Cemetery in Salem.

Fort Pickering, in Salem Massachusetts, was named for him, as was the World War II Liberty ship SS *Timothy Pickering*, lost off Sicily in 1943. The Pickering home in Salem remained in the family until the 1990s.

Charles Cotesworth Pinckney
(1746–1825)

XYZ Affair

Buried at St. Michael's Churchyard
Charleston, South Carolina

Military • Diplomat • US Constitution

Charles Cotesworth Pinckney was a South Carolina aristocrat who served as an officer in the Continental Army and later signed the US Constitution. He then served as the US Minister to France, ran once for vice president (1800), and ran twice for president as the Federalist candidate, losing to Thomas Jefferson (1804) and then James Madison (1808).

Pinckney was born on February 25, 1746, in Charleston, South Carolina, the son of the wealthy planter Charles Pinckney, later the colonial Chief Justice of South Carolina, and his wife, Eliza (née Lucas) Pinckney, a planter and agriculturalist who helped develop indigo cultivation in the area. Younger brother Thomas Pinckney and first cousin Charles Pinckney both later served as Governors of South Carolina.

From 1753 to 1758, the elder Pinckney was the colony's agent to England and the family lived in London. The elder Pinckney lobbied Parliament and the Court on behalf of the South Carolina planters. The Pinckney boys were enrolled in the Westminster School and remained when the family returned to South Carolina. Pinckney studied at Christ Church, Oxford, in 1763 and studied law at Middle Temple in 1764. He next studied botany for a year, assisting French botanist André Michaux,

Charles Cotesworth Pinckney (1746–1825)

Charles Cotesworth Pinckney

for which he was honored by having a plant species named for him: *Pinckneya pubens*. He also studied chemistry in France before attending the prestigious military academy at Caen. He completed his studies in 1769 when he was admitted to the English bar. He briefly practiced law in England before starting legal practice in Charleston.

In 1770, Pinckney was elected to the colonial legislature, representing St. John's Colleton Parish. He also became a vestryman and warden for the Episcopal church and by 1772, was a lieutenant in the militia, eventually rising to colonel.

In 1773, Pinckney served as a regional attorney general. On September 28, 1773, he married Sarah Middleton, the daughter of Henry Middleton, who later was a President of Congress, and sister of Arthur Middleton, a signer of the Declaration of Independence. Together, they had four children and Pinckney was now connected to the South Carolina gentry involved in the Revolution, including the Middletons, Rutledges, and William Henry Drayton.

As the Revolution neared, Pinckney was a member of the new South Carolina provincial congress, replacing the colonial body. He participated in the various revolutionary committees and prepared Charleston's defense. After the Battles of Lexington and Concord, he volunteered for service in the Continental Army. As captain, he was the senior commander of the Grenadiers of the 1st South Carolina Regiment. When British General Sir Henry Clinton attacked Charleston by sea in June 1776, Pinckney helped lead the defense in the Battle of Sullivan's Island, though he did not participate directly. Later that year, Pinckney was promoted to colonel and took control of the entire regiment.

Wanting to be in the action, in 1777, Pinckney took his regiment north to Philadelphia to join General Washington. He arrived in time to participate in the Battles of Brandywine and Germantown. During this time, he met Alexander Hamilton and James McHenry, who later became important political allies.

The following year, Pinckney headed South, participating in the successful repulse of Loyalist militia and British regulars in Florida. However, the Patriots failed to reach St. Augustine due to logistical problems and were defeated at the Battle of Alligator Creek Bridge. Due to disease and disorganization, only half of the Patriot forces made it home.

Later, in 1778, Major General Benjamin Lincoln was sent south to defend Savannah, Georgia, from British occupation. Lincoln placed Pinckney in charge of his Continental brigades. In October 1779, Pinckney participated in an American and French attack on Savannah that failed, resulting in numerous casualties.

In 1780, at Fort Moultrie, Pinckney defended Charleston from a British attack. Unfortunately, on May 7, the fort fell and Charleston was captured on May 12, when Lincoln surrendered 5,000 men. Both Pinckney and General William Moultrie were placed under house arrest, and the British attempted to lure them away. Said Pinckney at this time, "If I had a vein that did not beat with the love of my Country, I myself would open it. If I had a drop of blood that could flow dishonorable, I myself would let it out."

Pinckney remained in captivity until he was exchanged in Philadelphia in 1782. Upon his release, he rejoined the army, but the fighting had ended. At the conclusion of hostilities in November 1783, he was breveted to brigadier general.

Sadly, his wife, Sarah, died in 1784. The following year, Pinckney was wounded in a duel with Daniel Huger, leading him to advocate for anti-dueling laws. In 1786, Pinckney married Mary Stead, a daughter of wealthy Georgia planters. The couple had three daughters.

Pinckney returned to his legal practice and a seat in the South Carolina legislature, where he and his brother Thomas became political powers who advocated for the slave-owning gentry. He opposed Edward Rutledge's attempt to end the importation of slaves out of concern for the South Carolina economy. He was also involved in resolving the border with Georgia and signed the Convention of Beaufort to that effect. Regarding his militia service, Pinckney was promoted to major general of one of two divisions of the South Carolina militia.

In favor of a stronger central government, Pinckney represented South Carolina at the Constitutional Convention in 1787, along with younger cousin Charles Pinckney and two others. He argued to include slaves to be counted for the basis of representation and claimed that the Northwest Ordinance of July 1787 permitted slaveowners to reclaim their fugitives anywhere in the new nation. Boasted Pinckney, "We have obtained a right to recover our slaves in whatever part of America they may take refuge, which is a right we had not before."

Pinckney believed it impractical to elect representatives by popular vote and felt senators, as members of the wealthy gentry, need not be paid. He also played a key role in requiring treaties to be ratified by the Senate and in the continuation of the slave trade for another twenty years, extending it to 1808. Said Pinckney about slavery, "While there remained one acre of swampland uncleared of South Carolina, I would raise my voice against restricting the importation of negroes . . . the nature of our climate and the flat, swampy situation of our country, obliges us to cultivate our lands with negroes, and that without them South Carolina would soon be a desert waste . . ." However, he recognized the irony of our founding documents when he said, "Bills of rights generally begin with declaring that all men are by nature born free. Now, we should make that declaration with a very bad grace, when a large part of our property consists in men who are actually born slaves."

He also wanted no limitation placed on the size of the federal standing army.

Pinckney played a prominent role in ratifying the new Constitution in South Carolina in 1788. When the new President, George Washington, offered him his choice of the War Department or State Department in 1789, Pinckney declined both. Instead, he focused on the framing of a new state constitution in 1790. He then retired from politics and devoted himself to religious and charitable works, including establishing a state university, improving the Charleston library, and promoting scientific agriculture. The town and district of Pinckneyville in South Carolina were named in his honor in 1791. He was also appointed to the American Philosophical Society in 1789.

In 1796, Pinckney accepted President Washington's call to be the Minister to France following the Jay Treaty with Great Britain, which angered France, now amid a revolution. The French had directed their navy to seize American merchant ships trading with Great Britain. When Pinckney arrived in France, the French informed him that no American minister would be recognized. This outraged Pinckney. The next year, President Adams appointed him as one of three commissioners, including Elbridge Gerry and John Marshall, to negotiate a treaty with the French. When the French, led by Foreign Minister Tallyrand, requested a bribe to facilitate negotiations, Pinckney angrily exploded, "No, no, not a sixpence!" He urged his government to raise "millions for defense but not one cent for tribute." He broke off discussions and then headed home without a deal, taking Marshall with him, leaving the more moderate Gerry behind. This event, known as the XYZ Affair after the related documents were published in 1798, strained the Adams presidency and led to the Quasi-War with France. Upon returning home, Pinckney accepted an appointment as a major general in the army, commanding all forces south of Maryland until the peace was finally negotiated in the summer of 1800.

In 1800, the Federalists, coordinated by Alexander Hamilton, selected Pinckney as their vice-presidential nominee, hoping he would help carry the South. However, the Adams-Pinckney ticket narrowly lost to Jefferson-Burr, 73 to 64. Hamilton had schemed to use the Electoral College results to supplant Adams with Pinckney, but Pinckney had declared he would accept no votes intended for Adams.

In 1804, Pinckney was put up as the Federalist candidate against the popular Thomas Jefferson. Neither party ran a campaign, and Jefferson won in a landslide, 162 to 14 electoral votes. Pinckney even lost South Carolina, making him the first major party candidate to lose his home state.

With Jefferson out of the picture in 1808, Pinckney ran again for president as a Federalist, this time against James Madison, a Democratic-Republican. A potential war was looming with France or Britain, and someone with military experience might appeal to the electorate. While the Federalists won Delaware and most of New England, Madison prevailed in a closer election, 122 to 47.

For the remainder of his life, Pinckney focused on his plantations and legal practice. He was the President-General of the Society of the Cincinnati from 1805 until his death. He was elected to the American Antiquarian Society in 1813.

Pinckney died on August 16, 1825, in his 79th year. He was buried at St. Michael's Churchyard in Charleston, South Carolina. His tombstone is engraved, "One of the founders of the American Republic. In war, he was a companion in arms and friend of Washington. In peace, he enjoyed his unchanging confidence."

Pinckney is honored in many ways:

- Castle Pinckney, a fort in Charleston Harbor.
- Pinckney Island National Wildlife Refuge, on the site of the Pinckney family's plantation.
- C. C. Pinckney Elementary school in Fort Jackson, South Carolina.
- Charles Pinckney Elementary School school in Mount Pleasant, South Carolina.
- Pinckney Elementary school in Lawrence, Kansas.
- SS *Charles C. Pinckney*, World War II, a 422-foot liberty ship built in Wilmington, North Carolina.

- Pinckney Street on Beacon Hill in Boston and in Madison, Wisconsin.
- Pinckneyville, Illinois, and Pinckney, Michigan.
- Pinckney Highway (SC 9) in Chester, South Carolina.
- In the television comedy series *The Epic Tales of Captain Underpants*, Charles Cotesworth Pinckney is often brought up as something of a running gag when one of the cast yells at a painting of him, "Darn you, Charles Cotesworth Pinckney!"

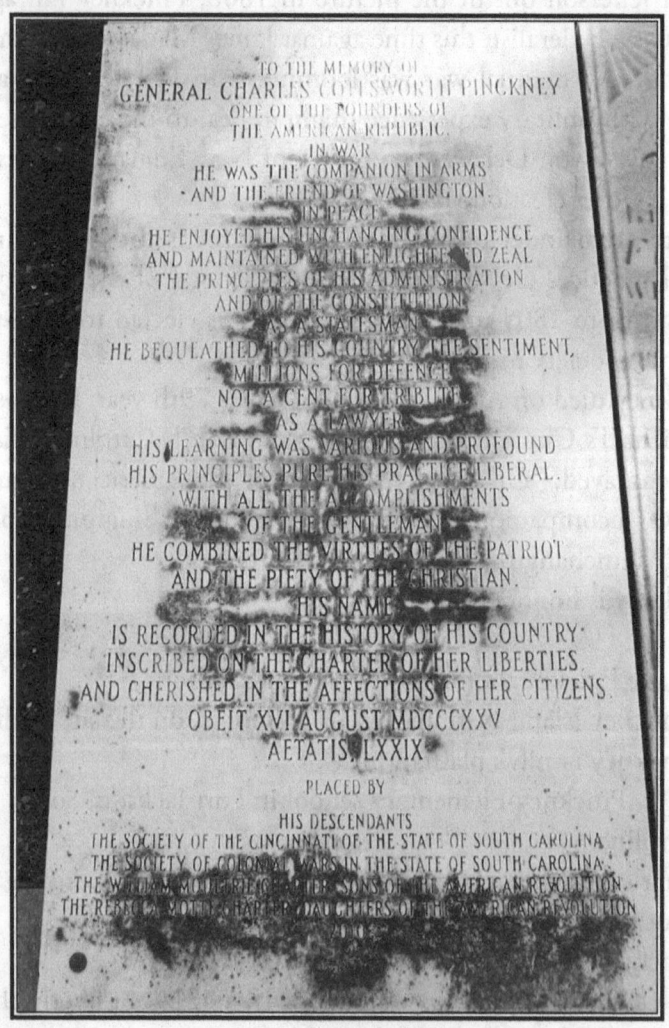

Charles Cotesworth Pinckney

Molly Pitcher (Mary Ludwig)
(1744 or 1754–1832)

Sergeant Molly

Buried at Old Graveyard,
Carlisle, Pennsylvania.

Revolutionary War Heroine

Molly Pitcher was a nickname given to a woman who fought in the Battle of Monmouth, during the American Revolutionary War. Her real name was Mary Ludwig. There is disagreement among scholars about several essential details of her life, beginning with her date of birth. Her cemetery marker indicates that she was born on October 13, 1744, but others point to evidence suggesting it may have been October 13, 1754. Her father is believed to have been a butcher (but may have been a dairy farmer). There is little doubt that Mary was raised as a hard worker. In 1768, she was sent to Carlisle, Pennsylvania, to become a servant in the home of Dr. William Irvine. The following year she married a local barber named William Hays.

Five years later, on July 12, 1774, in a meeting in the Presbyterian Church in Carlisle, Mary's employer (Dr. Irvine) organized a town boycott of British goods as a protest of the Tea Act of 1773. Mary's husband's name (William Hays) appears on a list of people who were charged with enforcing the boycott. In 1775, when the Revolutionary War began, William Hays enlisted in the Colonial Army.

After her husband's enlistment, Mary at first stayed in Carlisle. She then went to live with her parents near Philadelphia (so that she could be closer to her husband's regiment). During the winter of 1777, Mary joined her husband at the Continental Army's winter camp at Valley

Molly Pitcher at the Battle of Monmouth

Forge. She joined a group of "camp followers," who were led by Martha Washington. These women were of great importance to the army. As a general rule, women were not allowed to fight as soldiers. Instead, they cooked and washed the soldiers' clothes. They gathered and preserved food and supplies, and they repaired uniforms, blankets, and other items. They cared for the sick, wounded, and dying soldiers.

In the spring of 1778, the Continental Army was retrained under Baron von Steuben. During this time, William Hays trained as an artilleryman. Mary Hays and other camp followers served as "water girls" during the training, carrying water to drilling infantry troops. Artillerymen also needed a constant supply of water to cool down the hot cannon barrels and to soak the rag ("rammer rag") tied to the end of the ramrod with which they cleaned sparks and gunpowder out of the barrel after each shot.

The term "Molly Pitcher" was commonly used by Continental Army soldiers. It resulted from a combination of the name "Molly" (a

Molly Pitcher (Mary Ludwig) (1744 or 1754–1832)

widely-used nickname at the time for women named Mary or Margaret) and the term "pitcher" (the containers of water women carried on the battlefield).

The Battle of Monmouth took place on June 28, 1778, in modern-day Freehold, New Jersey. The Continental Army under General George Washington attacked the rear of the British Army column commanded by Lieutenant General Sir Henry Clinton as they left Monmouth Court House. With the temperature above 100 degrees that day, both sides lost almost as many men to heatstroke as to the enemy. It was during that battle that Mary Ludwig Hays earned the nickname "Molly Pitcher," becoming one of the most popular female images of the Revolutionary War.

Just before the battle started, Mary found a spring to serve as her water supply. (There are currently two different places within Monmouth Battlefield State Park that are marked as the "Molly Pitcher Spring.") She spent the early part of the day carrying water under heavy fire from British troops. Sometime during the battle, Mary saw her husband collapse either from heat exhaustion or because he was wounded (but regardless managed to survive). For the rest of the day, Mary stepped in and continued to "swab and load" the cannon using her husband's ramrod. She continued to do this until the battle was over. According to accounts, at one point, while loading a cartridge with her feet far apart, a British musket ball flew between her legs and took off the lower part of her petticoat. Mary supposedly said, "Well that could have been worse" and went back to swabbing and loading. Later that evening, the fighting stopped, and the British forces retreated and moved on. The Battle of Monmouth was seen as a significant victory for Americans.

Mary's legendary heroism was noted, and she was commissioned as a sergeant by General Greene (or by some accounts by George Washington himself). From that day forward, she was known as "Sergeant Molly." An old Revolutionary rhyme tells the story:

> Moll Pitcher, she stood by her gun
> And rammed the charges home, sir;
> And thus on Monmouth bloody field
> A sergeant did become, sir.

Until the close of the Revolutionary War, Molly Pitcher remained with the army and proved to be a beloved and valuable helping hand. After the war, she and her husband returned to Carlisle, and Mary went back to work as a domestic servant. In 1780, they had a son, John L. Hays. In 1786, William Hays died, and Mary married John McCauley, another veteran of the Revolutionary War. McCauley was a stone cutter. The marriage was reportedly not a happy one, and sometime between 1807 and 1810, John McCauley disappeared. It is not known what became of him.

Mary Ludwig Hays McCauley was known throughout Carlisle as Molly Pitcher. She lived in a house on the corner of North and Bedford Streets, which has since been demolished. In 1822, the state legislature awarded Molly Pitcher a sum of $40 and subsequent annual payments of $40 each "for the rest of her life."

On January 22, 1852, Mary died in Carlisle and was buried in the Old Graveyard with military honors. Her grave was unmarked, and her obituary did not mention her war contributions.

In 1856, Mary's son John L. Hays died. His obituary noted that he "was a son of the ever-to-be-remembered heroine, the celebrated 'Molly Pitcher' whose deeds of daring are recorded in the annals of the Revolution and over whose remains a monument ought to be erected."

On July 4, 1876, the 100th anniversary of the Declaration of Independence, the citizens of Carlisle erected a white marble monument over Mary's grave. It commemorates "Molly Pitcher, the heroine of Monmouth."

To complicate the story, there is another similar heroic story of a woman in the Revolutionary War. Margaret Corbin was the wife of John Corbin of Philadelphia, who was also an artilleryman in the Continental Army. On November 12, 1776, John Corbin was killed defending Fort Washington in northern Manhattan. Margaret took his place at his cannon and continued to fire it until she was wounded. In 1779, she was awarded an annual pension by the Continental Congress. She was the first woman in the United States to receive a military pension. She is buried at West Point. Her nickname was "Captain Molly."

So the name "Molly Pitcher" comes down to us as a symbol of courage and resourcefulness under fire. The story of Molly Pitcher was told

Monument to Molly Pitcher

for many generations. It inspired women of her time and captured the hearts of America. In 1928, Molly Pitcher was honored with an overprint on a U.S. postage stamp reading "MOLLY PITCHER" in capital letters. In 1978, the 200th anniversary of the Battle of Monmouth, Molly was pictured on an imprinted stamp on a postal card. She was further honored in World War II with the naming of the Liberty Ship SS *Molly Pitcher*. On its maiden voyage, it was torpedoed on March 17, 1943, by a German U-Boat about 500 miles west of Lisbon, Spain.

The stretch of U.S. Route 11 between Shippensburg and the Pennsylvania-Maryland state line is known as the "Molly Pitcher Highway." There is a Molly Pitcher Ale House on 2nd Avenue and 85th Street in Manhattan, a Molly Pitcher Brewing Company in Atascadero,

California, and a Molly Pitcher Inn in Red Bank, New Jersey, not far from the site of the Battle of Monmouth.

Statue of Molly Pitcher

Peyton Randolph
(1721–1775)

The First President

Buried at Wren Chapel at the College of William and Mary,
Williamsburg, Virginia

Continental Association

Peyton Randolph was the Attorney General and Speaker of the House of Burgesses in colonial Virginia prior to the American Revolution. He was early to the Patriot cause despite his connections to the colonial government. He was elected to both the First and Second Continental Congresses and served as the first President of those bodies. As such, he signed the Continental Association.

Randolph, born on September 10, 1721, at Tazewell Hall in Williamsburg, Virginia, the son of Sir John Randolph and his wife, Susannah (née Beverly or Beverley) Randolph. The Randolphs were wealthy plantation owners, and Sir John was a barrister who also served as Speaker of the House of Burgesses from 1734 to 1736 and as the Virginia colony's Attorney General. Sir John's father had also been the Speaker of the House, and the family had a long history of public service back to Sir Thomas Randolph (1523–1590), who was an advisor to Queen Elizabeth I.

Randolph had two brothers and one sister. The eldest brother, Beverley Randolph (1719–1764), married Agatha Wormeley (1721–1786) in 1742. Sister Mary Randolph (1720–1768) married Colonel

Peyton Randolph

Philip Ludwell Grymes (1721–1761), a member of the Virginia House of Burgesses, in 1742. The younger brother, John Randolph (1727–1784), married Ariana Jennings in 1750.

Sir John died in 1736, when Randolph was only 15, leaving the four children with their widowed mother. Soon after, Randolph attended the College of William and Mary in Williamsburg but did not graduate. In late 1739, he traveled to England to study law at the Middle Temple of Gray's Inn, a prominent law school. On February 10, 1744, after completing his studies, he was accepted by the London bar.

Randolph returned to Virginia and, in 1746, married Elizabeth Harrison of the Berkeley plantation, the sister of Benjamin Harrison, who would later sign the Declaration of Independence and be the grandfather and great-great-grandfather of two presidents. Peyton and Elizabeth had no children and lived on Nicholson Street in Williamsburg.

Based on a recommendation of John Hanbury, an English friend, Randolph was appointed the Attorney General for Virginia in 1748, despite the reservations of Royal Governor William Gooch. Randolph was also elected to the House of Burgesses.

In 1753, Randolph became embroiled in a dispute with Royal Governor Robert Dinwiddie when he was asked by the House of Burgesses to travel to England at the government's expense, including his salary, to oppose a land patent fee imposed by the governor before the British Board of Trade. The fee would be charged to colonists wishing to expand their land holdings. Normally, as Attorney General, Randolph was to represent the governor rather than the legislature. The governor and his council were outraged and replaced Randolph with George Wythe. Randolph arrived in London near the end of 1754 but was unable to sway the Board. However, when Randolph returned in a few months, the governor reinstated him, and the fee was dropped. This was an early instance of the colonists protesting taxation from overseas.

Following Braddock's defeat in 1755, Randolph led the "Associators," 300 militiamen who rallied to defend Virginia. On May 3, 1756, he wrote Colonel George Washington:

> Some public-spirited Gentlemen have done me the honor to fix upon me as their leader till we can come to the place where you command, when we shall be very glad to follow such orders, as you shall think most conducive to the public good.

After the French and Indian War in 1765, when Parliament was attempting to recoup the cost of the war from the colonists via the Stamp Act, the Virginia House of Burgesses selected Randolph to draft a petition to the King opposing it. Patrick Henry had raised his own objections to the Act, and most of them were accepted, superseding Randolph's more conservative petition. The amended petition was ignored by the King, and the tax was imposed.

This roiling of the colonial powers put Randolph in a position of disfavor with the governor. As he became Speaker of the House in 1766 following the death of John Robinson, he resigned from the Attorney General position and was replaced by his brother John, a Loyalist. Randolph then focused on his role in the House of Burgesses, leading a committee to collect and revise the laws of the colony in 1769. Said Thomas Jefferson of Randolph's performance as Speaker:

> Altho' not eloquent, his matter was so substantial that no man commanded more attention; which, joined with a sense of his great worth gave him a weight in the House of Burgesses which few ever attained.

In reaction to the discontent regarding the Townshend Acts (1767), Governor Lord Botetourt dissolved the House of Burgesses on May 17, 1769. Randolph and other members walked to Raleigh Tavern and formed an Association, which ultimately led to non-importation agreements and boycotts of English goods. Randolph led this opposition and also issued a statement of support for the Boston Port Act in 1773 as chair of the new Committee of Correspondence.

On September 5, 1774, Randolph, George Washington, Benjamin Harrison, Edmund Pendleton, Richard Henry Lee, Patrick Henry, and Richard Bland were sent to Philadelphia as delegates to the First Continental Congress. Randolph was nominated to the President of the Congress and was unanimously approved. The Congress asked for the repeal of the Coercive Acts and signed the Continental Association. Randolph then resigned as President, to head back to Virginia. He was replaced by Henry Middleton after a term of forty-seven days.

Following Patrick Henry's "give me liberty or give me death" speech in March 1775, at which Randolph presided, Royal Governor Lord Dunmore had the Royal Marines remove the gunpowder and muskets from the armory in Williamsburg on April 21, 1775. Unknown to anyone at the time, the first shots had been fired at Lexington and Concord. Randolph and the Associators were angered by this, and Patrick Henry threatened a military response. Carter Braxton helped to negotiate a payment for the arms from the governor to avoid a confrontation.

The Second Continental Congress was called on May 10, 1775, and Randolph was once again elected its President. However, in June, when Lord Dunmore called the House of Burgesses back in session, Randolph resigned from Congress and headed home. Thomas Jefferson took his seat in Congress, and John Hancock became President. As the Speaker of the Virginia House, Randolph rejected the offer of reconciliation from Lord North, who was trying to divide the colonies by reconciling with

Peyton Randolph (1721–1775)

The crypt under the Wren Chapel at the College of William and Mary containing the grave of Peyton Randolph.

them individually. The Continental Congress rejected it as well. As Lord Dunmore fled that June, Randolph led the formation of a Committee of Safety.

When the Continental Congress met again in Philadelphia in September 1775, Randolph returned as a delegate despite being in ill health. John Adams was concerned that Randolph might want his seat back as President when he wrote that Randolph "Sits very humbly in his Seat, while our new [President] continues in the Chair, without Seeming to feel the Impropriety." On October 22, 1775, while dining with Thomas Jefferson, Randolph suffered a five-hour-long "fit of apoplexy" and died. Said one Philadelphia newspaper (likely Franklin's):

> Last Sunday died of an apoplectic stroke, in the fifty-third year of his age, the Hon. Peyton Randolph, Esq; of Virginia, late President of the Continental Congress, a general who possessed the virtues of humanity in an eminent degree, and joining with them the

The approximate location in the Wren Chapel under which is Randolph's crypt.

soundest judgment, was the delight of his friends in private life, and a most valuable member of society, having long sided, and with great . . . integrity discharged the most honourable public trusts.

The entire Congress attended his funeral in Philadelphia on October 24, 1775. Carter Braxton was then called as a replacement for the Virginia delegation in Congress. Randolph's body was returned to Williamsburg and buried in the vault beneath the chapel at the College of William and Mary. When he died, in addition to his house in Williamsburg, Randolph also owned several pieces of land in town, two plantations in James City County, and more than 100 slaves.

The memorial plaque in the Wren Chapel dedicated to the Randolphs.

In honor of Randolph, the Congress named one of the first naval frigates the USS *Randolph* and a fort on the Ohio River as Fort Randolph. Randolph County, North Carolina; Randolph, Massachusetts; and Randolph County, Indiana, were named to his honor. During World War II, the aircraft carrier USS *Randolph* was named for him. The Peyton Randolph House in Colonial Williamsburg was declared a National Historic Landmark in 1970.

In October 1859, there was a fire in the chapel area of the college. Randolph's was the only vault damaged, but the newspaper reported his coffin was in excellent condition.

George Read
(1733–1798)

Triple Signer

Buried at Immanuel Episcopal Churchyard,
New Castle, Delaware

**Continental Association • Declaration of Independence
U.S. Constitution**

George Read was a highly active member of the Continental Congress from Delaware during the Revolutionary period. A politician from New Castle, he signed the Continental Association, Declaration of Independence, and the U.S. Constitution, one of only three statesmen to have signed all three documents. Read also served as President of Delaware, US Senator from Delaware, and the Chief Justice of Delaware.

George Read was born September 18, 1733, in Cecil County, Maryland, the son and eldest of eight children of John Read, an Irish immigrant, and his wife, Mary (née Howell) Read. The elder Read was born in Dublin, Ireland, the son of a wealthy Englishman from Berkshire, Hertfordshire, and Oxfordshire. He came to Maryland and Delaware to seek his fortune after his father's death, purchased a large estate in Cecil County, Maryland, and founded Charlestown with six associates. The goal was to establish a rival market to Baltimore further south and establish the Principio Company, an ironworks. The Washingtons were also interested in this venture. For many years, John Read was a member of the Maryland colonial legislature, held military offices, and later retired to his plantation in New Castle County, Delaware.

George Read (1733–1798)

George Read

Soon after George Read was born, the family moved to New Castle, Delaware, settling near the village of Christiana. Read attended school at the Reverend Francis Allison's Academy in New London, Pennsylvania, along with Thomas McKean. He then studied law with John Moland and was admitted to the Pennsylvania Bar in 1753. The next year, he returned to New Castle and opened a law practice.

In 1763, Read married Gertrude Ross Till, the daughter of the Reverend George Ross, the rector of the Immanuel Church in New Castle. She was also the widowed sister of George Ross, a future signer of the Declaration of Independence. Together, they had four children, John, George Jr., William, and Mary. The couple lived on The Strand in New Castle. Their home is presently now the Read House and Gardens managed by the Delaware Historical Society is a restoration built by the son following an 1824 fire. Read was later described by a descendant as "tall, slightly and gracefully formed, with pleasing features and lustrous brown eyes. His manners were dignified, bordering upon austerity, but courteous, and at times captivating. He commanded entire confidence, not only from his profound legal knowledge, sound judgment, and impartial decisions but from his severe integrity and the purity of his private character."

At this time, colonial governor John Penn appointed Read the Crown Attorney General for three Delaware counties, succeeding John Ross. He served in this position until 1774. He also served in the Colonial Assembly of the Lower Counties for twelve sessions.

Read was very outspoken from the start regarding the difficulties with Britain. He spoke out against the Boston Port Bill and, along with McKean, Dickinson, and others, led Delaware against the crown. Read was appointed to the First Continental Congress in 1774. While he signed the Continental Association, he was not an early advocate for outright independence. Instead, he was a signer of the Olive Branch Petition, seeking reconciliation with the king. When Congress voted for independence on July 2, 1776, Read voted against it. This prompted the need for Ceasar Rodney to quickly ride to Philadelphia to flip Delaware in favor. However, when it came time to sign the document, Read was there with his pen.

Explaining Read's thinking at the time, historian Charles Goodrich wrote in 1842, "It has already been noticed that when the great question of independence came before Congress, Mr. Read was opposed to the measure, and ultimately gave his vote against it. This he did from a sense of duty: not that he was unfriendly to the liberties of his country or was actuated by motives of selfishness or cowardice. But he deemed the agitation of the question, at the time premature and inexpedient. In these sentiments, Mr. Read was not alone. Many gentlemen in the colonies, characterized for great wisdom, and a decided patriotism, deemed the measure impolitic and would have voted had they been in Congress, as he did. The idle bodings of these, fortunately, were never realized." Read changed his vote after Romney arrived to make Delaware unanimous.

Following independence, Delaware elected Read its Speaker of the Legislative Council of the Delaware General Assembly, effectively the governor. He, with the assistance of Thomas McKean, drafted Delaware's Constitution of 1776. Following the capture of President John McKinly in Wilmington and his narrow escape from Philadelphia, Read returned home and took the office of President. During the occupation of Philadelphia from 1777 to 1778, Read worked to recruit soldiers to protect Delaware. The assembly was moved to Dover. Ceasar Rodney succeeded Read as President of Delaware but Read continued to serve in the legislature through 1788.

In 1786, Read represented Delaware at the Annapolis Convention, the precursor to the Constitutional Convention. He then represented Delaware in Philadelphia the next year. Read was an early proponent of a strong central government. He was for the abolition of the individual states, but with little support, shifted to policies that protected the smaller states. Said one of the delegates of Read, "his legal abilities are said to be very great, but his powers of oratory are fatiguing and tiresome to the last degree; his voice is feeble and his articulation so bad that few can have patience to attend him." Nevertheless, Delaware was the first state to ratify the Constitution, in large part thanks to Read.

Following the U.S. Constitution's ratification, Read was elected one of the first two senators from Delaware, serving from 1789 until he resigned in 1793 to become Chief Justice of the Delaware Supreme Court.

George Read died at his home in New Castle, Delaware, on September 21, 1798, and is buried at the Immanuel Episcopal Church Cemetery, nearby. His gravestone reads, "Member of the Congress of the Revolution, The Convention that framed the Constitution of the U.S. and of the first Senate under it. Judge of Admiralty, President and Chief Justice of Delaware and A signer of the Declaration of Independence."

Regarding the family legacy, brother Thomas Read was an officer in the Continental Navy during the Revolution. Another brother, James, was an officer in the Continental Army and was later active in managing the navy under the Articles of Confederation. George Read's son George Read Jr. served as the first U.S. Attorney for Delaware and his grandson George Read III served as the second. Another son, John, was a noted lawyer and banker of Philadelphia. George Read's great-granddaughter, Louisa, married Maj. Benjamin Kendrick Pierce, the brother of future President Franklin Pierce.

Joseph Reed
(1741–1785)

President of Pennsylvania

Buried at Laurel Hill Cemetery,
Philadelphia, Pennsylvania.

Military • Continental Congress • Articles of Confederation

Joseph Reed served in the Continental Congress and signed the Articles of Confederation. He was one of George Washington's aides-de-camp early in the Revolutionary War and held the ranks of colonel and adjutant-general. Given his background, money, education, and marriage, he was an unlikely revolutionist. He was an enigma to many as he at first believed that reconciliation with Britain was both desirable and possible. His reluctance to commit to the cause made him seem to be trying to be on the winning side for his gain. George Washington was a big supporter of Joseph Reed, but Reed even turned on Washington when things weren't looking very good for the general.

Joseph Reed was born in Trenton, New Jersey on August 27, 1741. He was the son of Andrew Reed, a merchant, and Theodora Bowes. Reed's ancestors had come to America from Northern Ireland and were well established by the time Joseph was born. The family moved to Philadelphia from Trenton shortly after Joseph's birth, and he was enrolled at Philadelphia Academy. He received his bachelor's degree in 1757 at the age of sixteen from the College of New Jersey, which became Princeton University. Soon after, he studied law under Richard Stockton

Joseph Reed (1741–1785)

Joseph Reed

the able, eloquent Princetonian who was acknowledged to be one of the best lawyers and who would become a signer of the Declaration of Independence. In 1763 Reed went to England to study law at the prestigious Middle Temple in London. He studied there for two years often attending debates in the House of Commons. During this time he met an Englishwoman named Esther deBerdt. They married in May of 1770. Reed returned to America with his wife and widowed mother-in-law in October of 1770. He set up a law practice in Trenton at first but soon moved to Philadelphia. There the couple had five children. Esther started an organization called the Daughters of Liberty, to raise money in support of the war. She died in September 1780, and Ben Franklin's daughter Sarah Bache took over the organization.

Reed focused on becoming a leading lawyer in Philadelphia and confronted suspicions that he was a Loyalist as he had marital and familial ties with the mother country. He slowly came to feel that independence was the only course for the colonies to take. In the two years before the war, he worked as a member of Philadelphia's Committee of Correspondence and as president of Pennsylvania's second Provincial Congress.

When the army was formed in April 1775, Reed became a lieutenant colonel. On June 19, 1775, four days after George Washington was elected commander in chief, he was asked to join Washington's staff. He joined Washington in Cambridge and was appointed as his secretary. Three months later, Reed departed, pleading the press of cases pending in his law practice. Washington requested that he return, but Reed was reluctant to do so. In March 1776, Washington offered him the job of Adjutant General, and he reluctantly accepted. He performed well and became one of Washington's most trusted officers. His judgment in military matters was consistently good and his advice to Washington excellent. However, to many, he seemed irresolute and wavering, wondering which current would become the mainstream.

After the loss of Fort Washington, the last outpost in colonial hands on Manhattan Island, Reed along with other generals, questioned Washington's judgments, especially allowing New York City to be dangerously open to invasion. Reed had not told Washington of his feelings but wrote to General Charles Lee, a letter that was a stunning criticism of Washington and praised Lee. Unhappily for all involved, when Reed was absent from headquarters, Washington opened a communication from Lee to Reed that indicated that they were both questioning Washington's abilities. This was extremely upsetting to Washington as Reed was one of his most trusted and relied upon officers. The aftermath was an awkwardness between the two that could not be repaired. The intimate relationship they had once was gone for good. Washington remained professional however and allowed Reed to continue. As a former resident of Trenton and Princeton, Reed knew that area well and supplied Washington with vital information before and during the battles of Trenton and Princeton. Three weeks after the victory at Princeton, Reed resigned as Adjutant General and then curiously volunteered as an aide without pay in time to serve at the battles of Brandywine, Germantown, and Monmouth.

In 1777, Reed was offered the positions of brigadier general and Chief Justice of the Supreme Court of Pennsylvania. He declined both

Joseph Reed (1741–1785)

in favor of being elected as a delegate to the Continental Congress. In 1778 he was one of five Pennsylvania delegates to sign the Articles of Confederation. Also that year he was elected to the equivalent position to Pennsylvania Governor, President of the Supreme Executive Council of Pennsylvania, with an almost unanimous vote. He was re-elected to this position twice. During his administration, he helped oversee the passage of a statute that abolished slavery in Pennsylvania. He also was successful in getting Revolutionary War soldiers placed on half-pay for life. Also during this time, he pressed charges against Benedict Arnold for corruption and military malpractice while he was in command at Philadelphia. The subsequent court-martial largely exonerated Arnold,

The grave of Joseph Reed

but his resentment over this matter is thought to have fueled his later traitorous behavior.

Also in 1778, he was caught up in a scandal in which he was accused of traitorous correspondence with England. Until his name was cleared long after his death, some people questioned his loyalty which may be why he took such a strong stance against Loyalists. He was very strongly anti-Loyalist, advocating in Congress for property seizure and treason charges against anyone who sympathized with the Crown. As President of Pennsylvania, Reed oversaw numerous trials of suspected Loyalists. After James Wilson defended 23 people accused of treason, a mob, stirred up by Reed's speeches, attacked Wilson in what was to become known as the "Battle of Fort Wilson." The arrival of militia saved Wilson and his friends after one casualty from inside Wilson's house. A number of the mob were arrested, but Reed pardoned and released them.

After Reed's term as President of Pennsylvania ended in 1781, he returned to practicing law. He was again elected to Congress in 1784 but declined to serve because of deteriorating health. Joseph Reed died at his house in Philadelphia on March 5, 1785. He was initially buried in the Arch Street Presbyterian Burial Grounds in Philadelphia but was removed to Laurel Hill when that cemetery was abolished in 1868.

Paul Revere
(1735–1818)

"Listen, my children, and you shall hear..."

Buried at Granary Burying Ground
Boston, Massachusetts

Militia Officer • Courier • Industrialist

Paul Revere was quite a guy—smart, talented, brave, dependable, creative, and industrious. He was known and respected in the Boston area but was transformed into a national folk hero by Henry Wadsworth Longfellow's poem "Paul Revere's Ride." His life was long and productive, involving industry, politics and community service. He played a number of important roles in the American Revolution.

Paul Revere was born in North End Boston on or about January 1, 1735. His father, Apollos Rivoire, was a French Huguenot immigrant who changed his name after arriving in America. He was a goldsmith. He married Deborah Hitchborn in 1729, and the couple had twelve children, of which Paul was the third.

He attended the North Boston Writing School between the ages of seven and thirteen after which he became an apprentice to his father. His father died in 1754 when Paul was nineteen, leaving him to support his mother and siblings. Two years later, in 1756, Revere was commissioned as a second lieutenant in the Massachusetts Artillery and sent to fight the French in upstate New York. He only served a short while, and when he returned in November 1756, he began in earnest to build the

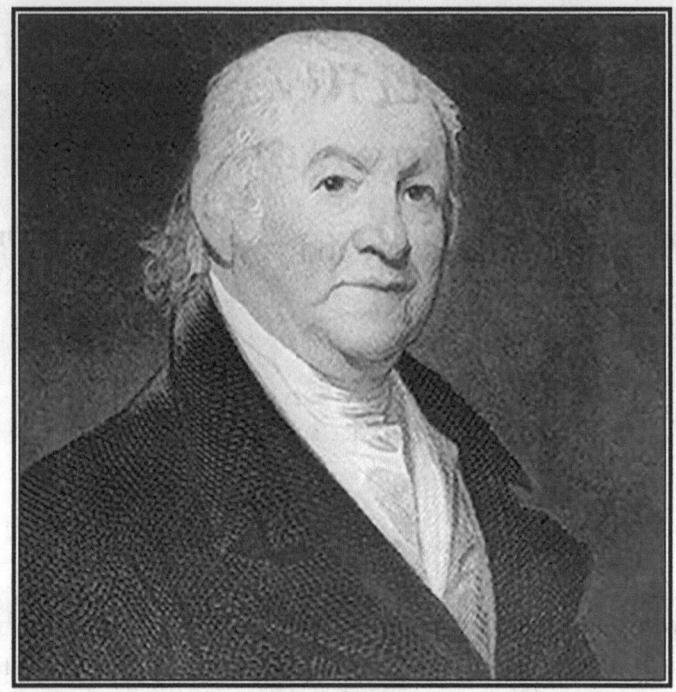
Paul Revere

family silver business. He returned with neither laurels nor war stories that would entertain.

In August 1757, Revere married Sarah Orne. The couple had eight children. Soon after Sarah died in 1773, Revere married Rachel Walker, with whom he also had eight children.

Revere's primary vocation was as a silversmith. His shop produced pieces from simple spoons to magnificent tea sets. His work was well regarded during his lifetime and is highly prized today. He supplemented his income by working as a copperplate engraver. He also tried his hand at dentistry, opening his own office in Boston in 1768. Being a skilled craftsman, he was good at making artificial teeth. One of his customers, who became a good friend, was Joseph Warren, a prominent doctor and a major general in the Continental Army.

In the years leading up to the Battles of Lexington and Concord Revere worked tirelessly for the patriot cause. He was a member of the Freemasons, the Mechanics Union, the Sons of Liberty and other groups. He became a nexus in the social networks of the Revolution. He gathered intelligence by watching the movements of British soldiers and was a courier for the Boston Committee of Correspondence and the Massachusetts Committee of Safety, riding express to the Continental Congress in Philadelphia.

In November 1773, the merchant ship *Dartmouth* arrived in Boston carrying the first shipment of tea made under the terms of the Tea Act, which authorized the British East India Company to ship tea bypassing colonial merchants. Revere and Joseph Warren organized a watch over the ship so that it would not be unloaded. Revere took his turn at guard duty. He was a ringleader when, on December 13, 1773, he and fifty other patriots boarded the ships in the harbor and dumped the tea.

His activism extended beyond Boston when he began work as a courier and rode from Boston to New York and to Philadelphia to spread information about activities in the colonies. After the British seized a supply of the colony's gunpowder, he organized a system to detect and warn others of British troop movements. He once rode fifty miles to Portsmouth, New Hampshire, to warn the locals there of an impending seizure.

When Joseph Warren and his associates learned the British were moving troops out of Boston and planned to arrest Sam Adams and John Hancock in Lexington, Revere was sent to warn them and locals in Concord where weapons and supplies were being stored. At about 10 PM on April 18, 1775, Revere set out on horseback. A soldier named William Dawes had been sent about an hour earlier on a different route with the same objective. Revere arrived first, and Dawes about half an hour later. Adams and Hancock, being warned, were able to avoid arrest. As Revere and Dawes set out to warn Concord, they were joined by Dr. Samuel Prescott, who was on his way home in Concord. Ironically Prescott was the only one to make it. A British mounted patrol intercepted the three riders. They captured Revere, but Dawes and Prescott escaped. Dawes, however, was thrown from his horse as he fled and made his way back to Lexington. Prescott made it to Concord after riding through woods and swamps. The Battles of Lexington and Concord would spark the Revolutionary War the next day. The first shot fired in Lexington

A romantic depiction of Paul Revere's nighttime ride to warn of the approaching British.

became known as "the shot heard round the world." The ride has been commemorated most notably by Henry Wadsworth Longfellow's 1861 poem, "Paul Revere's Ride," which shaped popular memory of the event despite its factual inaccuracies. The famous opening verse began:

> LISTEN, my children, and you shall hear
> Of the midnight ride of Paul Revere,
> On the eighteenth of April, in seventy-five;
> Hardly a man is now alive
> Who remembers that famous day and year.

After Lexington and Concord, Revere felt it unsafe to return to Boston and boarded in Watertown, Massachusetts. He was denied a commission in the newly formed Continental Army. He found other ways to help, however, such as manufacturing gunpowder. Gunpowder was in short supply, and Revere managed to build a gunpowder mill in present-day Canton, Massachusetts. The mill produced tons of gunpowder for the Patriot cause. Tragically, he was also called to do some dental work. His friend General Joseph Warren was killed at the Battle of

Bunker Hill on June 17, 1775. Nine months later, in early 1776, Revere was called upon to help identify his friend. Months had passed since the battle, but Revere recognized the artificial teeth and dental prosthetic he had implanted.

He returned to Boston in 1776 and was commissioned a major of infantry in the Massachusetts Militia and, in May, transferred to Artillery. In November, he was promoted to Lt. Colonel and stationed at Castle William, defending Boston Harbor. In the summer of 1779, he was appointed commander of the field artillery in a large expedition to dislodge the British from a new base they had established on Penobscot Bay. Forty-five American ships sailed into Penobscot Bay, and the British

Revere's tomb marker

were grossly outnumbered; the Americans did not attack. Land and sea commanders squabbled over control and could not agree on strategy or tactics. The arrival of British reinforcements led to the destruction of the entire Massachusetts fleet. An orderly retreat up the Penobscot River turned into a panicked rout. The American land forces became scattered, and most made their way back to Boston on foot. A variety of charges were made against Revere. In September 1779, a Board of Inquiry held hearings on the matter, and the results were inconclusive,

Paul Revere's monument

but he was asked to resign his post. The Board did find Commodore Dudley Saltonstall, the commander of the expedition, to be primarily responsible and he was dismissed from the Navy for ineptitude. Revere was unhappy with this outcome and determined to receive a proper hearing; he petitioned the Massachusetts government seven times for a court-martial before one was finally convened in February 1782. The court, consisting of one general and twelve captains ruled that Revere be found not guilty of all charges. He accepted the result as a vindication of his honor. While his conduct as a military officer was perhaps less than exemplary, the circumstances were unusual, and neither he nor his forces were professional military men.

Revere lived for almost forty years after the war, becoming renowned as a craftsman. Pioneering in a number of areas, he designed and printed the first issue of Continental paper currency, cast cannons and bells in bronze and built the first copper-rolling mill in America. One of his largest bells still rings in Boston's Kings Chapel. He provided copper sheeting for the dome of the State House and the hull of the USS *Constitution* when it was re-coppered in 1803.

Paul Revere died on May 10, 1818, at the age of 83, at his home on Charter Street in Boston. He is buried in the Granary Burying Ground on Tremont Street.

George Ross
(1730–1779)

Lawyer, Colonel, and Congressman

Buried at Christ Church Burial Ground,
Philadelphia, Pennsylvania.

Continental Association • Declaration of Independence

George Ross was a founder from Pennsylvania who was a signer of the Continental Association (1774) and the Declaration of Independence (1776). He served as a Judge of the Admiralty Court of Pennsylvania, a colonel in the Continental Army and Vice-President of the Pennsylvania Constitutional Convention.

George Ross was born to a man of the same name and Catherine Van Gezel in New Castle, Delaware on May 10, 1730. George Sr. was an Episcopal Church clergyman. George Jr. received his education at home and went on to study law at the age of 18 under the supervision of his older brother, who had a law practice in Philadelphia. In 1750, after only two years of study, he was admitted to the Pennsylvania bar at the age of 20. The next year Ross set up his law practice in Lancaster, Pennsylvania and soon married one of his first clients, Anne Lawler. The couple would have a daughter and two sons.

He practiced law for several years and attained a good reputation. In 1756, Ross was chosen to be the Crown Prosecutor. At that time he was a Tory and loyal to the King. Ross served in that position for twelve years and in 1768 was elected to the provisional legislature. It was while

George Ross (1730–1779)

George Ross

serving there that he was able to better understand the colonial struggle against the Crown and its taxation policies, and he began to change his views.

He often opposed the Royal Governor, and while he had opposed American independence, in 1774, he changed his mind and began to support the patriot cause. As his passion for the patriot cause grew and became known, Ross was elected to the Continental Congress, receiving more popular votes than anyone except Ben Franklin. He served on the Committee of Safety overseeing the defense of the colonies.

In 1776 he was re-elected to the Continental Congress, appointed a colonel in the Continental Army, and was vice president of the State Constitutional Convention where he helped draft the Pennsylvania Bill of Rights. However, he stopped short of signing the controversial Pennsylvania Constitution of 1776, ending the rule of the Penn family and establishing Pennsylvania as an independent commonwealth. Ross believed the constitution was too radical. That same year he joined the Continental Congress after the historic vote for independence but was present on August 2 for the signing. He was the last of the Pennsylvania delegation to affix his signature.

He was re-elected to the Congress again in 1777 but resigned that same year because of poor health. He would not be out of public service for long however as in 1778, he was elected Vice President of the Pennsylvania Assembly, and he accepted a judgeship in the Pennsylvania Court of Admiralty. While serving on the court, he was involved in the controversial decision regarding *United States vs. Peters*. A congressional court of appeals overruled his decision in the case involving a dispute between a sailor from Connecticut, Gideon Olmstead, and the state of Pennsylvania regarding the spoils from a captured ship, the British sloop *Active*. Olmstead was among a group of captive American sailors who overtook the sloop while they were being pressed into service. The sloop was then captured by American privateers who planned to sell the ship for a profit. The higher court ruled the captured sailors deserved a share, but the Pennsylvania Court disagreed. Ross refused to acknowledge the

The grave of George Ross

authority of the higher court to counter state decisions because a jury had been involved.

Perhaps Ross's most famous contribution to the new nation was not his alone. George had a niece, Betsy Ross (born Elizabeth Phoebe Griscom in 1752). She acquired her famous last name when she married Ross's nephew, John Ross. John and Betsy had a sewing business in Philadelphia, and Betsy was an excellent seamstress. The story told by Betsy's descendants was that one day in May of 1776, a three-member committee from the Continental Congress came to call upon her. Those representatives, General George Washington, Robert Morris, and George Ross, asked her to sew the first American flag based on a design Washington had drafted. The stars and stripes created by Ross would eventually be officially adopted by the Congress on June 14, 1777, as the official banner of the new nation.

Unfortunately, in 1779, at the age of 49, George Ross died from a violent attack of gout and didn't live to see independence. On his deathbed, Ross said that he was sure he was going to a place where "there were the most excellent wines." He was buried at Christ Church in Philadelphia.

Edward Rutledge
(1749–1800)

Youngest to Sign the Declaration

Buried at Saint Philips Episcopal Church Cemetery
Charleston, South Carolina

**Continental Congress • Signer of the Continental Association &
Declaration of Independence • Military**

Edward Rutledge was a young lawyer from a privileged South Carolina family who, along with his brother John and his law partner, Charles Cotesworth Pinckney, became intimately involved in the independence movement. Rutledge signed the Continental Association and was the youngest to sign the Declaration of Independence. Later, he was the governor of South Carolina.

  Rutledge was born in Charleston, Christ Church Parish, South Carolina, on November 23, 1749, the youngest of seven children of Dr. John Rutledge and his wife, Sarah (née Hart) Rutledge. The elder Rutledge was a physician of Scots-Irish roots. The mother was of English heritage.
  Young Edward was educated by private tutors, including David Smith, who taught him seven languages. Rather than following in his father's footsteps to become a physician, like his older brothers John and Hugh, he studied law at the Middle Temple, one of the four Inns of Court in London. Rutledge was admitted to the English bar in 1772 and returned to Charleston to open a law practice.

Edward Rutledge (1749–1800)

Edward Rutledge

Rutledge was a noteworthy lawyer from the start. Soon after opening his practice in 1773, he won the release via grounds of *habeus corpus* of Thomas Powell, the newspaper publisher who had been imprisoned by the authorities for printing an article critical of the colonial government. The following year, Rutledge was named one of five delegates to the First Continental Congress from South Carolina.

On March 1, 1774, Rutledge married Henrietta Middleton, the daughter of fellow Continental Congressman Henry Middleton. The couple had three children: Henry, Edward, and Sarah. Later that year, on October 20, Rutledge and his brother John were among the five signers of the Continental Association from South Carolina, which also included his father-in-law, Henry Middleton, Christopher Gadsden, and Thomas Lynch, Sr. Though the junior member of the delegation at that time, with the retirements of Gadsden and Middleton from Congress and the debilitating stroke that hit Lynch, Edward Rutledge soon became the lead representative.

Rutledge was an early proponent of a national constitution as the Congress debated independence. He was concerned the independent states would flounder without one. Thus, he initially resisted Richard Henry Lee's motion for independence in June 1776, believing the colonies were not ready. Though Rutledge had told John Adams he was in favor of independence when it came time to vote, South Carolina and Pennsylvania voted in the negative. Delaware was tied as a delegate was absent, and New York had no instructions and could not act. Rutledge, however, intimated he would change his vote to the majority should it be needed to pass the resolution. The next day, Delaware's delegates were all present and voted in the affirmative, providing a sufficient majority to declare independence. South Carolina then reversed its vote, adding to the majority. Edward Rutledge was then the youngest delegate to sign the Declaration of Independence.

Also, in June 1776, Rutledge was named to the Board of War for the colonies, overseeing the Continental Army. The Congress attempted to parley with the British, seeking to avoid further warfare. Benjamin Franklin had written a letter to Admiral Richard Howe, suggesting a meeting. Howe and his brother William had been named peace commissioners to seek a resolution from further hostilities. Known as the Staten Island Conference, the meeting was held on September 11, 1776, at the home of Colonel Christopher Billop on Staten Island. John Adams and Edward Rutledge served in the delegation with Franklin. The British had just captured New York City, and Howe felt he did not have the authority to negotiate such a resolution. Thus, the meeting ended in failure.

Rutledge left the Congress and returned home in November 1776. In 1778, he was elected to a seat in the South Carolina legislature. He also volunteered to serve in the South Carolina militia, in the Charleston Battalion of Artillery, attaining the rank of captain. When he was re-elected to the Continental Congress in 1779, he refused the seat on account of his military service. In February 1779, Rutledge participated in General William Moultrie's successful battle with the British at Port Royal Island, also known as the Battle of Beaufort.

The British invaded South Carolina in 1780, sacking Charleston in May. Rutledge and fellow co-signers of the Declaration of Independence, Arthur Middleton and Thomas Heyward, were captured and imprisoned at St. Augustine, Florida. They were finally exchanged for other prisoners in July 1781.

Upon his release in 1782, Rutledge was returned to the South Carolina legislature, serving in 1782, 1786, 1788, and 1792 as the representative from Saint Philip and Saint Michael Parishes. He advocated for the taking of Loyalist property. Three times, he was named a presidential elector and aligned with the Federalists, though, in 1796, he voted for Southerners Jefferson and Pinkney.

In 1788, Rutledge attended the state's convention to ratify the US Constitution, voting in the affirmative. During this time, Rutledge also became a wealthy plantation owner.

Rutledge was nominated to be a justice on the US Supreme Court by George Washington in 1794, but he declined. Four years later, despite declining health, Rutledge was elected governor of South Carolina. Historian Robert T. Conrad wrote of Rutledge's appearance in 1846:

> The person of Mr. Rutledge was above the middle size, and inclining to corpulency; his complexion was florid and fair, and if not what would be termed a handsome man, the expression of his countenance was universally admired. He lost the greater part of his hair early in life, the remainder being perfectly white, and curling on his neck; so that had it not been for the goodness of his teeth, and the smoothness of his visage, and the fine flow of his spirits, he would have been considered a much older man than he was . . . Being latterly afflicted with gout, his gait was infirm, and he walked with a cane: before he was debilitated by this disease, his step was steady and quick, his arms usually folded across his breast, or his hands interlocked behind. His general demeanor was serene and composed, and when in a sitting posture, he usually rested his chin upon his hand, as if in serious contemplation.

As governor, Rutledge returned home to Charleston due to his gout. En route, on January 23, 1800, Rutledge suffered a stroke and died at age 50. Some contemporaries suggest the cause of death was apoplexy out of concern for George Washington's recent passing the prior month.

Rutledge was laid to rest in Charleston at Saint Philip Episcopal Church. A stone at his tomb reads: "Beneath this Stone are Deposited the Remains of His Excellency Edward Rutledge Esq. Late Governor of this State, whom it pleased the almighty to take from this life Jany 23rd 1800 at the age of Fifty years."

The Edward Rutledge House in Charleston, since 1971, is a National Historic Landmark and is privately owned and operated as a bed and breakfast, the Governor's House Inn.

Edward Rutledge appears in Trumbull's paintings of the Declaration of Independence, standing on the far right.

Grave of Edward Rutledge

John Rutledge
(1739–1800)

"The Dictator"

Buried at Saint Michaels Episcopal Church Cemetery
Charleston, South Carolina

**Continental Congress • Signer of the Continental Association &
US Constitution • US Supreme Court**

John Rutledge was a lawyer from a privileged South Carolina family who, along with his brother Edward, represented South Carolina in the Continental Congress. Rutledge signed the Continental Association and the US Constitution. He was also the first governor of newly independent South Carolina and later one of the first associate justices of the US Supreme Court. In 1795, he briefly became the second Chief Justice of the US Supreme Court.

Rutledge was born in Charleston, Christ Church Parish, South Carolina, on September 17, 1739. He was the oldest of seven children of Dr. John Rutledge and his wife, Sarah (née Hart) Rutledge. The elder Rutledge was a physician of Scots-Irish roots who had arrived with his brother, Andrew, in 1735. His mother was of English heritage and was only fifteen when he was born. Her father had dowered a large estate with the marriage, so the children were raised with great advantages.

Young John was educated by his father until his death in 1750. He was then tutored by an Anglican priest, Reverend Andrews. Next, John was admitted to the Middle Temple, one of the four Inns of Court of

John Rutledge

the English judicial system in London, on October 11, 1754, at only fifteen. In 1756, Rutledge was an understudy with James Parsons, a local barrister in Charleston and his uncle, Andrew Rutledge, also an attorney. Upon finishing two years of study, Rutledge returned to England and was called to the English bar in 1760. He won several cases in the English courts before he returned to Charleston in 1761 to open his law practice. He also sought his first political office. He was first elected to the South Carolina Provincial Assembly in 1762, representing Christ-Church Parish in the Charleston area. He served until the start of the American Revolution.

On May 1, 1764, Rutledge married Elizabeth Grimké. Together, they had ten children, eight of whom lived to adulthood. Daughter Elizabeth later married Henry Laurens, Jr., the son of the President of the Continental Congress.

John Rutledge (1739–1800)

To reimburse the Crown for the cost of the French and Indian War, Parliament implemented the Stamp Act in March 1765. The stamps were to be affixed to various paper products throughout the Americas. This was met with strong resistance, including John Rutledge from South Carolina. He, Thomas Lynch, and Christopher Gadsden were appointed to meet in New York with other colonies in protest. This Stamp Act Congress penned a petition to Parliament. Rutledge, Edward Tilghman, and Philip Livingston were charged with the task. A portion of it read it was "the undoubted right of Englishmen, that no taxes be imposed on them but with their own consent, given personally, or by their representatives." The petition was unsuccessful, and chaos ensued throughout the colonies, including the destruction of stamps and persecution of Loyalists. In South Carolina, due to the absence of stamps, all legal proceedings came to a standstill. Ultimately, the act was repealed in 1766.

Rutledge continued his law practice during the intervening years and enriched himself via his plantations. By the early 1770s, tensions increased with Britain. When the Crown clamped down on Massachusetts following the Boston Tea Party in December 1773, many across the colonies rallied in sympathy. In July 1774, South Carolina met in Charleston and declared Henry Middleton, John Rutledge, Christopher Gadsden, Thomas Lynch, and Edward Rutledge would be delegates to the First Continental Congress to be held in Philadelphia in September. John, the elder Rutledge, was the chairman of the delegation.

At the Continental Congress, John Rutledge was very conservative, seeking reconciliation with Great Britain. Unlike his brother, he was against a move to independence at the time. It was at Rutledge's suggestion, after much debate on apportionment based on populations, that the colonies each simply received one vote. Ultimately, Congress passed the Continental Association, to which Rutledge and his brother were signers.

At the Second Continental Congress the following year, both Rutledges signed the Olive Branch Petition, seeking reconciliation with Great Britain. Rutledge urged the creation of new governments in the colonies based on constitutions, and in November 1775, returned to South Carolina to help draft the state's constitution, the first such document in the colonies. This was enacted in early 1776, and Rutledge was elected president (governor) of the state in March. He faced his first crisis in June when an attack by the British on Charleston. General Charles Lee had urged Moultrie's retreat from the unfinished fort on Sullivan Island, but Rutledge penned a short note, "General Lee wishes you to evacuate the fort. You will not without an order from me. I would sooner cut off my hand than write one." Moultrie was victorious, some say, thanks to the walls being made of palmetto trees and sand, which diminished the force of the cannonballs. Thus, the palmetto tree later became the state symbol.

Rutledge served as governor through his resignation in 1778 and then again from 1779 to 1782, earning the name "Dictator John" for his autocratic rule. In 1780, when the British captured Charleston, Rutledge escaped, functioning as a one-man government in exile until the Continental Army liberated the state. Following the victory at Cowpens and Nathanael Greene's taking of Charleston, John Mathewes then succeeded Rutledge as governor in 1782. Rutledge returned to the Continental Congress. In 1784, Rutledge was elected chief judge of the South Carolina Court of Chancery.

In 1787, Rutledge was a delegate to the Constitutional Convention in Philadelphia. He was a proponent of a strong chief executive and the limitations of the judiciary. He also was against landownership as a criterion for voting rights. During the deliberations, Rutledge was one of the primary authors of what became the Great Compromise, also known as the Connecticut Compromise, addressing how representation would be apportioned. It was agreed the Senate would have an equal number of representatives while the House would be based on population. Though the Southern delegates argued for fully counting slaves for the purpose of apportionment, it was agreed to reduce the ratio to three-fifths, thereby achieving political balance, North and South. It was also agreed that the international slave trade would not be prohibited before 1808. Additionally, the South Carolina delegates saw that the Fugitive Slave Clause was added to further protect slavery by requiring slaves to be returned to their states of labor. Rutledge signed the US Constitution and returned home to lead the effort of its adoption.

In the first presidential election, Rutledge received six electoral votes. Newly elected President George Washington appointed Rutledge as one of the four associate judges on the new US Supreme Court. Rutledge was unable to travel to the new capital in New York City, so he traveled a circuit, hearing local cases. After two years of this, on account of his health, Rutledge resigned. He had also been named South Carolina's Chief Justice of the Court of Common Pleas, which he accepted in March 1791. Another factor in his decision may have been the declining health of Elizabeth, his wife, who died in 1792. This loss deeply affected Rutledge, who is said to have fallen into depression and alcoholism and was beginning to suffer financial distress.

In 1795, when Chief Justice John Jay's resignation appeared imminent given his election as the governor of New York, Rutledge informed President Washington he would be willing to take the position. Washington agreed to the offer and asked the Senate to confirm Rutledge, not knowing of Rutledge's personal issues. Before leaving for Philadelphia, Rutledge denounced the recent Jay Treaty, preferring war with England over its adoption, and took his seat for the August term while the Senate was in recess.

While chief justice, two important cases were decided. In *United States v. Peters*, the Court ruled that federal district courts had no jurisdiction over crimes committed against Americans at sea. In *Talbot v. Janson*, the Court held that a citizen of the United States did not waive all claims to U.S. citizenship by either renouncing citizenship of an individual state or by becoming a citizen of another country. This set the precedent for the possibility of multiple citizenship.

Upon the Senate's return to session, many senators had difficulty with Rutledge's feelings about the Jay Treaty and were concerned about his mental and financial state that was being discussed in the newspapers. On December 15, 1795, the Senate voted 14 to 10 against Rutledge as Chief Justice. Disgraced, Rutledge first attempted suicide on December 26, 1795, by jumping off a wharf in Charleston Harbor. He was rescued by two slaves who saw him drowning. Rutledge then resigned on December 28, 1795, before his term would have lapsed. He left for home, the shortest-tenured Chief Justice in US history at only 138 days. He also resigned from the South Carolina Supreme Court citing health reasons. Rutledge did serve one more term in the South Carolina House of Representatives but was very frail in his retirement.

GRAVES of our FOUNDERS

John Rutledge died in Charleston on July 18, 1800, at the age of 60. He was interred at St. Michael's Episcopal Church in Charleston. His grave inscription says, "On the 18th of July Anno Domini 1800 Departed this Life in the 61st Year of His Age. John Rutledge. Signer of the US Constitution." Said one Charleston newspaper:

Grave of John Rutledge

John Rutledge (1739–1800)

In the times that tried men's souls, and when the greatest abilities were requisite, Carolina looked to her John Rutledge, and confined her most important interests to his talents and virtues. Nor was she disappointed. What could be done by any man for his country, invaded, distressed, and over-run, was done for South-Carolina by this, her highly favored son. As a public speaker, he charmed and transported all who heard him: his eloquence would not suffer by a comparison with the most famous orators of antiquity.

One of Rutledge's houses has been renovated and is open to the public as the John Rutledge House Inn.

James Smith
(1719–1806)

York's Radical Revolutionary

Buried at First Presbyterian Memorial Gardens,
York, Pennsylvania.

Declaration of Independence • Continental Congress

James Smith organized a volunteer company of militia in York County. It was the first volunteer company raised to oppose the British, and he was among the first of colonial leaders to call for a continental congress to discuss the problems with the home country. He served as a delegate from Pennsylvania to the first and second Continental Congresses and signed the historic Declaration of Independence.

Exactly when James Smith was born is open to question. He was born in Ulster, Northern Ireland but would never admit to the year. In 1805 a fire destroyed his office and all his official papers. We know the family emigrated to America in 1727 and that James was a young boy. They settled in Chester County, Pennsylvania and James' father John died in 1761.

Young James was tutored in the classical education of the day by local clergy and attended the Philadelphia Academy (later known as the University of Pennsylvania). There he came to study under the distinguished provost Dr. Allison. He studied Latin and Greek and excelled at the art of surveying, which at that time was of great importance.

When he completed his studies at the Philadelphia Academy, he decided to study law under his brother George and in the office of Thomas

James Smith (1719–1806)

James Smith

Cookson in Lancaster, Pennsylvania. He was admitted to the Pennsylvania Bar in 1745 and began a practice in Shippensburg, Pennsylvania but soon moved the practice to the flourishing town of York, Pennsylvania.

In 1760 at the age of 41, Smith married a woman from New Castle, Delaware, Eleanor Armor. They would have five children, four of whom would die without having children. James Smith has no living descendants.

Smith early perceived the gathering storm and was among the first Pennsylvanians to speak out fearlessly on the side of the patriots from Massachusetts and Virginia. In 1774 he attended a provincial assembly where he presented a paper he had written entitled "Essay on The Constitutional Power of Great Britain Over The Colonies In America." In that paper, Smith recommends that the colonies boycott all British goods. He felt that such action would pressure the British Parliament to back away from some of their oppressive laws.

Later that same year, Smith organized a volunteer militia company in York which elected him captain. It was the first volunteer corps raised in Pennsylvania. In soon increased in size to a regiment and he was appointed its colonel, a title which in respect to him was honorary, sine he never assumed actual command.

Emerging as one of the regions radical leaders, he was elected a delegate to the state convention in Philadelphia in January 1775. He concurred in the spirited declaration of that convention that "if the British administration should determine by force to effect a submission to the

The grave of James Smith

late arbitrary acts of the British Parliament, in such a situation, we hold it our indispensable duty to resist such force, and at every hazard to defend the rights of liberties of America." These were strong words considering that many Pennsylvanians hoped for some form of "accommodation" with the mother country. Also, in Pennsylvania, many of the delegates and citizens were Quakers and against any violence.

Smith did not take part in the debates in the Continental Congress that led to independence. He was added to Pennsylvania's delegation on July 20, 1776, by a provincial convention in time to sign the Declaration of Independence on August 2, 1776. On the evening of August sixth, he rode off to York with a printed broadside copy to read to the public in the town square.

Smith continued to serve in Congress and the state assembly through 1778. He lent his law office in York to the Board of War in 1777 when Congress had to flee Philadelphia and move operations there. He was elected a Brigadier General of the state militia in 1781 and resumed his law practice when the war ended.

In 1785, Smith was elected to Congress again but declined to serve because of his age. He never said how old he was and any legal papers that might have shed light on his age were destroyed in the aforementioned fire about a year before his death. Smith died on July 11, 1806, and was buried in the First Presbyterian Memorial Gardens in York, Pennsylvania. His grave marker says he was ninety-three.

Haym Solomon
(1740–1785)

Financier of the Revolutionary War

Buried at Mikveh Israel Cemetery,
Philadelphia, Pennsylvania.

Financier

When this man was born on April 7, 1740, in Poland no one would have predicted that he would one day be considered a founder of a new nation. Yet this man from a Sephardic Jewish family came to the new world where he made his fortune. He then actively supported the patriot cause. While aiding Robert Morris, he became the man who may well have been the prime financier of the American side during the Revolution. All this came at considerable risk for he was captured by the British and only avoided a death sentence by escaping. He remains one of the lesser-known founders but one to whom this country owes much, perhaps independence itself. His name was Haym Solomon.

Solomon was descendent of Spanish and Portuguese Jews who migrated to Poland after Ferdinand and Isabella expelled the Jews in those regions in the same year Columbus found his way to America. Solomon left Poland while still young, and during his travels, in Western Europe, he studied finance and became fluent in eight languages including German. His mastery of the German language would serve both him and the patriot cause well during the Revolution.

Solomon arrived in America in 1772 and settled in New York where his financial knowledge allowed him to start a business and become

Haym Solomon (1740–1785)

Haym Salomon

active as a dealer in foreign securities. He developed a strong friendship with Alexander McDougal, who was a wealthy and powerful man of Scottish descent known to be a leader against British rule. His relationship with McDougal resulted in his embrace of the Patriot cause, and soon Solomon became an active member in New York's Sons of Liberty. On September 20, 1776, a fire broke out in New York that destroyed 493 homes many of which the British had intended to use to house its troops. The English authorities blamed the sons for the fire and began to arrest the known members arbitrarily. Solomon was among those who were arrested by the English authorities accused of setting the fire.

Facing brutal prison conditions aboard an English ship, Solomon utilized his German. He showed the English he could converse with the Hessian soldiers who had been contracted by King George III. He worked as an interpreter in return for an upgrade to both his living conditions and his diet. Knowing that the English didn't understand German, he used his time with the Hessian soldiers encouraging them to desert. It's been estimated that he was successful in approximately 500 cases. After 18 months of imprisonment on the English prison ship, Solomon was paroled.

In 1778 he was again arrested and charged with being an American spy. The English confiscated his properties and sentenced him to be hanged. With the help of the Sons of Liberty and a bribed guard, he was able to escape. He made his way to Philadelphia, where his wife and child joined him. Once settled in Pennsylvania he reopened his brokerage business and rebuilt his fortune. By 1781 he was the American agent to the French consul and the paymaster for French forces in North America. It was during this period that Solomon provided financial support and loans with no interest to James Monroe, Thomas Jefferson, James Madison, and James Wilson. Most of these loans were never repaid.

Solomon's business continued to grow and eventually became the largest depositor in the Bank of North America run and owned by a signer of the Declaration of Independence, Robert Morris. The revolutionary government had appointed Morris to the post of Superintendent of Finance, and it was his responsibility to manage the economy. As the young nation faced one financial crisis after another, Morris turned to Solomon for help. Morris kept a detailed diary and the name Haym Solomon appears in it more than 75 times.

In 1781 General George Washington saw an opportunity to win the war that he had been fighting for more than half a decade. The British General Charles Cornwallis had suffered a series of defeats. He had retreated with his forces to Yorktown, Virginia where he waited for the British Navy to supply both supplies and reinforcements. The French fleet, however, defeated the English fleet and positioned themselves outside of the Chesapeake Bay effectively blocking any aid that could reach him by sea. With both the anticipated support and escape to the sea lost Cornwallis could only hope to escape by land. Instead, he decided to wait for help from British forces stationed in New York, and this presented Washington with the opportunity he saw and wished to use to his advantage.

Unfortunately for the American general, his army was underpaid, undersupplied, and underfed. Washington and his troops lacked the funds necessary to move south where they could trap the British force against the sea. The revolutionary treasury was empty, and Washington required funds to transport and feed his army. Washington appealed to Morris, who turned to Solomon for help. Within a day, the necessary funding was secured. Washington then led his forces south where they boxed in Cornwallis and forced his surrender. The siege of Yorktown proved to be the decisive battle in the successful American Revolution.

The end of the war did not mean that all was well financially in the young nation. By August of 1782, the United States Treasury was once again empty. The country had no credit left, and the economic situation was a threat to make meaningless the victories won on the American Revolution battlefields. Morris, as he detailed in his diary, once again turned to Haym Solomon for help. In the estimation of the Harvard historian Professor Albert Bushnell Hart, "Solomon's credit was better than that of the whole thirteen United States." Haym Solomon again did what was necessary for his country, and through his efforts, this crisis was averted.

After the war, Solomon did indeed turn his attention back to his business and his family. Though still a young man, his health deteriorated. Some believe that he had contracted tuberculosis during the time he was imprisoned by the British. He also suffered severe financial reverses, and when he died on January 6, 1785, he was bankrupt. Not a single loan drawn from his fortune and granted to the United States government and multiple revolutionary era figures was ever repaid. He was laid to rest in the Mikveh Israel Cemetery on Spruce Street in Philadelphia. His family could not afford a tombstone, and the grave was never marked. Thus the exact location is unknown. There are two plaque memorials at the site. There is also a sculpture, the Herald Square Monument located in Chicago, that shows George Washington flanked by Solomon and Morris and grasping hands with both men. The inscription at the base of the monument quotes the first President, "The Government of the United States, which gives to bigotry no sanction, to persecution no assistance, requires only that they who live under its protection should demean themselves as good citizens, in giving it all occasions their effectual support."

Solomon today remains one of the lesser-known founders who deserves far more recognition for his efforts on behalf of the new nation. It is not an exaggeration to state that without his assistance, the chances of the American Revolution ending successfully would have been greatly diminished. Like many of his contemporaries, current Americans remain in his debt.

Memorial to Haym Solomon in the cemetery where he is believed to be buried

John Sullivan
(1740–1795)

Irish General

Buried at Sullivan Family Cemetery
Durham, New Hampshire

**Continental Congress • Continental Association
Major General • Governor**

John Sullivan was an Irish American lawyer from New Hampshire who became a Continental Congressman, Major General, Governor of the Granite State, and Federal judge. He was a signer of the Continental Association and led several military engagements during the Revolution, including the Delaware Crossing and Sullivan's Expedition against the Iroquois, who were loyal to the British.

Sullivan, born on February 17, 1740, in Somersworth, New Hampshire, was the third son of Irish settlers from the Beara Peninsula, County Cork, John Owen "Eoghan" O'Sullivan and his wife Margery (née Browne) O'Sullivan. His father was a schoolteacher, the son of minor gentry in the Irish penal colony, Philip O'Sullivan. Because they were Catholics, they were reduced to peasants, though retaining their property. Upon emigrating to Maine, then in Massachusetts, John became a Protestant. Sullivan's brother, James Sullivan, was later a governor of Massachusetts, and brother Benjamin served in the Royal Navy and died before the American Revolution. Another brother, Captain David Sullivan, was kidnapped by the British on February 14, 1781, and later died of disease.

John Sullivan

Sullivan received a limited education in New Hampshire but studied law under attorney Samuel Livermore from 1758 to 1760. Soon after his admission to the New Hampshire bar in 1760, he married Lydia Worcester. The couple had six children, four of whom survived infancy: Lydia, John, James, and George (who later served as a United States Representative from New Hampshire).

Sullivan first practiced law beginning in 1763 in Berwick, now in Maine, and then moved to Durham, New Hampshire in 1764. For the next eight years, he grew his practice and expanded into milling. He joined the St. John's Lodge of Freemasons in Portsmouth in 1767 and remained a member for the rest of his life, rising to be the first Grand Master of the Grand Lodge of New Hampshire.

In 1772, Sullivan was appointed as a major in the New Hampshire colonial militia by his friend, Governor John Wentworth. In 1773, his law practice included Alexander Scammell. As tensions rose with the British,

Sullivan was at odds with the governor and supported the Patriots. On July 21, 1774, he was appointed the delegate from Durham to the first Provincial Congress of New Hampshire. This assembly then sent him and Nathaniel Folsom to the First Continental Congress, where they arrived in time for the first meeting on September 5, 1774. They both signed the Continental Association on October 20, 1774.

Amid the gunpowder controversies, upon his return, Sullivan led a raid to take cannon and muskets on December 15, 1774, near Portsmouth. In January 1775, the New Hampshire Congress sent Sullivan and John Langdon to the Second Continental Congress. They arrived in time to discuss the hostilities at Lexington and Concord and the formation of the Continental Army. George Washington was appointed Commander in Chief, and Sullivan was made a Brigadier General. He left Philadelphia on June 27, 1775, to join the new Continental Army at the Siege of Boston. According to local legend, his troops used the password "St. Patrick" until the British left.

Following Britain's evacuation of Boston in the spring of 1776, Washington sent Sullivan to Quebec to replace John Thomas, who had died from smallpox. Sullivan inherited a division stricken with illness and unable to take Trois-Rivières, instead falling back to Crown Point. Congress sought a scapegoat for the failed invasion and attempted to pin the defeat on Sullivan. However, he was exonerated and then promoted to Major General on August 9, 1776.

Sullivan next joined Washington at Long Island and was put in command of half of the defense in tandem with senior officer Israel Putnam on August 23, 1776. During the Battle of Long Island on August 27, there was confusion in command; Sullivan personally fought bravely against the Hessians at Battle Pass, pistols in each hand. To no avail, he was captured by the British.

While in captivity, the Howe brothers, General and Admiral, convinced Sullivan to attend a peace conference with the Congress. Sullivan was sent as a peace delegate and managed to have the meeting. John Adams, however, shut it down, referring to Sullivan as a "decoy duck." The peace conference failed, and Sullivan returned to captivity until exchanged for Lieutenant General Richard Prescott.

Sullivan returned to the army in time to help lead the attack on Trenton on December 26, 1776, which led to the capture of many Hessians. He then performed well at the Battle of Princeton. At Brandywine in September 1777, Sullivan's troops were surprised by the British but left the field in an orderly manner, reinforced by Nathanael Greene. At Germantown, Sullivan's men were routing the British light infantry, but then heavy fog and delayed movements prevented victory and caused confusion, leading to friendly fire on his troops.

In early 1778, Sullivan led Continental troops and militia at Rhode Island, working together with the French Navy to capture Newport, which was held by the British. The French Admiral d'Estaing found his ships damaged and scattered in a storm, leaving Sullivan to himself. Sullivan's troops then fought a retreat in Rhode Island. Sullivan felt the French had dishonored him.

Next, in the summer of 1779, Sullivan led an expedition against the Iroquois in Pennsylvania and upstate New York. The Six Nations had been hostile to the colonists, raiding settlements. Sullivan and three thousand men gathered in northeastern Pennsylvania and marched towards Tioga in upstate New York, adding another one thousand men on the way.

At one point, Sullivan pushed his troops so hard that his horses became unusable and had to be killed. The spot where this occurred is known as Horseheads, New York. Due to Congress's tepid reaction and Sullivan's mounting financial issues back home, he retired from the military and returned to New Hampshire, where he was seen as a hero.

Sullivan was again elected to the Continental Congress by the legislature in November 1780, though it was against his wishes. Sullivan reluctantly returned to Congress and was immediately embroiled in dealing with the status of Vermont, whether it should be part of New York, New Hampshire, or independent. A possible alliance with the British in Canada also loomed, leading to Vermont becoming a separate state. Sullivan became embroiled in controversy when he borrowed money from the French minister to Congress that was likely not to be repaid. Sullivan, in turn, was accused of favoring the French in Congress, tarnishing his reputation. As the war came to an end, Sullivan was involved in deciding on peace negotiators who would favor the French, including Benjamin Franklin. One of his last acts was to vote Robert Livingston to the position of Secretary of Foreign Affairs over John Adams, who had been lobbying for it. He then resigned from Congress a month early, on

John Sullivan memorial

General John Sullivan's house in Durham, New Hampshire.

August 11, 1781. Though historian George Bancroft, one hundred years later, declared that Sullivan had taken French bribes and shown them favor, there was no direct proof, and Sullivan was exonerated by other historians.

Back in New Hampshire, Sullivan was named New Hampshire's Attorney General, serving from 1782 until 1786. He was also elected to the state assembly and served as its speaker. Sullivan was one of the 31 founding members of The Society of the Cincinnati in New Hampshire on November 18, 1783. He was elected the first President of the New Hampshire Society, serving until 1793.

He led the ratification of the US Constitution in New Hampshire on June 21, 1788. He was then President (now Governor) of New Hampshire in 1786 when he quelled the Exeter Rebellion, also known as the Paper Money Riot, in the midst of Shay's Rebellion by calling up over two thousand militia. He led the state again in 1787 and 1789.

Sullivan was appointed a US District Court Judge for New Hampshire by President Washington on September 24, 1789, and confirmed by the Senate on September 26. However, due to poor health, he was not seated until 1792.

John Sullivan (1740–1795)

Justice Sullivan died at home in Durham, New Hampshire, on January 23, 1795, and was interred in the family cemetery behind the house. Said his obituary in the *American Minerva*:

> The character of that hon. Gentleman is the part he took in his Country's interest, when great and patriotic exertions were necessary; His tried and distinguished abilities in various high, and important offices; and his public and private virtues, are all well known to his Fellow-citizens of United America.

Counties in New Hampshire, Missouri, New York, Pennsylvania, and Tennessee are named for him. The towns of Sullivan in New Hampshire

Grave of John Sullivan

and New York are named after him. Bridges in New Hampshire and Pennsylvania carry his name, as does a street in Greenwich Village in Manhattan. The Sullivan Trail follows some of Sullivan's 1779 Expedition in northeast Pennsylvania and Sullivan Way in Trenton is named for him.

Sullivan's father outlived him, dying at 104 in June 1795. A statue honoring Sullivan was erected in 1894 in Durham. His house, known as The General John Sullivan House, is privately owned and occupied and is on the National Register of Historic Landmarks.

Artemas Ward
(1727–1800)

First Commander-in-Chief

Buried at Mountain View Cemetery
Shrewsbury Center, Massachusetts

**Major General • Colonial Governor • Continental Congress
United States House of Representatives**

Artemas Ward was a member of a noteworthy New England family who served as a colonel in the Massachusetts Militia during the French and Indian War. Following Lexington and Concord, he answered the patriot call and was initially the first commander-in-chief of colonial forces. During the Siege of Boston in 1775, prior to Washington's arrival, Ward was the commanding officer of the patriot forces there, coordinating the arrival and positioning of cannon and the defense of Bunker and Breed's Hills. While he commanded from his headquarters, he was the planner of the defense that proved tenacious for the advancing Redcoats. He was then appointed one of the four major generals subordinate to George Washington. After the British left Boston, Ward returned to civilian life and was active politically, ultimately serving in the Continental Congress and then the Second and Third Congresses in the House of Representatives. In his writings about the American Revolution, President John Adams eulogized Ward as: "universally esteemed, beloved and confided in by his army and his country."

Artemas Ward, the son of Colonel Nahum Ward and his wife Martha (née How or Howe) Ward, the sixth of seven children, was born on

GRAVES of our FOUNDERS

Artemas Ward

November 26, 1727, in Shrewsbury, Massachusetts. The elder Ward was deeply involved in the community and was credited as one of the founders of Shrewsbury. He was a lawyer who served in several political offices, including selectman, representative in the General Court, Justice of the Peace for Worcester County, and Judge of the Court of Common Pleas as well. He was also a land developer, farmer, merchant, and sea captain. Martha's father had also been a sea captain. The Ward family was one of the first to settle on Massachusetts Bay, descended from William Ward, a Puritan, who arrived in Sudbury and then Marlborough.

Young Artemas attended the local common schools, sharing a private tutor with his siblings. He graduated from Harvard in 1748 with a bachelor's degree. He followed this with a master's degree in 1751 and taught for a while at Harvard. While in graduate school, on July 31, 1750,

Artemas Ward (1727–1800)

Ward married Sarah Trowbridge (1724–1788), a daughter of Reverend Caleb Trowbridge and Hannah Walter of Groton, Massachusetts. The Trowbridges were descendants of Cotton and Increase Mather. The young couple soon returned to Shrewsbury, where Ward opened a general store. Over the next fourteen years, the couple had eight children: Ithamar (1752), Nahum (1754), Sara (1756), Thomas (1758), Artemas Jr. (1762), Henry Dana (1768), Martha (1760), and Maria (1764).

Ward continued to study law after Harvard and became involved in the community politically. His first office was as a township assessor for Worcester County in 1751. Next, in 1752, at only age 25, he was elected as a justice of the peace and to the Massachusetts Provincial Assembly, also known as the "General Court," serving many terms in that body.

During the French and Indian War, between 1755 and 1757, Ward alternated between military and political duties. In 1755, Major Ward was in the 3rd Regiment of soldiers drawn from Worcester County, garrisoning the western frontier of the colony. In 1757, he was promoted to colonel of the regiment, which now included Middlesex and Worcester Counties.

Following the war, in 1762, Ward was named a justice on the Court of Common Pleas, rising to Chief Justice over the next thirteen years. During the Stamp Act crisis, Ward was very vocal in the General Court, speaking out second only to James Otis. He was on the taxation committee with Sam Adams and John Hancock. Given his protesting nature, in 1767, Royal Governor Francis Bernard revoked Ward's military commission. The following year, the governor voided Ward's election to the General Court, but Ward would not be silenced. Soon, he was back among the Governor's Council under Thomas Hutchinson, especially at the time of the Boston Tea Party in 1773.

Following the Boston Port Act, Parliament's response to the Boston Tea Party, on October 3, 1774, the 3rd Regiment of Massachusetts Militia resigned en masse from British service. They unanimously elected Ward as their leader and marched to Shrewsbury to inform him. Governor Hutchinson then abolished the assembly, but patriots established Committees of Safety across the colony. The new Provincial Congress then, on October 27, 1774, appointed Ward as General and Commander-in-Chief of all Massachusetts Militia.

As the Second Continental Congress met in early 1775, following Lexington and Concord, they appointed Artemas Ward as Commander-in-Chief of all colonial forces. Ward had been ill at home and missed the initial battle but quickly rallied in his new role to organize the forces to counter the British occupation of Boston. It was Ward who drilled the various militia groups who arrived to resist the Crown's invaders. It was Ward, who planned the defenses, including the movement of cannon and men to Bunker and Breed's Hills. It was Ward who assigned Israel Putnam to these defenses. While the battle on June 17, 1775, was a loss for the rebels, it cost the British dearly, sending the message that any suppression of the Americans was going to be difficult.

On June 19, as the Continental Congress met in Philadelphia, they selected George Washington of Virginia to be the Commander-in-Chief for all Continental forces and sent him to Boston to take over from Ward, who remained in command until July 2, 1775. Ward was retained, with Charles Lee, Philip Schuyler, and Israel Putnam as major generals under Washington. Horatio Gates was named adjutant-general. Over the intervening months, Washington held the British in check, besieging the British in Boston. In November, he sent Henry Knox to retrieve the captured cannon from Fort Ticonderoga and reposition them on the Dorchester Heights above Boston. The cannons were in place by January 1776, under Ward's command. Soon after, the British ended their occupation of Boston on March 17, 1776.

As the British left Boston, Washington soon followed them to New York. Ward remained behind, in command of the forces around Boston, until March 1777, when he resigned from the army citing ill health.

Almost immediately after the British left the area, while still in command of the local military forces, Ward returned as Chief Justice of the Court of Common Please for Worcester County. In 1777, after resigning from the military, he was named a member of the Massachusetts Executive Council until 1779, serving as its President, making him the colony's governor until the new Massachusetts constitution was adopted in 1780. He was also elected to the state House of Representatives, serving until 1785, rising to Speaker in his final year.

When Continental Congressman Timothy Edwards resigned on June 2, 1779, the Massachusetts legislature selected Ward as his replacement.

Grave marker of Artemas Ward

However, Ward did not take his seat until the following year. Ward served in the Continental Congress, now back in Philadelphia, from January 1780 until May 1782. During this time, the Articles of Confederation were adopted.

Ward returned to Massachusetts and continued his role in the legislature. As Speaker of the House and Justice of the Peace of the Worcester Court in 1786, he was involved in suppressing Shays Rebellion, facing down the rebels at his courthouse steps.

Following the signing of the U.S. Constitution in September 1787, Ward remained in Massachusetts in the courts. But in November 1790, he ran for and won a seat in the Second and then the Third U.S. Congresses, serving in the House of Representatives from 1791 until 1795. Ward was one of only nine representatives to vote against the Eleventh Amendment to the Constitution concerning states' rights and the judiciary.

Ward returned home to Shrewsbury in March 1795. In December 1797, he retired from his judicial duties. He died at his home on October

28, 1800, at the age of 72. He was laid to rest at Mountain View Cemetery in Shrewsbury.

Ward has been remembered in a number of ways. In 1778, the town of Ward was named after him. However, in 1837, following complaints to the postal services, the town's name was changed to Auburn because Ward was too similar to nearby Ware, Massachusetts.

The Artemas Ward House, the original home of Nahum Ward, remains as a museum at 786 Main Street, Shrewsbury, Massachusetts.

In Washington, D.C., on the campus of American University, Ward Circle is at the convergence of Massachusetts and Nebraska Avenues. In 1938, a ten-foot marble statue of Ward was erected in this circle, modeled after a painting by Charles Wilson Peale. At its base is inscribed "Artemas Ward, 1727-1800, Son of Massachusetts, Graduate of Harvard College, Judge and Legislator, Delegate 1780-1781 Continental Congress, Soldier in Three Wars, First Commander of the Patriotic Forces." American University has since named the home of its School of Public Affairs the Ward Circle Building in honor of Artemas Ward.

Sources

Books, Magazines, Journals, Files:

Alexander, Edward P. *Revolutionary Conservative: James Duane of New York*. New York: Ams Press, 1978.

Anthony, Katharine Susan. *First Lady of the Revolution; The Life of Mercy Otis Warren*. Port Washington, N.Y.: Kennikat Press, 1972.

Appleby, Joyce. *Inheriting the Revolution: The First Generation of Americans*. Cambridge, Massachusetts: Harvard University Press, 2000.

Atkinson, Rick. *The British Are Coming: The War for America, Lexington to Princeton, 1775-1777*. New York: Henry Holt & Co. 2019.

Bordewich, Fergus M. *The First Congress: How James Madison, George Washington, and a Group of Extraordinary Men Invented the Government*. New York: Simon and Schuster Paperbacks, 2016.

Boudreau, George W. *Independence: A Guide to Historic Philadelphia*. Yardley, Pennsylvania: Westholme Publishing, LLC. 2012.

Bowen, Catherine Drinker. *Miracle at Philadelphia: The Story of the Constitutional Convention May to September 1787*. Boston, Massachusetts: Little, Brown & Company, 1966.

Breen, T.H, *George Washington's Journey: The President Forges a New Nation*. New York: Simon & Schuster. 2016.

Brookhiser, Richard. *Gentleman Revolutionary: Gouverneur Morris The Rake Who Wrote the Constitution*. New York: Free Press, 2003.

———. *John Marshall: The Man Who Made the Supreme Court*. New York: Basic Books. 2018.

Brush, Edward Hale. *Rufus King and His Times*. New York: N.L. Brown, 1926.

Chadwick, Bruce. I Am Murdered: *George Wythe, Thomas Jefferson, and the Killing That Shocked a New Nation*. Hoboken, New Jersey: John Wiley & Sons, 2009.

Chambers, II, John Whiteclay. *The Oxford Companion to American Military History*. Oxford: Oxford University Press, 1999.

Commager, Henry Steele & Richard B. Morris. *The Spirit of 'Seventy-Six: The Story of the American Revolution as Told by Participants*. New York: Harper & Rowe, 1967.

Cole, Ryan. *Light-Horse Harry Lee: The Rise and Fall of a Revolutionary Hero*. Washington, D.C.: Regnery History. 2019.

Conlin, Joseph R. *The Morrow Book of Quotations in American History*. New York: William Morrow and Company, Inc., 1984.

Daniels, Jonathan. *Ordeal of Ambition*. Garden City, New York: Doubleday & Company, Inc., 1970.

Dann, John C. *The Revolution Remembered: Eyewitness Accounts of the War for Independence*. Chicago: University of Chicago Press, 1980.

DeRose, Chris. *Founding Rivals: Madison vs. Monroe: The Bill of Rights and the Election that Saved a Nation*. New York: MJF Books, 2011.
Drury, Bob & Tom Clavin. *Valley Forge*. New York: Simon & Schuster. 2018.
Ellis, Joseph J. *Revolutionary Summer: The Birth of American Independence*. New York: Alfred A. Knopf, 2013.
———. *The Quartet: Orchestrating the Second American Revolution, 1783-1789*. New York: Alfred A. Knopf, 2015.
———. *His Excellency: George Washington*. New York: Alfred A. Knopf, 2004.
Flexner, James Thomas. *George Washington in the American Revolution, 1775-1783*. Boston: Little, Brown & Company, 1967.
Flower, Lenore Embick. "Visit of President George Washington to Carlisle, 1794." Carlisle, Pennsylvania: The Hamilton Library and Cumberland County Historical Society, 1932.
Gerlach, Don R. *Proud Patriot: Philip Schuyler and the War of Independence, 1775-1783*. Syracuse, N.Y.: Syracuse University Press, 1987.
Goodrich, Charles A. *Lives of the Signers of the Declaration of Independence*. Charlotteville, N.Y.: SamHar Press, 1976.
Griffith, IV, William R. *The Battle of Lake George: England's First Triumph in the French and Indian War*. Charleston, South Carolina: The History Press, 2016.
Grossman, Mark. *Encyclopedia of the Continental Congress*. Armenia, New York: Grey House Publishing, 2015.
Hamilton, Edward P. *Fort Ticonderoga: Key to a Continent*. Boston: Little, Brown & Company, 1964.
Isenberg, Nancy. *Fallen Founder: The Life of Aaron Burr*. New York: Penguin Group, 2007.
Kennedy, Roger G. *Burr, Hamilton, and Jefferson: A Study in Character*. New York: Oxford University Press, 1999.
Kiernan, Denise & Joseph D'Agnese. *Signing Their Lives Away: The Fame and Misfortune of the Men Who Signed the Declaration of Independence*. Philadelphia: Quirk Books, 2008.
———. *Signing Their Rights Away: The Fame and Misfortune of the Men Who Signed the United States Constitution*. Philadelphia: Quirk Books, 2011.
Klarman, Michael J. *The Framers' Coup: The Making of the United States Constitution*. New York: Oxford University Press, 2016.
Langguth, A. J. *Patriots*. New York: Simon and Schuster, 1988.
Larson, Edward J. *A Magnificient Catastrophe*. New York: Free Press, 2007.
Lee, Mike. Written *Out of History: The Forgotten Founders Who Fought Big Government*. New York: Penguin Books, 2017.
Lewis, James E., Jr., *The Burr Conspiracy: Uncovering the Story of an Early American Crisis*, Princeton: Princeton University Press, 2017.
Lockridge, Ross Franklin. *The Harrisons*. 1941.
Lomask, Milton. *Aaron Burr: The Years from Princeton to Vice President, 1756-1805*. New York: Farrar Straus Giroux, 1979.
Lossing, Benson J. *Pictorial Field Book of the Revolution*. New York: Harper Brothers. 1851.

SOURCES

Maier, Pauline. *American Scripture: Making the Declaration of Independence.* New York: Alfred A. Knopf, Inc., 1997.

McCullough, David. *John Adams.* New York: Simon & Schuster, 2002.

Meltzer, Brad & Josh Mensch. *The First Conspiracy: The Secret Plot to Kill George Washington.* New York: Flat Iron Books. 2018.

Middlekauff, Robert. *The Glorious Cause: The American Revolution, 1763-1789.* Oxford: Oxford University Press, 2005.

Miller, Jr., Arthur P. & Marjorie L. Miller. *Pennsylvania Battlefields and Military Landmarks.* Mechanicsburg, Pennsylvania: Stackpole Books, 2000.

Millett, Allan R. & Peter Maslowski. *For the Common Defense: A Military History of the United States of America.* New York: The Free Press, 1984.

Moore, Charles. *The Family Life of George Washington.* New York: Houghton Mifflin, 1926.

Nagel, Paul C. *The Lees of Virginia: Seven Generations of an American Family.* Oxford: Oxford University Press, 1990.

O'Connell, Robert L. *Revolutionary: George Washington at War.* New York: Random House. 2019.

Racove, Jack N. *Revolutionaries: A New History of the Invention of America.* New York: Houghton Mifflin Harcourt, 2011.

Raphael, Ray. Founding Myths: *Stories That Hide Our Patriotic Past.* New York: MJF Books, 2004.

Rossiter, Clinton. *1787 The Grand Convention.* New York: The Macmillan Company, 1966.

Seymour, Joseph. *The Pennsylvania Associators, 1747-1777.* Yardley, Pennsylvania: Westholme Publishing, LLC. 2012.

Schweikart, Larry & Michael Allen. *A Patriot's History of the United States from Columbus's Great Discovery to the War on Terror.* New York: Penguin, 2004.

Sharp, Arthur G. *Not Your Father's Founders.* Avon, Massachusetts: Adams Media, 2012.

Stahr, Walter. *John Jay: Founding Father.* New York: Diversion Books, 2017.

Taafee, Stephen R. *The Philadelphia Campaign, 1777-1778.* Lawrence, Kansas: University of Kansas Press, 2003.

Tinkcom, Harry Marlin, *The Republicans and the Federalists in Pennsylvania, 1790-1801.* Harrisburg, Pennsylvania: Pennsylvania Historical and Museum Commission. 1950.

Ward, Matthew C. *Breaking the Backcountry: The Seven Years' War in Virginia and Pennsylvania, 1754-1765.* Pittsburgh, Pennsylvania: University of Pittsburgh Press, 2003.

Weisberger, Bernard A. *America Afire: Jefferson, Adams, and the Revolutionary Election of 1800.* New York: HarperCollins, 2000.

Wood, Gordon S. *The Radicalism of the American Revolution.* New York: Vintage Books, 1993.

———. *Empire of Liberty: A History of the Early Republic, 1789-1815.* New York: Penguin Books, 2004.

———. *Revolutionary Characters: What Made the Founders Different.* New York: Penguin Books, 2006.

———. *The Americanization of Benjamin Franklin.* Oxford: Oxford University Press, 2009.

Wright, Benjamin F. *The Federalist: The Famous Papers on the Principles of American Government: Alexander Hamilton, James Madison, John Jay.* New York: Metro Books, 2002.

Zobel, Hiller B. *The Boston Massacre.* New York: W. W. Norton & Company, 1970.

Video Resources:

Guelzo, Allen C. The Great Courses: *America's Founding Fathers* (Course N. 8525). Chantilly, Virginia: The Teaching Company, 2017.

Online Resources:

Archives.gov – for information on the Constitutional Convention.
CauseofLiberty.blogspot.com – for information on Daniel Carroll.
ColonialHall.com – for information about the signers of the Declaration of Independence.
DSDI1776.com – for information on many Founders.
FamousAmericans.net – for information on many Founders.
FindaGrave.com – for burial information, vital statistics and obituaries.
FirstLadies.org – for information on Abigail Adams.
Newspapers.com – Hundreds of newspaper articles were accessed—too numerous to mention here.
NPS.gov – for information on various park sites.
TeachingAmericanHistory.com – for information on Charles Pinckney and George Wythe.
TheHistoryJunkie.com – for information on multiple Founders.
USHistory.org – for information on multiple Founders.
Wikipedia.com – for general historical information.

Index

Adams, Abigail, 10, 15, 75, 205
Adams, Andrew, 24–27
Adams, John, 6, 8–10, 12, 14–18, 20–21, 23, 28, 31, 48–49, 51, 69, 75, 85, 114, 124–25, 136, 142, 146, 149, 181, 200, 202–203, 205–206, 225, 228, 237–42, 246, 261, 268, 281, 306, 327, 329, 333, 335
Adams, John Quincy, 126,
Adams, Samuel, 9, 24, 28–34, 48–49, 146, 203, 205–206, 237, 241, 295
Addison Burial Ground, 161, 164
Albany Rural Cemetery, 251, 256
Alien and Sedition Acts, 17, 261
Allen, Ethan, 35–40, 204
Alsop, John, 122
American Revolution, 28, 30, 32–33, 35, 37, 41, 43, 49, 51, 53, 63, 67, 74, 76, 80, 87–88, 98, 104–106, 111, 113, 120, 122, 131, 136, 165–66, 172–74, 177, 184, 186, 188–90, 192, 195, 199–200, 206–207, 212, 217, 222, 224–25, 229, 234, 237, 241–43, 246, 248, 259, 266, 271, 273–74, 287–88, 291, 293, 295, 310, 320, 323–25, 333
Andre, John, 159
Annapolis Convention, 68, 111–12, 212, 287
Annapolis Tea Party, 110
Armstrong, John Jr., 45
Armstrong, John Sr., 41–45
Arnold, Benedict, 37, 184, 186, 198, 233, 291
Articles of Confederation, 1, 24–26, 28, 32, 61, 65, 92, 115–16, 161, 163, 182, 188, 190, 199, 202, 205, 212, 217, 219–20, 254, 287–88, 291, 337
Asante, Molefi Kete, 50
Attucks, Crispus, 46–50
Augustus Lutheran Church Cemetery, 229, 234

Bache, Richard, 245
Bacon, Sir Francis, 15
Bancroft, George, 330
Barbary Pirates, 12, 19, 57
Barry, John, 51–60
Bartlett, Josiah Dr., 61–66
Bassett, Richard, 67–71
Battle of Alligator Creek Bridge, 266
Battle of Beaufort, 306
Battle of Bemis Heights, 198
Battle of Bennington, 65, 198
Battle of Brandywine, 44, 101, 117, 131, 232, 266, 290, 328
Battle of Bunker Hill, 204, 296–97

Battle of Combahee River, 191
Battle of Derna, 19
Battle of Germantown, 44, 101, 117, 131, 232, 266, 290, 328
Battle of Long Island, 158, 327
Battle of Monmouth, 101, 206, 232, 272–73, 275–76, 290
Battle of Princeton, 54, 68, 117, 158, 290, 328
Battle of Rhode Island, 173
Battle of Sullivan's Island, 44, 266
Battle of Trenton, 54, 68, 117, 156, 158, 290, 328
Battle of Turtle Gut Inlet, 53
Battle of White Plains, 197
Bee, Thomas, 220
Before George, 1
Biddle, Charles, 72
Biddle, Edward, 72–77, 225
Biddle, James, 72
Biddle Nicholas, 72
Bill of Rights, 12, 207–208, 214–15, 225
Blair, James, 212
Blair, John Jr., 78–82
Bland, Richard, 83–87, 280
Boston, 24, 28, 30–34, 37, 46, 48, 54, 79, 111, 147, 150–52, 157, 163, 166, 169–71, 173, 197, 200, 202–204, 206, 237, 240–41, 259, 293–98, 327, 333, 336
Boston Massacre, 31, 46–47, 49, 63, 104, 166, 168, 196, 203
Boston Relief Committee, 68
Boston Tea Party, 31, 34, 63, 111, 166, 173, 204, 311, 335
Boudinot, Elias, 88–94, 164
Bowen, Jacob, 135
Brack, Danae, 245
Bragg, Braxton, 99
Brands, H. W.,12
Braxton, Carter, 3, 95–99, 280, 282
Brearley, David, 100–103, 253
Broad Street Church Cemetery, 257, 263
Broadwater, Jeff, 212
Brodie, Fawn M., 7–8
Brown, William,46
Bruton Parish Churchyard, 78, 82
Burr, Aaron, 15, 17–18, 20–21, 107, 120, 125, 130, 132–33, 142, 256, 269
Butler, Pierce, 104–107

Cadwalader, John, 54
Caesar, Julius, 15
Caldwell, James, 168

343

GRAVES of our FOUNDERS

Calhoun, John C., 126
Carroll, Charles Of Carrollton, 108–14, 143
Carroll, Daniel, 173
Carlisle, Pennsylvania, 41–45, 271, 274
Chalmers, James, 246
Charleston, 195, 199, 220–21, 231, 233, 264–66, 269, 304, 306–10, 312–14
Chase, Samuel, 110, 112
Chericoke Plantation, 95, 97–99
Chesapeake Patriots, 1
Chief Pontiac, 43
Christ Church Burial Ground, 300, 303
Christ Church Episcopal Cemetery, 104, 107
Circular Congregational Church Burying Ground, 217, 221
Clingan,, William, 115–19, 225
Clinton, DeWitt, 125, 128
Clinton, George, 20, 120–29, 141–42
Coercive Acts, 68, 163, 280
Committee of Correspondence, 31, 76, 85, 89, 122, 136, 180, 280, 290, 295
Concord, 25, 32, 37, 64, 86, 89, 97, 122, 150, 181, 197, 219, 257, 259, 266, 280, 294–96, 327, 333, 336
Congressional Cemetery, 127
Conrad, Robert T., 307
Constitutional Convention, 12, 68, 78, 80, 100, 102, 104, 106–107, 113, 132, 192, 207, 212, 253, 267, 287, 312
Continental Association, 1, 28, 31, 72, 75, 83, 85, 134, 136, 139, 141, 144, 147, 175, 180, 277, 280, 284, 286, 300, 304–305, 309, 311, 325, 327
Continental Congress, 5, 8, 12, 24–25, 31–32, 34, 37–38, 41, 43–44, 56, 61, 63–65, 74, 83, 85, 87–89, 95, 97, 108, 112–13, 116, 120, 122, 130, 134, 136, 141, 146–48, 156, 160–61, 163, 175, 180–81, 190, 192, 202, 204–205, 211–12, 217–19, 222, 225, 231, 246–48, 253, 277, 280–81, 284, 286, 288, 291, 301–306, 309–12, 316, 319, 325, 327–28, 336–37
Conway Cabal, 113, 202
Cole, Joseph, 174
Cosway, Maria, 13
Cresap, Michael, 163
Crothers, Jane, 47–48
Crown Point, 37

D'Agnese, Joseph, 110
Dana, Francis, 205–206
David, William Richardson, 58
Dawes, William, 295
Dayton, Johnathan, 130–33, 226, 253
Deane, Silas, 75, 146–47, 247
Declaration of Independence, 1, 3, 5, 9, 11, 28, 32, 61, 64, 66, 74, 95, 97, 105, 108, 110, 113–14, 129, 138–39, 141, 175, 178, 182, 209–10, 224, 243, 246, 265, 284–85, 287, 289, 300, 304, 306, 308, 316, 319, 322
Dickinson, John, 9, 43, 69, 181–82, 274, 278, 286
District of Columbia, 14
Doughoregan, Manor Chapel, 108, 114
Drayton, William Henry, 147, 266
Dulany, Daniel, 110
Duane, James, 122
Dyer, Eliphalet, 134–38, 146

Edwards, Timothy, 336
Ellery, William, 181–82
Ellsworth, Oliver, 58, 256
Embargo Act of 1807, 20, 262

Fairfax Resolves, 210
Faneuil Hall, 48, 203
First Presbyterian Memorial Gardens, 316, 319
Fleming, David, 9, 14
Floyd, William, 139–43
Folsom, Nathaniel, 327
Fort Charlotte, 219
Fort Clinton, 123
Fort Duquesne, 43, 74
Fort Edward, 198
Fort Henry, 224
Fort Lee, 246
Fort Montgomery, 123
Fort Moore, 219
Fort Moultrie, 266
Fort Niagara, 74
Fort Pitt, 156–57, 160
Fort Ticonderoga, 198, 205, 336
Fort Washington, 163, 165, 274, 290
Franklin, Benjamin, 9–10, 12, 55, 88, 112, 178, 182, 205–206, 245–46, 289, 301, 306, 329
French And Indian War, 30, 35, 41, 43, 73, 104–105, 120, 130, 136, 189–90, 196, 218, 279, 311, 333, 335
French Revolution, 12, 16–17, 248, 260

Gadsden, Christopher, 144–49, 181, 219–20, 305, 311
Gallatin, Albert, 19, 127
Garrick, Edward, 46, 167
Gates, Horatio, 44, 198, 205, 336
General Braddock, 43
General Burgoyne, 91, 198
General Carleton, 124
General Clinton, 148, 199, 266, 273
General Cornwallis, 10–11, 54, 148–49, 184, 186, 191, 199–200, 233, 322
General Gage, 32, 197
General Howe, 90, 152, 306
Gerry, Elbridge, 205, 214, 261, 268

344

INDEX

Goldfinch, John, 167
Goodrich, Charles, 286
Gotham Graves, 1
Granary Burial Ground, 28, 33, 46, 48, 237, 241, 293, 299
Grand Army of the Republic Cemetery, 166, 174
Greene, Jerome, 236
Greene, Nathanael, 220, 231–32, 246, 273, 312
Green Mountain Boys, 35–37
Green Mountain Cemetery, 35, 39
Groom, Winston, 6, 14

Hacker, Hoysted, 56
Hale, Nathan, 150–55
Hamilton, Alexander, 2, 6, 14–15, 17–18, 20, 55, 69, 107, 120, 124, 130, 132, 225–26, 234, 256, 260–61, 266, 268–69
Hancock, John, 32–33, 48, 53, 61, 64, 113, 168, 190, 202, 205, 241, 280, 295, 335
Hand, Edward, 156–60
Hanson, John, 92, 161–65
Hanson, Peter Contee, 163, 165
Harrison, Benjamin, 278, 280
Hart, Albert Bushnell, 323
Haslet, John, 68
Hawkes, James, 173
Hays, William, 271–72, 274
Heath, James E., 187
Hemings, Madison, 7
Hemings, Betty, 7, 11
Hemings, James, 13
Hemings, Sally, 11, 13
Henry, Patrick, 7, 11, 80, 97, 211, 279–80
Hewes, Joseph, 51
Hewes, George Robert Twelves, 166–74
Heyward, Thomas Jr., 146, 218, 306
Hollywood Cemetery, 99
Hopkins, Esek, 53, 181
Hopkins, Stephen, 175–83
Howe, Robert, 199
Hull, William, 153
Huntington, Samuel, 163
Hutchinson, Thomas, 28, 238, 240–41
Hutson, Richard, 220
Hyland, William G. Jr., 208, 210

Immanuel Episcopal Churchyard, 284, 287
Independence Hall, 59
Intolerable Acts, 31, 63, 79
Irvine, William, 271

Jackson, Andrew, 126
Jay, John, 80, 82, 120, 122–23, 142, 260, 313
Jay Treaty, 16, 227, 261, 268, 313
Jefferson Jane Randolph, 5
Jefferson, Peter, 5

Jefferson, , Thomas, 2–3, 5–23, 58, 83, 87, 98, 107, 114, 120, 124–25, 127, 132–33, 142, 200, 210–11, 216, 226, 234, 246, 249, 260–62, 264, 269, 279–81, 307, 322
Johnson, Samuel, 163
Johnson, William, 232
Jones, John Paul, 51, 58
Jordan Point Plantation, 83, 87

Kennedy, John F., 23
Keystone Tombstones, 1
Kieran, Denise, 110
Kilbourn, Dwight C., 26
Kilmeade, Brian, 19
King George III, 8, 38, 74, 112, 145, 321
King, Martin Luther Jr., 50
King, Rufus, 125
Kinloch, Francis, 220
Kittanning, 41, 43, 45
Knox, Henry, 37, 57, 197, 199, 260, 336

Lafayette, James Armistead, 184–87
Lafayette, Marquis de, 184–87, 199, 233
Langdon, John, 64, 327
Langguth, A. J., 9
Larson, Edward J.,17
Laurel Hill Cemetery, 288, 292n
Laurens Family Cemetery, 188
Laurens, Henry, 148, 188–94, 220, 247–48
Laurens, John, 55
Lee, Charles, 44, 231, 290, 312, 336
Lee, Francis, 181
Lee, Harry, 199, 206
Lee, Richard Henry, 112, 280, 306
Leslie, Alexander, 259
Lewis, James E., 20, 132
Lexington, 25, 32, 37, 64, 86, 89, 97, 122, 150, 181, 197, 219, 257, 259, 266, 280, 294–96, 327, 333, 336
Lincoln, Abraham, 195, 200
Lincoln, Benjamin, 195–201, 238, 266
Livingston, Philip, 122, 311
Livingston, Robert, 9, 122, 329
Livingston, Robert R.,19, 246
Livingston, William, 90, 253–54
Locke, John, 9, 15, 29, 210
Lomask, Milton, 109
Longfellow, Henry Wadsworth, 2, 293, 296
Lord Hillsborough, 191
Lord Mansfield, 240
Louisiana Purchase, 19–20, 132, 262
Lovell, James, 202–206
Lynch, Thomas, 146, 305, 311

Madison, James, 2, 12, 15–16, 21, 45, 80, 106, 120, 125, 127–28, 212, 214, 263–64, 269, 322

Malcolm, John, 170–71
Malone, Dumas, 7, 10
Marion, Francis, 106
Marshall, John, 19–20, 261, 268
Martin, John Blennerhassett, 187
Mason Family Cemetery, 207
Mason, George, 9, 207–16
Matthews, John, 217–21
Maxwell, Thompson, 168
McCauley, John, 274
McClene, John, 225
McDougal, Alexander, 321
McHenry, James, 266
McIntosh, Lachlan, 106, 193
McKean, Thomas, 164, 234, 285–86
McKensie, Frederick, 153
Merry, Anthony, 20
Middlekauff, Robert, 246
Middleton, Arthur, 105, 306
Middleton, Henry, 146, 219–20, 265, 280, 305, 311
Mifflin, Thomas, 228
Mikveh Israel Cemetery, 320, 323
Monroe Doctrine, 22
Monroe, James, 15, 19, 21–22, 187, 216, 225–26, 249, 322
Montgomery, Richard, 38
Monticello Graveyard, 5
Montresor, John, 153
Morris, Gouverneur, 214
Morris, Robert, 52, 98, 116, 247, 303, 320, 322–23
Mountain View Cemetery, 333, 338
Muhlenberg, Frederick Augustus Conrad, 222–29, 231, 234
Muhlenberg, John Peter Gabriel, 228–36

Napoleon, 19–20, 249
Nathan Hale Cemetery, 150, 154
New Jersey Patriots, 1
Newton, Isaac, 15
New York, 9, 14–15, 17, 20, 23, 36, 38, 69, 90–91, 100, 107, 120–22, 124–25, 127–29, 132, 138–43, 146, 152, 158, 166, 173, 177, 197–98, 224, 233, 243, 249, 251, 256, 259, 290, 293, 295, 306, 311, 313, 320–22, 328, 331–32, 336
New York Patriots, 1
North Burial Ground, 175, 182

O'Hara, Charles, 199
Old Dutch Churchyard, 120, 127
Old Graveyard, 41, 45, 271, 274
Old Ship Burying Ground, 195, 200
Olive Branch Petition, 75, 311
Otis, James Jr., 85, 178, 237–42, 335

Paine, Thomas, 9, 93, 243–50

Paine, Robert Treat, 205
Patterson, William, 102, 251–56
Penn, John, 182
Philadelphia, 8–9, 12, 14–15, 25, 31–32, 38, 44, 51–54, 57–59, 63–64, 67–68, 72–73, 75, 85, 88, 91–92, 94, 97, 101, 104, 106–107, 112–13, 115, 120, 122, 131–32, 135–36, 141, 144, 147, 156, 163–64, 181, 190, 194, 207, 210, 212, 219–20, 223–25, 230–32, 234, 245, 253, 259, 266–67, 271, 274, 280–82, 286–92, 295, 300, 303, 311–13, 318–20, 322–23, 327, 336–37
Pickering, Timothy, 256–63
Pierce, Franklin, 287
Pierce, William, 212, 253
Pinckney, Charles C., 17–18, 20, 106, 125, 261, 264–70, 304, 307
Pitcher, Molly (Mary Ludwig), 271–76
Pitt, Leonard, 169
Plains Cemetery, 61, 65
Powell, Thomas, 305
Prescott, Samuel, 295
Preston, Thomas, 47
Price, Thomas, 163
Private White, 46–47
Putnam, Israel, 327, 336

Randolph, Edmund, 212, 214, 260–261
Randolph, Peyton, 83–84, 86, 97, 277–83
Randolph, William, 83, 256
Read, George, 284–87
Reed, Joseph, 76, 116, 288–92
Revere, Paul, 2, 166, 293–99
Richman, Irving Berdine, 183
Roberdeau, Daniel, 116, 225, 246
Rodney, Caesar, 68, 286–87
Rodney, Thomas, 68
Ross, Betsy, 74, 303
Ross, George, 74, 285, 300–303
Rossiter, Clinton, 105, 212
Rush, Benjamin, 58, 98, 205, 245
Rutledge, Edward, 304–308, 311
Rutledge, John, 105. 146, 199, 219–21, 304–305, 309–15

Saint Mary's Episcopal Churchyard, 88, 94
Saint Michael's Church Cemetery, 100, 103
Saint Michael's Episcopal Church Cemetery, 309, 314
Saint Philips Episcopal Church Cemetery, 304, 307
Saratoga, 195, 200
Schuyler, Philip, 122–23, 198, 205, 336
Shay's Rebellion, 195, 200, 330, 337
Sheen, Martin, 66
Sherman, Roger, 9, 246
Skelton, Martha Wayne's, 7–8, 11

INDEX

Smith, James, 316–19
Smith, Joseph Bacardi, 116
Smith, Seymour Weyss, 165
Smith, William Jr., 121
Solomon, Haym, 320–24
Sons of Liberty, 24, 30, 146–47, 179, 294, 321–22
Stamp Act, 7, 30, 136, 145, 162, 178, 239, 279, 311, 335
Stark, John, 65, 198
Stephen, Adam, 44
Steuben, Baron von, 233, 272
St. James Episcopal Church Cemetery, 156, 160
St. John's Episcopal Church, 130, 133
St. Mary's Catholic Churchyard, 51, 58
St. Michael's Churchyard, 264, 269
St. Philip's Churchyard, 144, 149
Stockton, Richard, 88, 252, 288
St. Paul's Cemetery, 72, 76
Sullivan Family Cemetery, 325, 331
Sullivan, John, 325–32
Sugar Act of 1764, 85, 146, 162

Tallmadge, Benjamin, 140, 150–51
Tarleton, Banastre, 11
Taylor, Alan Shaw, 128
Tea Act, 111, 168, 271
Thatcher, Benjamin Bussey, 174
The Thomas Paine Gravesite, 243, 250
Thomas, John, 327
Thornton, Matthew, 64
Ticonderoga, 37–39
Tilghman, Edward, 311
Townshend Acts, 162, 280
Treaty of Paris, 88, 191
Trinity Lutheran Church, 228
Trumbull, John, 66, 200, 205, 308
Trumbull, Joseph, 75
Twain, Mark, 138

United States Navy, 51, 57–58, 60, 147
Upper Octorara Church Cemetery, 115, 119
US Constitution,1, 12, 18, 33, 41, 65, 67, 69, 78, 80, 92, 100, 103–104, 107–108, 130, 149, 192, 200, 207, 209, 214–16, 225, 251, 253–54, 260, 264, 268, 284, 287, 307, 309, 312, 314, 330, 337

Valley Forge, 38, 101, 113, 124, 131, 231, 271–72

Van Buren, Martin, 142
Van Cortland, Philip, 100
Virginia Dynasty, 5, 21
Virginia Resolves, 97

Ward, Artemas, 197, 333–38
Ward, Samuel, 178, 181
Warner, Seth, 37–38
War of 1812, 173, 263
Warren, James, 203–204
Warren, Joseph, 171, 294–96
Washington, George, 2, 8–9, 11–17, 32, 38, 41, 43–44, 54–55, 57, 68, 79–80, 88–92, 103, 113, 120, 123–25, 131, 140, 142, 147, 149, 152, 156, 158–60, 163–64, 172, 184–86, 197, 199–200, 202–207, 209–10, 212, 214, 225, 231–33, 247, 249, 255, 257, 259–61, 266, 268–69, 273, 279–80, 288, 290, 303, 307, 312–13, 322–23, 327, 330, 333, 336
Washington, Martha, 272
Wayne, Anthony, 44, 260
Weiser, Conrad, 223–24, 229
Wentworth, Bennington, 36
Wentworth, John, 63, 326
West Cemetery, 24, 26
Westernville Cemetery, 139, 142
Wharton, Thomas, 228
Whipple, William, 63
Whiskey Rebellion, 256
Wiencek, Henry, 13–14
Wilkinson, James, 20, 75
Wilmington & Brandywine Cemetery, 67, 70
Wilson, James, 292, 322
Windham Cemetery, 134, 137
Witherspoon, John Dr., 89
Woodland Hill Cemetery, 222, 228
Wren Chapel, 277, 281–83
Wynkoop, Henry, 225
Wythe, George, 6, 212, 279

Yeager, Don, 19
York Pennsylvania, 25, 136, 190, 194, 219, 316–19
Yorktown, 11, 38, 132, 149, 156, 159, 164, 184, 186–87, 191, 195, 199–201, 234, 322–23
Young, Alfred, 166, 17
Young, Thomas, 35, 39

Zabin, Serena, 47

www.ingramcontent.com/pod-product-compliance
Lightning Source LLC
Chambersburg PA
CBHW011742220426
43665CB00022B/2898